Harry S. Truman and the News Media

Harry S. Truman

and the
News
Media

CONTENTIOUS RELATIONS,
BELATED RESPECT

Franklin D. Mitchell

UNIVERSITY OF MISSOURI PRESS
COLUMBIA AND LONDON

Copyright © 1998 by
The Curators of the University of Missouri
University of Missouri Press, Columbia, Missouri 65201
Printed and bound in the United States of America
All rights reserved
5 4 3 2 1   02 01 00 99 98

Library of Congress Cataloging-in-Publication Data

Mitchell, Franklin D.
    Harry S. Truman and the news media : contentious re-
lations, belated respect / Franklin D. Mitchell
        p.   cm.
    Includes bibliographical references (p.   ) and index.
    ISBN 0-8262-1180-1 (alk. paper)
    1. Truman, Harry S., 1884–1972—Relations with jour-
nalists.   2. Press and politics—United States—History—
20th century.   3. United States—Politics and government—
1945–1953.   I. Title.
E814.M58   1998
973.918'092—dc21   98-6620
                                                                           CIP

♾™ This paper meets the requirements of the
American National Standard for Permanence of Paper
for Printed Library Materials, Z39.48, 1984.

Designer: Stephanie Foley
Typesetter: BookComp, Inc.
Printer and binder: Edwards Brothers, Inc.
Typefaces: Regency Script and Trump Medieval

For Susana, Giselle, Mark, and Gianfranco

CONTENTS

FOR A FULL GENERATION NOW, since his death in 1972, Harry S. Truman has been acclaimed by the American people as a national hero and one of the country's greatest presidents. Paradoxically, many of his contemporaries held him in low esteem, and the public, in an evaluation performance poll taken late in his administration, accorded Truman one of the lowest ratings of any modern president.[1]

The American news media played a primary role in the denigrating portrayal of the president. While a portion of the press supported Truman's policies, understood and lauded his leadership, and valued his personal character and integrity, a larger segment did not. To his detractors, Truman's rise to power in political alliance with the Pendergast machine of Kansas City tainted his record of public service long after 1939, when the combined efforts of reformers and the press crushed the corrupt boss and his organization. The conservative press in opposition to Truman's administration, principally the publishing empire of William Randolph Hearst, the McCormick-Patterson newspapers, the Scripps-Howard chain, and the newsmagazines of Henry R. Luce, contested the president for his efforts to preserve and expand the New Deal. Its opposition presented Truman with his greatest challenge in gaining election to a full term in 1948. His election triumph, the greatest upset in

1. Truman's performance rating dipped to 23 percent in November 1951, one point lower than President Richard Nixon's lowest rating and two points higher than the low accorded President Jimmy Carter. Robert H. Ferrell, *Harry S. Truman: A Life*, 358; Burton I. Kaufman, *The Presidency of James Earl Carter* (Lawrence: University Press of Kansas, 1993), 193.

American politics, produced as well the greatest miscalled election in journalistic history.

During the Truman presidential years of 1945–1953, the news media's coverage of the president and national life registered significant innovation and development but also stubborn resistance to change. The Washington news corps nearly doubled in size from a decade earlier in response to the growing importance of the federal government in the lives of the American people and the emergence of the United States as the ascendant global power. White males working for newspapers still dominated the news scene, but radio and television broadcasters and women and minority journalists gained power and influence during the immediate postwar period. These developments foreshadowed an expanding role for broadcast journalism in the news media at the expense of newspapers, photojournalism, and newsreels, as well as a greater democratization of the journalism profession.

Truman's full term occasioned the onset of a nuclear arms race in the developing Cold War, war in Korea and the recall of General Douglas MacArthur, failed efforts to secure legislative enactment of the administration's domestic Fair Deal, and the revelation of corruption in the federal government. News media reportage and editorials on these events and developments produced celebrated instances of acrimony and brought censure of the president and several members of his official family by elements of the fourth estate. By extension, press coverage of the first family and their kin was designed, in significant part, Truman believed, to diminish his power and the family's good name. The press—the "one-party press," according to Truman—had unfairly consigned him, he later wrote, to the company of "charlatans, demagogues, and traitors."[2] During the final years of his presidency, he pledged himself, with some seriousness, to spend the rest of his life "in an endeavor to cause a return to truthful writing and reporting."[3]

During his retirement of nearly two decades, however, Truman had too many other interests to sustain a quarrel with the press, and eventually the passage of time brought history's favorable verdict upon his personal qualities and his administration. When he died in 1972, the American people, recognizing the goodness of the man and the greatness of his presidency, made the old Missourian a

2. Truman to Richard Amberg, September 16, 1958, *St. Louis Globe-Democrat* folder, Box 26, President's Personal Name File, Truman Library.
3. Quoted in William Hillman, *Mr. President*, 229.

national hero. Even the press, in a remarkable change of sentiment and opinion, joined the public in its admiration of, and affection for, Old Harry. The journalistic tributes to Truman thus brought to a close a vibrant chapter of American history.

This story, told here in a blend of chronological narrative history and topically developed chapters, has been written with both general readers and academic specialists in mind. I hope that both audiences will find my account informative and interesting.

ACKNOWLEDGMENTS

THE IDEA FOR THIS BOOK originated in 1986, but some of the research that appears here was collected more than thirty years ago when I first initiated what became essentially annual visits of a few days' or a few weeks' duration to the Harry S. Truman Library in Independence, Missouri. Consequently, my original and greatest debt is to the members of the Truman Library staff who have assisted my research over the years. The library's founding director, the late Dr. Philip C. Brooks, and his colleagues—Philip Lagerquist, J. R. Fuchs, Harry Clark, Donna Clark, Carol Briley, Jerry N. Hess, Erwin J. Mueller, Mary Jo Minter, Anne Parman, Doris Pesek, Warren Ohrville, John Curry, Millie Carroll, and others—established a protocol and professionalism that served me and the first generation of Truman scholars exceedingly well. Benedict K. Zobrist, Larry Hackman, George Curtis, Raymond Gesselbracht, Dennis Bilger, Pat Dorsey, Anita Heavener, Niel M. Johnson, Sam Rushay, Randy Sowell, Pauline Testerman, and their colleagues continued (and continue) the library's tradition of friendly and efficient service. Liz Safly, ever-helpful librarian and unofficial custodian of the library's corporate memory, links the first and second generation of the Truman Library personnel. I salute them all.

Other institutions and persons have assisted my research for this book. The Harry S. Truman Library Institute twice granted timely seed money. The University of Southern California provided research funds and leave time. Hari Rorlich and Edward Comstock of the USC Doheny Library and Dace Taube of the USC Regional Cultural History Center assisted my use of microfilm and manuscript material in their respective departments. Christine Stilwell and

xiii

Rebecca Wright tracked down a few elusive matters in the newspaper holdings of the University of Missouri at Columbia while Souad Halila checked newsmagazines for similar material in Los Angeles. David Wigdor facilitated my research in several collections at the Library of Congress. Haroldine Helm made my stays at her home in Independence pleasant, especially during one memorable visit when her guests included Truman scholars from Austria, China, France, and Germany.

The bibliography affords one measure of my acknowledgment of the work of Truman scholars, journalists, and historians of journalism. I have drawn heavily upon the Truman biographies by Margaret Truman, David McCullough, Robert H. Ferrell, and Alonzo L. Hamby, the presidential histories by Cabell Phillips, Robert J. Donovan, and Donald R. McCoy, and the fine monographs on the 1948 campaign by Irwin Ross and the "Truman scandals" by Andrew J. Dunar. I have benefited, too, from the pioneering studies on Truman and the press by James E. Pollard and Herbert Lee Williams. James L. Baughman's *Henry R. Luce and the Rise of the American News Media* gave me the key to understanding the role of Luce's publications in the 1948 election and helped me to overcome a lack of access to the restricted papers of the publisher at the Time Inc., Archives and the Library of Congress.

My friends and fellow historians Monte M. Poen, Edwin J. Perkins, and Richard O. Davies read the first draft of the manuscript and offered many suggestions for its improvement. An outside reader for the University of Missouri Press gave valuable advice on matters of fact and style that merited my full consideration. Gail Suber formatted the manuscript. The errors and shortcomings that remain are of my own making.

At the University of Missouri Press, Clair Willcox, acquisition editor, and Jane Lago, managing editor, served as helpful liaison; John Brenner, editor, copyedited the entire manuscript. Design and production came under the expert direction of Stephanie Foley, Dwight Browne, and Nikki Waltz.

Along the way Richard S. Kirkendall inspired me by his example of archival research and Truman scholarship. Gerald Goodstone offered wise counsel at a critical time. Earlier, Wilma Sellers Johnson, Beverly Peterson Ansley, Darlene Goddard Kingsbury, Neil Alexander, and the now departed J. Joe Wright, Clarence E. Bundy, my uncle, T. N. Mitchell, and my parents, Worth and Laura Mitchell, in their respective ways and perhaps without always knowing it, encouraged my bent for history. Salvador and Juanita Alcala and

David Monicatti made their contribution through their friendship and by freeing me from nonwriting chores.

I am especially grateful to my wife and children, to whom I dedicate this book, for their love and support and for allowing me to be excused from family affairs by accepting my explanation, "I have a book to write."

Franklin D. Mitchell
Santa Monica, California

Harry S. Truman and the News Media

1

Before the White House Years

MOMENTOUS CHANGES IN communications technology transformed the American news media during the long lifetime of
Harry S. Truman. When Truman was born on May 8, 1884, in the
small Missouri town of Lamar, metropolitan newspapers, following
the example of Joseph Pulitzer and the *New York World*, were just
beginning to blend sensationalism and solid news reporting characteristic of the era's New Journalism. The wireless of Marconi and
his rivals loomed just over the horizon, but commercial radio's news
coverage did not begin until 1920 when KDKA in Pittsburgh broadcast the results of the presidential election. Television, successfully
demonstrated by several of its various "fathers" during the 1920s,
required more than two decades of development before it became
a national medium of news communication at midcentury. Television's predecessor, newsreels shown in motion picture theaters,
brought first the sights and then the sounds of the news until their
demise a few years before Truman's life drew to its close in 1972.

During the years of transformation in media communications,
Harry Truman, like many ordinary Americans, avidly followed the
news of his time. His rise in politics from precinct officer to the
presidency, however, changed his role from news consumer to the
nation's leading news maker. His developing political career as a
county administrator, U.S. senator, and vice president—two decades
of public service before he became president of the United States—

1

served as a long apprenticeship in shaping his relations with the press. During this period he received coverage in local, state, and national newspapers and newsmagazines that alternately boosted his political stock or threatened through adverse publicity to end his political career. As a result, he brought to the White House well-formulated views on the press based on extensive personal experience.

Truman's introduction to academic journalism came during his senior year of high school in Independence, Missouri. At the time, journalism's professional development extended upward into colleges and universities and down into high schools. The Independence School Board joined the national trend for the expansion of the high school curriculum by adding a year of courses and extracurricular activities to its schedule in the fall of 1900. The latter included the inauguration of the school's first yearbook under the editorship of Charles G. Ross with the uncredited assistance of classmate Harry Truman.[1]

When the two friends graduated in 1901, they went in quite different directions. Ross, eager to become a newspaperman, headed for the University of Missouri at Columbia to enroll in courses that later became the nucleus of the university's School of Journalism. Young Harry went neither to West Point, where he had hoped to be educated for a military career, nor to the state university. Poor eyesight barred his appointment to the military academy, and his aspirations for a university education did not match those of young Ross. Instead, Harry spent a leisurely summer visiting relatives before enrolling in practical business courses at Spalding's Commercial College in Kansas City. When the money ran out—his father had lost all of the family's considerable property in commodity trading by the spring of 1902—he spent the next few years in routine work, including the job of wrapper in the mailing room of the *Kansas City Star*, timekeeper for a construction crew of the Santa Fe railroad, and bank clerk. His prospects looked bleak indeed when contrasted with the rising star of Ross, who joined the faculty of Missouri's new "J" school in 1908 before eventually leaving to begin his long and distinguished career with the *St. Louis Post-Dispatch*.[2]

Harry left Kansas City in 1906 to join his parents and other

---

1. Ronald T. Farrar, *Reluctant Servant: The Story of Charles G. Ross*, 17, 19–20; David McCullough, *Truman*, 64.
2. Farrar, *Reluctant Servant*, 23–30, 44–47, 69–70, 116–21; Robert H. Ferrell, *Harry S. Truman: A Life*, 23–30; McCullough, *Truman*, 66–69.

family members in the operation of a six-hundred-acre grain and livestock farm in Jackson County, Missouri. For the next eleven years he experienced the drudgery of farm life, relieved by a host of social activities such as picnics, church parties, family visits, fairs, lodge meetings, vaudeville theater in nearby Kansas City, and, most importantly, starting in 1910, his courtship of Elizabeth Wallace.[3]

Harry Truman and Bess Wallace belonged to the last generation of Americans of the "horse and buggy" era of transportation and the first generation to enjoy the automobile. For four years after their courtship began in 1910, Harry relied upon a combination of conveyances—horse and carriage, the railroad, and an interurban trolley—for traveling the indirect distance of about twenty miles from rural Grandview to the Wallace residence in Independence. At times, he traveled by horse and carriage to the closest interurban station for the trolley ride to Independence via Kansas City. Other times he walked about a mile from his farm home to Grandview to catch the train before switching to the interurban streetcar for the remainder of the trip to Independence. At the end of a date he retraced his route, often arriving home long after midnight. Little wonder that he yearned for an automobile to free him from these cumbersome modes of travel and greatly enjoyed the convenience of the car he purchased in 1914.[4]

The Trumans, like most rural middle-class Americans of their day, had acquired a telephone years before buying their first automobile. The separate and sometimes inoperable telephone systems serving Jackson County permitted Harry and Bess to converse when the message required immediate communication, but the lack of privacy in telephoning, its cost, and Harry's aversion to talking on the telephone limited his use of this modern communication mode. All subscribers on the Trumans' "party line," alerted to a neighbor's telephone call by the central operator's ringing of an assigned number or the subscriber's cranking of the telephone to make a call, could "listen in." When the cost of monthly telephone service and toll calls to Kansas City mounted to ten dollars a month in 1913, an exorbitant amount for that time, the Trumans and their neighbors made plans to build and maintain their own lines.[5]

3. See Robert H. Ferrell, *Harry S. Truman: His Life on the Family Farms.*
4. Robert H. Ferrell, ed., *Dear Bess: The Letters from Harry to Bess Truman, 1910–1959*, 14–15, 17, 23, 57, 69, 92, 162.
5. Claude S. Fischer, *America Calling: A Social History of the Telephone to 1940* (Berkeley: University of California Press, 1992), 42–44, 47–48, 86–121;

By contrast, the postage for a letter, underwritten by the federal government through rural free delivery, cost only two cents. Moreover, letters allowed Harry and Bess to share in confidence their experiences, opinions, aspirations, and, of course, their affection and devotion. The correspondence they initiated during their courtship became a lifelong habit whenever they were absent from one another; the letters written by Harry and saved by Bess—Bess may have burned some of Harry's letters and the letters she wrote to him—constitute the most important source of information for biographers of the thirty-third president.[6]

Rural free delivery of mail, as relied upon by Harry and Bess during their courtship, thus ranked, after its inauguration nationwide in 1896, as equal to the telephone in its importance as a communications innovation. R.F.D.'s Monday-to-Saturday daily schedule, bringing postcards and letters to isolated rural Americans and carrying their outbound correspondence to near and distant points, also brought daily and weekly newspapers and mass-circulation magazines to their homes. The Truman household subscribed to a number of periodicals including *Adventure, American Magazine, Ladies' Home Journal, McClure's, Redbook,* and the *Saturday Evening Post.* Harry enjoyed the serialized stories that kept the reader in suspense until the next installment arrived or until the story ended. John Truman liked to read aloud to his son the exaggerated claims of successful farming endeavors featured in farm periodicals, but Harry viewed the farm papers as "run for the advertising money and not for the subscriber."[7]

While the daily *Kansas City Star* kept the Trumans abreast of world and national news along with current events in Kansas City and Missouri, the local weekly, the *Belton Herald,* informed them of civic affairs and the activities of their neighbors in the small town of one thousand residents. The *Herald* reported on the birth of babies (animals included, if the offspring was unusual in some way), marriages, deaths (with a report on the deceased's final illness, floral

---

Ferrell, ed., *Dear Bess,* 45, 47, 76–77, 86, 120, 128. For an amusing account of Harry "listening in" on a party line conversation and his aversion to talking on the telephone, see 20–21 and 134.

6. Ferrell, ed., *Dear Bess,* vii, viii, ix, 120.

7. Wayne Fuller, *RFD: The Changing Face of Rural America,* 292–93. The Trumans received mail addressed to Grandview, Missouri, R.F.D. #37. Envelope postmarked October 23, 1908, Item 3, Box 1, Mary Jane Truman Papers, Truman Library. Ferrell, ed., *Dear Bess,* 16, 62, 64, 79, 99, 100, 126.

tributes, and a respectful assessment of the late person's virtues),
and social activities such as family reunions or a routine visit of
relatives and friends, a meeting of the ladies' aid society, and other
news featuring the names of local residents and subscribers. If the
community was large enough to have ambition for growth—and
most communities with a few hundred inhabitants dreamed of being
larger and more prosperous—the local editor was the town's chief
booster. Civic improvements such as more hitching posts on the
town square or main street, bond issues for municipal utilities, and
sidewalks were perennial topics in small-town newspapers at the
turn of the century.[8]

Local officials and aspiring politicians read the newspapers with
an eye toward favorable publicity, and editors, eager to receive an
advertisement or a year's subscription from both Republican and
Democratic candidates, couched their partisanship so as to avoid
unduly offending an office-seeker or member of the opposition party.
But the editor of the *Belton Herald* angered John Truman in an
editorial in 1913 that indirectly referred to him, in his capacity
as one of the county's road supervisors paid for maintaining the
roads in his neighborhood, as "one of the henchmen of the Jackson County court." "I told him that was a very mild remark and
should be accepted as a compliment to a man who has a political
job," Harry wrote Bess. The fiercely independent farmer thought
otherwise; he journeyed to Belton, intent on giving a whipping to
the editor. Fortunately, the editor was away from the office when
John Truman called.[9]

Editors of that era could be combative, too. "Squeaky" Bill Southern, editor of the *Independence Sentinel* in Truman's hometown,
had a well-deserved reputation as a scrapper handy with both words
and weapons. The journalist Mary Paxton Keeley, who once lived
next door to Southern, offered this portrait of the feisty editor: "If
you combined a bantam rooster's size with a turkey gobbler's strut
and the voice of a rain crow, you might have a creature in minia-
ture who somewhat resembled him." Southern, Keeley avowed,
edited his newspaper "with the same tone of voice with which
he drew knives or pistols on those who annoyed him. He may not

8. This analysis is based on a reading of several issues of the *Belton Herald* for
1905 and 1911–1913, microfilm copy in the possession of the State Historical
Society of Missouri, Columbia. See especially the April 7, 1905, issue devoted
to boosting the town of Belton.

9. *Belton Herald*, April 24, 1913; Ferrell, ed., *Dear Bess*, 126.

have invented personal journalism, but he perfected its poisonous invective."[10]

If Truman did not later follow the advice he once offered to his father, he learned well the lesson of cultivating local newspaper editors in advancing his own political career. After deciding to enter politics in 1922, he visited William Southern, Jr., the nephew of "Squeaky" Bill and the publisher and editor of the *Independence Examiner*, to seek the newspaper's support. Southern unofficially endorsed Truman's initial bid for a seat on the Jackson County Court (the administrative body of three "judges" similar to a board of supervisors or county commissioners in other states) and supported his hometown citizen in Truman's subsequent campaigns for public office.[11]

The friendly relationship between Truman and Southern rested upon a set of shared values that shaped the lives of many Missourians in early-twentieth-century America. The moral code of the Ten Commandments and Christian ethics of the New Testament guided both men throughout their lifetime. Southern wrote and published a widely used Sunday School lesson for decades, and Truman read the Bible from his youth to old age. Civic and personal responsibility grew out of the biblical injunction to "Render unto Caesar the things that are Caesar's and to God the things that are God's." Other Scripture such as "Seest thou a man diligent in his labor? He shall not stand before mean men, he shall stand before the King" reinforced the Christian work ethic that Truman especially exemplified. Religion was more than a one-day-a-week affair solemnized by public rituals; religious beliefs guided one's private life and daily conduct.[12]

10. Loren Reid, *Hurry Home Wednesday: Growing Up in a Small Missouri Town, 1905–1921*, 53–54. See also William Lyon, *The Pioneer Editor in Missouri, 1808–1860* (Columbia: University of Missouri Press, 1964). Mary Gentry Paxton [Keeley], *Mary Gentry and John Gallatin Paxton, A Memoir*, 19.

11. The relationship between the Southerns and their respective newspapers and the younger Southern's support of Truman over the years is discussed in a retrospective of William Southern, Jr., in *Independence Examiner*, c. 1988, Vertical File, Truman Library.

12. William H. Taft, *Missouri Newspapers*, 304; *Kansas City Star*, February 6, 1955; *Independence Examiner*, c. 1988; for Truman's lifelong reading of the Bible, see Robert H. Ferrell, ed., *The Autobiography of Harry S. Truman*, 33 and Hillman, *Mr. President*, 104–6. The biblical passages, quoted from the King James version, are from Matthew 22:21 and Proverbs 22:29. For Truman's mature views on religion see Ferrell, ed., *Dear Bess*, 22–25.

Secular beliefs drawn from the American frontier experience informed Missourians, too. The first settlers of the state and their descendants made Missouri "the mother of the west" without surrendering sectional ties that extended either to the South or to the North. Missourians possessed a hardy skepticism summed up in the saying, "I'm from Missouri, you'll have to show me."[13]

Other beliefs needed only to be proclaimed and defended rather than examined rigorously. The Trumans and the Southerns and their kin acquired their Democratic politics as they had acquired their religion; they were born Democrats as they were Protestants. Their Protestant beliefs made them the keepers of their own conscience while their Democratic politics made them, like Thomas Jefferson and Andrew Jackson, champions of the people and the common man. Loyalty, valued as an independent virtue, also rooted Missourians to their cultural and political heritage. All these beliefs found continuous expression throughout Truman's life and significantly influenced his relations with the press.[14]

Similar religious and secular values were expressed in the editorials and news stories of Missouri's many country newspapers. The country editors recognized that the earnest politician from Independence spoke their language because his values were their values and his dreams their dreams. He met their expectations for honesty and integrity. They were impressed with the leadership Truman had brought to Jackson County government, which had gained for the county a modern highway system, new civic structures—a new courthouse in Kansas City and a remodeled courthouse in Independence—and the improvement of facilities and operations of the homes for the county's orphaned children and indigent aged citizens. Truman's vision of Kansas City and Missouri in the dawning air age—a belief fostered by the state's geographical location in the middle of the nation—may have caught the imagination of the small-town editors as well.[15]

13. Paul C. Nagel, *Missouri: A Bicentennial History*, 4–5, passim. The phrase, "I'm from Missouri, you'll have to show me," was popularized by Missouri congressman William Vandiver, in a speech in Philadelphia in 1902.

14. Independence and eastern Jackson County, part of the populous slave-holding area of Missouri, was settled by Kentuckians and other Upper South residents with strong ties to the Democratic party. McCullough, *Truman*, chapter one; Franklin D. Mitchell, *Embattled Democracy: Missouri Democratic Politics, 1919–1932*, 12–13.

15. Several Missouri small-town newspaper editorials published at the time of Truman's death in 1972, some written by editors who began their careers when Truman first entered politics, convey this relationship. See *Harry S.*

Understandably, when Truman tested the political water for the Democratic nomination for governor in 1932, some rural editors greeted his bid with warmth and enthusiasm. The editor of the *Odessa Democrat* gave him a glowing endorsement with a story headlined "Truman Would Make Ideal Candidate for Governor." Other Democratic editors around the state, following the practice of borrowing stories from one another, and having their own positive perception of Harry Truman, gave the endorsement wide circulation. Although the kingmaker of Missouri Democratic politics, Boss Thomas J. Pendergast of Kansas City, did not support his fellow Jackson Countian's gubernatorial bid, the publicity Truman gained made him better known to the voters around the state. Two years later, when Pendergast backed Truman for the senatorial nomination, the country press gave valuable support to the man of Independence.[16]

By contrast, Truman's move from local politics to the national scene with his nomination and election to the U.S. Senate in 1934 succeeded despite the opposition of the major newspapers of Kansas City and St. Louis. The *Kansas City Star* praised the efficiency and honesty that Truman had brought to county government but lambasted his ties with the Pendergast machine that controlled Kansas City and received patronage dispensed by the Truman-led court. The *St. Louis Globe-Democrat* also emphasized Truman's connections with Pendergast as much for the power the Kansas City machine gave to the western part of the state at the expense of St. Louis and eastern Missouri as for the machine's corruption of the political process.[17]

Truman, Late a President of the United States: Memorial Tributes Delivered in Congress, 43–56; Richard S. Kirkendall, *A History of Missouri: Volume V, 1919 to 1953*, 45–48, 51, 141–42; Richard Lawrence Miller, *Truman: The Rise to Power*, 280–81.

16. The newspaper practice of borrowing, called "clipping," is discussed in Reid, *Hurry Home Wednesday*, 58–59. Pendergast originally supported Francis M. Wilson, unsuccessful Democratic gubernatorial candidate of 1928 who had been renominated by his party in 1932. When Wilson died six weeks before the general election, Pendergast engineered the nomination of Guy B. Park. Franklin D. Mitchell, "Who is Judge Truman?: The Truman-for-Governor Movement of 1931," 5. Ferrell, ed., *Autobiography*, 67–68; Eugene Francis Schmidtlein, "Truman the Senator," 80–81; Truman extolled the influence of the rural press in a retrospective letter to Robert C. White II, publisher of the *Mexico* (Mo.) *Ledger*. Herbert Lee Williams, *The Newspaperman's President: Harry S. Truman*, 20.

17. Margaret Truman, *Harry S. Truman*, 84, 88; Schmidtlein, "Truman the Senator," 36–38, 49, 84.

The *St. Louis Post-Dispatch,* largest daily metropolitan newspaper in St. Louis and second to the *Kansas City Star* in statewide circulation, rivaled the *Star* as the chief critic of the Pendergast machine. When a decade of Republican control of state government ended with the onset of the Great Depression and voter preference for Democratic candidates, the *Post-Dispatch* editors interpreted the gubernatorial election of Guy B. Park, the Pendergast-backed candidate, as an extension of the boss's power to the statehouse.[18] With this logic, the newspaper regarded the 1934 senatorial contest as a test of Pendergast's influence that could, if his choice of candidate was elected, extend to the floor of the U.S. Senate. The key to this formula in the Democratic primary rested on the character of the candidate from Independence: Was Harry Truman his own man?

An intriguing morality play was acted out against this political background when Charlie Ross accepted the invitation of Joseph Pulitzer II, publisher of the *Post-Dispatch,* to assume the responsibility for the newspaper's editorial page. Guiding Ross and his *Post-Dispatch* colleagues was the founder's creed. After Joseph Pulitzer's death in 1911, the independent newspaper published the senior Pulitzer's "platform" on the masthead of every issue. In Pulitzer's words, these were the cardinal principles of the *Post-Dispatch:*

> always fight for progress and reform, never tolerate injustice or corruption, always fight demagogues of all parties, never belong to any party, always oppose privileged classes and public plunderers, never lack sympathy with the poor, always remain devoted to the public welfare, never be satisfied with merely printing news, always be drastically independent, never be afraid to attack wrong, whether by predatory plutocracy or predatory poverty.[19]

In this spirit *Post-Dispatch* reporter Paul Y. Anderson won the Pulitzer Prize in 1928 for his investigative reporting of the Teapot Dome scandal, and in 1932 Ross won the same coveted award for his incisive analysis of the country's plight in the Great Depression. Ross's professional reputation as Washington correspondent of the

---

18. The *Kansas City Star,* with a daily circulation of 294,000, was the largest metropolitan newspaper in Missouri. The *Post-Dispatch* circulation of 237,000 made it the second-largest metropolitan newspaper in the state; *Time* (August 13, 1934): 22–25; Lyle W. Dorsett, *The Pendergast Machine,* 90–101; Alfred Steinberg, *The Man from Missouri: The Life and Times of Harry S. Truman,* 105, 110–11.

19. Daniel W. Pfaff, *Joseph Pulitzer II and the Post-Dispatch,* 76.

Post-Dispatch was large when he returned to St. Louis to assume his editorial assignment.[20]

Ross began his editorial duties on July 11, 1934, less than a month before the August 4 primary election when Missouri Democrats would choose one of the three major Democratic contenders to be the party's U.S. senatorial candidate: Congressman John Cochran of St. Louis, Congressman Jacob "Tuck" Milligan of Richmond, near Kansas City, or Harry Truman of Independence.[21]

Ross's editorial colleagues knew Tom Pendergast and Kansas City machine politics better than he; as an observer of the national scene from Washington since 1918, he had lost touch with state and local politics. Only Ross, however, was personally acquainted with Truman and the details of his early life that later appeared in the *Post-Dispatch*. He knew Truman as his able but intellectually outdistanced classmate—Ross led the class of 1901 in scholarship—who lacked a college education. Truman's enlistment in the National Guard in 1905 and combat service during World War I may not have surprised Ross, for he had played at soldiering with Harry during the Spanish-American War and knew of his friend's early ambition for a military career. Truman's entry into local politics and his program of public works that modernized Jackson County with new highways and civic buildings were the real enactment of assignments on Greek and Roman statecraft and model bridge building projects of the students of ancient civilization and Latin in Independence High School. Now Truman's bid for statesmanship as a U.S. senator, something that Ross had never dreamed about, would vault him over Ross in their respective careers.[22] Ross found the rationale for opposing and belittling his former classmate as the handpicked candidate of a corrupt political boss.

Ross's behind-the-scenes maneuvers against Truman were complicated by the policy of the *Post-Dispatch* to take no position on the merits of primary candidates, reserving its endorsement or opposition for the general election after the voters had made their selection in the primary. During the last three weeks of the campaign Ross

20. Farrar, *Reluctant Servant,* 88–89, 94–98.
21. Ibid., 112–15, 116–17; Margaret Truman, *Harry S. Truman,* 84–85.
22. Ferrell, ed., *Autobiography,* 11–12; Henry A. Bundschu, a classmate of Truman and Ross at Independence High School, wrote in a biographical account of Truman that "Charlie himself says he might be credited with being more literary but Harry Truman is gifted with political sagacity and wisdom which exceeds anything that he, Ross, has ever dreamed of. "Harry S. Truman: The Missourian," reprinted in the *Kansas City Star,* December 26, 1948.

tried unsuccessfully to persuade Pulitzer to change policy given his belief that the race was between Congressman Cochran and Judge Truman, with the victor destined to win the November election. He wanted to oppose Truman because he believed Truman was not a free and independent man: he was "Pendergast's creature" who would extend the power of the boss to the U.S. Senate. "The issue being what it is," Ross informed Pulitzer, "I should like your authority to say in the *Post-Dispatch* if and when I think advisable before the end of the campaign that the interest of the state would be best served by nominating Cochran." He reminded Pulitzer that the *Post-Dispatch* had departed from its policy of neutrality in the primary campaign of 1932 by calling for "the defeat of the Pendergast candidate . . . for the same reasons that we would now oppose Truman."[23]

Pulitzer, on vacation in Maine, telegraphed Ross that he preferred to avoid saying "vote for Cochran" and to "rest our case with the voters for a forthright vigorous unequivocal expose of the disqualification of Truman as a boss-picked and boss-controlled candidate." He reinforced the point by adding, "I should like to see you go the limit in opposing Truman but falling short of giving Cochran our endorsement." Having stated his preference, but recognizing Ross's desire to back Cochran, Pulitzer asked Ross to convene the editorial board for a consideration of his views and to wire back the recommendations of the editors.[24]

Ross faithfully reported to Pulitzer on the deliberations of the board. O. K. Bovard considered all candidates "a sorry lot," but found "nothing in the record to show that Truman would not be as good a senator as the other candidates." Bovard therefore argued strongly that the newspaper remain neutral on the candidates. Clark McAdams wanted to attack Truman as a boss-candidate and back Cochran as the best qualified. George Johns believed that while the *Post-Dispatch* could oppose Truman as a boss-controlled candidate without endorsing Cochran, he advised that the newspaper report on the candidate without indicating a preference. "My own feelings after hearing conflicting views," Ross advised, "is that for the present we should comment on utterances [of the candidates] from time to time in order to expose any false statements and clarify issues." This

23. Ross to Pulitzer, telegram, July 25, 1934, Microfilm Reel 95, Joseph Pulitzer II Papers, Library of Congress.
24. Pulitzer to Ross, telegram, July 26, 1934, Microfilm Reel 95, Pulitzer Papers, Library of Congress.

course, Ross observed, would "leave the way open to denunciation of Truman as boss-controlled if on further thought you believe it desirable."[25]

Pulitzer gave the situation much thought, even to the extent that he believed it had been unwise for the *Post-Dispatch* to have labeled Governor Park the "creature of Pendergast." He had not forgotten that Ross had initially asked for an explicit endorsement of Cochran and an outright rejection of Truman. "However creditable you think Cochran's record on the whole has been," he wired Ross, "I don't believe you have any great amount of confidence based on his record which is the only thing that counts, that he will become a really good senator."[26]

"As to Truman," Pulitzer concluded, "I must confess that I am not as well informed as I should be. But is not about the worst thing that can be said against him the charge that Pendergast picked him? You and Mac [McAdams]," he conceded, "may be eternally right in believing that he will prove to be just a 'creature' to quote Mac's favorite word, of Pendergast." Pulitzer continued,

> Yet unless his record is such as to indicate without the slightest doubt that he will be the servile creature of the man who picked him, and that his vote in consequence will be against the public's interest, I question—and the Lord knows I have no fondness for Mr. Pendergast—whether your opinion, righteous as it is, is sufficient ground on which to base an editorial attack against Truman and either an outspoken or implied support of Cochran.[27]

Ross ended the preprimary exchange of views between the editors and the publisher by conceding that "it is not possible to say of Judge Truman that his record is 'such as to indicate without the slightest doubt that he will be a servile creature of the man who picked him.'" This evaluation came as close as Ross could manage for a positive assessment of the character and integrity of Truman. The *Post-Dispatch* thus remained neutral in the Democratic primary election.[28]

25. Ross to Pulitzer, telegram, July 28, 1934, Microfilm Reel 95, Pulitzer Papers, Library of Congress.

26. Pulitzer to Ross, telegram, July 29, 1934, Microfilm Reel 95, Pulitzer Papers, Library of Congress.

27. Ibid.

28. Ross to Pulitzer, telegram, August 1, 1934, Microfilm Reel 95, Pulitzer Papers, Library of Congress.

In the August primary Truman received a comfortable forty-thousand-vote plurality over Cochran and Milligan. The lopsided margin compiled for him in Kansas City and Jackson County, augmented by strong support in the state's predominantly rural counties, produced the victory.[29]

There is no record of a congratulatory telegram from Ross to Truman. There is instead the damning postprimary editorial that would have been Ross's responsibility to write. The editorial charged that Truman, "an obscure man," was named the Democratic senatorial nominee "because Tom Pendergast willed it so." Measuring the county judge against eminent senators from Missouri—"Benton and Blair, Cockrell and Vest, Stone and Jim Reed"—the editorial found him severely wanting. The unsigned, belittling sketch of Truman, headlined "Career of Truman, Ex-Rail Hand," may have been written by Ross as well; certainly the information of the article revealed an intimate knowledge of the early life of Truman that Ross knew better than his colleagues.[30]

Moreover, Ross intended to give no support to his former classmate in the general election contest between Truman and the incumbent, conservative Republican Roscoe C. Patterson. "The results of the recent primaries," he wrote to Pulitzer, "leave no doubt as to the attitude we should take on the relevant election in the fall. The choice, as you know, lies between Truman who was put over by Pendergast, and Patterson, and it looks like a case of 'a plague o' both your houses.'" Consequently, the *Post-Dispatch* withheld its editorial support from both candidates in the November election.[31]

During Truman's first term Ross and the *Post-Dispatch* promoted the fiction that the Missourian was "the senator from Pendergast." The phrase gained popularity in the St. Louis newspaper after its reporter Spencer McCulloch wrote an account of his personal interview with Tom Pendergast. According to McCulloch, the Kansas City boss boasted that some senators represented special interests so his "office boy" would represent him. Years later, Truman penciled his version of the interview in a draft of his biography written by Jonathan Daniels: "What TJP really told our lying friend [McCulloch] . . . was that steel, railroads [and] utilities had senators—his

29. Ferrell, ed., *Autobiography*, 67–68. Truman won, in addition to Jackson County, forty counties and ran second in sixty; Schmidtlein, "Truman the Senator," 80–81.

30. Editorial, *St. Louis Post-Dispatch*, August 8, 1934.

31. Ross to Pulitzer, August 10, 1934, Microfilm Reel 95, Pulitzer Papers, Library of Congress; Editorial, *St. Louis Post-Dispatch*, November 4, 1934.

candidate represented the people. I heard the conversation," Truman recalled, and McCulloch "wrote the lie as the P.D. wanted it." Truman also challenged the reporter's labeling of him as Pendergast's "office boy," insisting that Boss Tom had never treated him in this manner. "I think you make too much of the office boy thing," he wrote on the margin of Daniels's manuscript. "I never even heard of it!" Truman had indeed heard similar insults, of course, from his opponents in the 1934 Democratic senatorial primary, and he once complained, after Roosevelt had solicited his vote on a matter, that he was "tired of having the President treat me like an office boy." Daniels diplomatically incorporated Truman's version of these matters in a chapter of his biography titled "The Gentleman from Pendergast."[32]

At the time Ross and the *Post-Dispatch* never let their readers forget Truman's ties with the Pendergast machine. In mid-February 1938 an unsigned *Post-Dispatch* editorial censured Truman for criticizing President Roosevelt's reappointment of anti-Pendergast U.S. District Attorney Maurice Milligan. The editorial, echoing Ross's earlier belief of Truman's subservience to Pendergast, reinforced its point with Daniel Fitzpatrick's cartoon of Truman as Edgar Bergen's dummy Charlie McCarthy seated on the lap of Boss Pendergast. The caption read "Charlie McTruman Does His Stuff."[33]

Only after Ross returned to Washington in January 1939 to become a contributing columnist for the *Post-Dispatch* did he make amends with Truman. He invited his former classmate to his home for Sunday breakfast to renew their friendship and to clear the air arising from his role in the 1934 editorials and reportage on Truman's first senate term. Ross took the initiative for renewing the friendship while his journalist friend, James McAtee, offered an explanation of the 1934 pieces. In a letter to Bess that described the affair, Harry reported that "Charlie had a program of our graduation on May 30, 1901, and he is a sentimentalist just as I am. He got it out and passed it around and he didn't write that editorial but had to publish it or get fired. And the St. Louis outfit [apparently the Democratic leaders there] were sore at him because he wouldn't

32. Steinberg, *The Man from Missouri*, 114; Manuscript biography of HST, 237, 243, Box 83, Jonathan Daniels Papers, University of North Carolina, Chapel Hill; Jonathan Daniels, *The Man of Independence*, 172, 174, 179–80.

33. Steinberg, *The Man from Missouri*, 80; *St. Louis Post-Dispatch*, February 16, 1938.

endorse Cochran in 1934. McAtee told me that—not Charlie."[34] Ross would have had a different story to tell; nevertheless, the explanation satisfied Truman and allowed him to retain his belief— mistaken in this case—that editors and reporters were required to write what their publishers wanted written.

Truman ardently desired to perform well as a senator, and his major first-term committee assignment and voting record produced that result. His appointment to the Interstate Commerce Committee chaired by the progressive Democrat from Montana, Burton K. Wheeler, allowed him to prove his worth on the committee as it dealt with the difficult problem of restoring the financially strapped railroads to a sound, honest operating basis. His letters to Bess reported the compliments paid him by senior colleagues and favorable press notices in the *New York Times* and other metropolitan newspapers; both contributed to his growing reputation as one of the workhorses of the Senate. In addition, the votes he cast for New Deal measures pleased his constituents who benefited from the New Deal's recovery, relief, and reform agenda.[35]

But while Missourians could, and did, find much in Truman's first-term record to warrant his renomination and reelection, developments in the state from 1935 onward involving Tom Pendergast and his Kansas City machine on the one hand, and the reform governorship of Lloyd C. Stark and the governor's bid to win Truman's seat in the U.S. Senate on the other, pointed instead to his political demise.[36]

The fall of the House of Pendergast and the concomitant rise of Governor Stark accelerated in 1937 when Stark fired the state commissioner of insurance, who had taken bribes from insurance companies doing business in Missouri and shared the money with Boss Tom. Pendergast had lived well on the graft of Jackson County, but after his addiction to betting on horse races led to large losses, his reliance on insurance bribe money to keep himself solvent proved

34. Ferrell, ed., *Dear Bess*, 434. McAtee was apparently James McAtee, a former journalism student of the University of Missouri in the early 1930s and, in 1939, the executive secretary of Sigma Delta Chi, the professional fraternity of journalism. Information supplied by the University of Missouri School of Journalism, Rebecca Wright to author, February 2, 1994.

35. Ferrell, ed., *Dear Bess*, 382, 403, 409, 415; Alonzo L. Hamby, *Man of the People: A Life of Harry S. Truman*, 213–27.

36. I have relied heavily upon the biographies of Truman by Robert Ferrell, Alonzo Hamby, and David McCullough for my condensed account of these developments.

to be his undoing. In April 1939 a grand jury indicted him for evading income tax. The following month Pendergast pleaded guilty to income-tax evasion; he received a fifteen-month prison sentence (reduced from three years due to his age and ill health), fines, and a bill for back taxes totaling well over eight hundred thousand dollars, along with a stipulation barring him from all political activity during a five-year probation period.

The Kansas City machine, stripped of its leader, had been weakened earlier when a body of reformers appointed by Governor Stark purged the Kansas City voter registration rolls of tens of thousands of fraudulently entered registrants. The conviction of numerous Kansas City Democrats on vote fraud and racketeering charges in 1938 further thinned the ranks of the organization. The only thing left, in the view of the state's major newspapers and anti-machine reformers, was the retirement of the "senator from Pendergast."[37]

Still, Truman steadfastly refused to renounce his friendship with Tom Pendergast and break his political ties with the remnant of the Kansas City political organization as demanded by several newspapers and some politicians. Even if he had, it probably would not have satisfied the reform-minded press that had played its own important part in the fall of Pendergast and the buildup of Governor Stark. President Roosevelt, although no admirer of Stark, personally told Truman in early 1939 that he wanted Missouri politics cleaned up; later he sent word to the senator of an awaiting appointment to the Interstate Commerce Commission as a way of removing an encumbrance to the national ticket in Missouri. Seasoned political observers in the state, along with most major newspapers in Missouri, shared the *Post-Dispatch*'s blunt evaluation of Truman's chances of nomination: "He is a dead cock in the pit."[38]

Thus, prominent in the history of Truman's uphill battle of 1940, and even more so in his memory, was the nearly united opposition of the state's metropolitan newspapers—the *Kansas City Journal*

37. Hamby, *Man of the People*, 228–47, especially 233. See also the valuable discussion in Ferrell, *Harry S. Truman: A Life*, 140–53, and McCullough, *Truman*, 235–52. Maurice Milligan, who got into the senatorial race in part because he thought that Truman would not enter, remarked, "How could a Pendergast man get anywhere without a Pendergast?" His candidacy soon faded and the race became essentially a contest between Stark and Truman. Steinberg, *The Man from Missouri*, 168, 172–74.

38. Steinberg, *The Man from Missouri*, 166; Ferrell, ed., *Autobiography*, 83–84; McCullough, *Truman*, 241, 244; Ferrell, *Harry S. Truman: A Life*, 147–49; Hamby, *Man of the People*, 235.

the major exception—to his renomination and reelection. Failing to persuade the voters of the righteousness of their position—the *Post-Dispatch*, for example, had warned that Truman's nomination would bring "shrill rejoicing among all the forces of evil in Missouri"—the opposition press viewed the outcome much as did the *St.Louis Globe-Democrat*, which called his victory a "calamitous result."[39]

The Missouri press judgment notwithstanding, Truman's senatorial colleagues accorded him a warm reception when he walked onto the Senate floor for the first time after his nomination. Several senators had helped Truman by campaigning for him in Missouri or by releasing letters of support to the press to aid his candidacy. Their effusive affirmation of Truman in the Senate chambers demonstrated, biographer Alfred Steinberg wrote, that "he now belonged, independent and secure, no longer the creature of Tom Pendergast." The ratifying vote of confidence for Truman came from the Missourians who contributed to his forty-thousand-plus margin in the general election.[40]

Truman's national visibility and standing increased sharply during his second term as the result of his origination and chairmanship of the Senate Special Committee to Investigate the National Defense Program. The disclosures linked to the disclosures of the Truman Committee, as it became popularly known, saved taxpayers billions of dollars during World War II by exposing fraud in the manufacture of shoddy goods and materials for the military and by cutting bureaucratic red tape that slowed production. The *New York Times* and other metropolitan eastern newspapers gave Truman frequent favorable front-page treatment in coverage of the national defense committee hearings beginning in 1942.[41]

Truman's even-handed and energetic committee leadership continued to elicit much positive press comment, and in March 1943 *Time* made Truman the subject of a cover issue. The magazine

39. Steinberg, *The Man from Missouri*, 171, 177–78. Robert Ferrell has pointed out that in addition to the *Kansas City Journal*, Truman received backing from the *Jefferson City Daily Capitol News, Dade County Advocate*, the weekly newspaper in Harrisonville, and *Labor*, voice of railroad unions, which blanketed the state with a half-million copies of a special issue touting Truman. *Harry S. Truman: A Life*, 150; Hamby, *Man of the People*, 238.

40. Steinberg, *The Man from Missouri*, 166–79; Ferrell, ed., *Autobiography*, 73–74.

41. Ferrell, ed., *Dear Bess*, 477, 484. See also the numerous entries for Truman in the *New York Times Index* for 1942–1944.

praised the chairman and the work of his committee, reversing its earlier description of Truman as a "fox-faced little senator." *Time's* cover portrait was anything but fox-faced; rather it depicted Truman with a set jaw and determined look, a man of steel rather than cunning. And while Truman complained to friends that the *Time* portrait had made him appear to be twenty years older than his real age, he wrote a letter to *Time* publisher Henry R. Luce to thank him for the favorable article of the cover-page issue.[42]

Continuing favorable press coverage of Truman and his committee delighted the Missouri senator. In a letter of June 22, 1943, to his wife, he wrote: "The *Time* and *Life* came in to see me. They are getting an article for *Life* on your old man. Ain't it awful? *Time, Life, Saturday Even'Post, Click*—what can I do?" A few weeks later he noted that *Business Week* "has a big write-up on the committee . . . *Life* is getting out a special issue—ain't it awful?"[43]

In view of Truman's growing prominence and reputation, some Democratic power brokers began to think of him as a replacement for Vice President Henry A. Wallace in the 1944 presidential election. Senator Joseph Guffey (D-Pa.) broached the subject in the summer of 1943 by asking the senator for his opinion of Wallace. Truman replied, "Henry is the best Secretary of Agriculture that we ever did have." Guffey laughed at this indirect criticism of Wallace and asked if the Missourian would help the ticket if it became necessary by accepting the nomination for vice president in 1944. In a letter to Bess describing the conversation, Harry wrote: "I told him in words of one syllable that I would not—that I had only recently become a Senator and that I wanted to work at it for about ten years."[44]

Despite this reassurance, Bess still worried about the prospect that Harry might be named as President Roosevelt's running mate in 1944. Both she and her husband, aware of insider reports of the president's ill health and yet confident of his reelection, believed that the Democratic vice-presidential nominee would likely complete FDR's fourth term. Harry, in a letter to his daughter Mar-

42. *Time*, March 8, 1943, cover page, 3–15; Ferrell, ed., *Dear Bess*, 471; Truman to Brown Harris, March 13, 1943, Senatorial File, Harry S. Truman, Box 166, Truman Library; Truman to Luce, March 13, 1943, Senatorial File, Harry S. Truman, Box 166, Truman Library.

43. Ferrell, ed., *Dear Bess*, 492, 494.

44. Ibid., 495. Guffey, an ardent admirer of Wallace, in fact became a conduit of political information to the vice president and backed him for renomination. John Morton Blum, ed., *The Price of Vision: The Diary of Henry A. Wallace, 1942–1946* (Boston: Houghton Mifflin, 1973), 361, 363–64, 368–71.

garet written shortly before the opening of the Democratic National Convention, acknowledged the gathering momentum for his nomination and how he "hoped to dodge it. 1600 Pennsylvania is a nice address," he added, "but I'd rather not move in through the back door—or any other door at sixty." Margaret Truman, from her unique perspective as family member, intimate eyewitness, and biographer of her parents, revealed during their lifetime that her mother "bitterly opposed" the nomination. But she did not fully unravel Bess's opposition until after the death of her father and mother. Bess feared that press inquiry into the life and family of the vice-presidential candidate would redisclose and revive the greatest traumatic experience of her life: the death of her father by suicide in 1903.[45]

At the time of his passing, David W. Wallace's suicide had received a full account in local newspapers. The *Independence Examiner*, duly noting the special qualities of the handsome and likable man, graphically described how Wallace had fired a pistol into his head early in the morning in the upstairs bathroom while the family still slept.[46]

Life for Madge Gates Wallace and her four children, particularly eighteen-year-old Bess, would never be the same. Madge's parents, now aged but comfortably well-off, provided immediate comfort by opening their large Victorian home in Independence to the bereaved family; shortly after they provided them with the means for a year's stay in Colorado. The shattered widow and children benefited greatly from this generosity, but once back home in the Gates house, they withdrew psychically into the classic defense of suicide victims: a conspiracy of silence. This undeclared commitment to silence, especially bonded in the close emotional relationship of Bess and her mother, eventually extended to Harry after his marriage to Bess.[47]

45. Margaret Truman, *Bess W. Truman*, 223, 225; Margaret Truman, *Souvenir: Margaret Truman's Own Story*, as quoted in Robert H. Ferrell, *Choosing Truman: The Democratic Convention of 1944*, 115, note 47; Margaret Truman, *Bess W. Truman*, 227–28.

46. Margaret Truman, *Bess W. Truman*, 17–21.

47. Ibid., 19–21. The psychiatric profession has been slow in studying the impact of suicide upon the victim's survivors. Albert Cain's pioneering work, *Survivors of Suicide* (1972) was the first study that established the traumatic and long-lasting effect upon people who "survive" the suicide death of someone close to them. Cain's book and the "conspiracy of silence" of survivors is discussed in Edward J. Dunne, John L. McIntosh, and Karen Dunne-Maxim, eds., *Suicide and Its Aftermath* (New York: W.W. Norton, 1987). For the emotionally

In turn, Margaret's parents successfully shielded her from the circumstances surrounding her grandfather Wallace's death until after Truman's vice-presidential nomination. Only then did Margaret's aunt, Natalie Wallace, assuming that the press would dig up the story of David Wallace's suicide, break the family's silence by informing her niece how her grandfather had died. When Margaret asked her father to confirm the fact, Harry, firmly clutching his daughter's arm, gave her a stern admonition: "Don't you *ever* mention this to your mother." Then he angrily hurried off to upbraid his sister-in-law for her revelation.[48]

Margaret remained silent on her grandfather's suicide until she published her biography of Bess Wallace after the death of both parents.[49] With the benefit of knowing how this important personal dynamic bore on the lives of Bess and Harry and her mother, it is easier to understand the resistance the Missouri senator offered to efforts to make him the party's vice-presidential candidate.

In opposition, Robert Ferrell, whose book, *Choosing Truman: The Democratic Convention of 1944*, is the fullest account of the 1944 Democratic vice-presidential nomination, has found Margaret's psychological interpretation unconvincing and unsupported by explicit evidence prior to Truman's nomination. After weighing numerous factors influencing Harry and Bess in the politics of 1944, he emphasized the prenomination explanation Truman gave to his Kansas City friend, Tom Evans, for not wanting to be drawn into the spotlight by the vice-presidential nomination: the placement of Bess on his senate office payroll.[50]

According to Evans's oral history, Truman had summoned his friend to Chicago to help spread the word among the delegates to the Democratic National Convention that he did not want the nomination. Evans, puzzled why Truman, unlike other ardent seekers of the vice-presidential nomination, did not want the office, asked the senator to explain his position. Truman confided that he did not want to "drag . . . a lot of skeletons out of the closet."

Evans pressed on, asking Truman, "What are these skeletons?"

"Well," Truman replied, "the worst thing is that I've had the boss [Mrs. Truman] on the payroll in my Senate office and I'm not going

---

dependent relationship of Madge Wallace to her daughter Bess, see *Bess W. Truman*, 162 and Hamby, *Man of the People*, 37, 199.

48. Margaret Truman, *Bess W. Truman*, 233–34.

49. Ibid., 235.

50. Ferrell, *Choosing Truman*, 57–61.

to have her name drug over the front pages of the paper and over the radio."

Evans quickly dismissed Truman's concern by pointing out that he could name a dozen senators and forty or fifty congressmen who had their wives or relatives on the payroll. When he inquired about other "skeletons" in the family closet, Truman changed the subject by citing his lack of money for a campaign. Although Evans assured him that he and his friends could raise the money, their conversation ended with Truman still adamantly opposed to his nomination. All this changed, of course, when President Roosevelt, in effect, commanded him to be his running mate.[51]

As Truman had feared, the press revealed Bess's place on his office payroll a few days after his nomination. The disclosure, appearing July 24 in a Republican newspaper, the *New York Herald Tribune*, was later embellished to include tart-tongued Clare Boothe Luce's cutting reference to Mrs. Truman as "Overtime Bess." *Time* tagged the story to an otherwise charming account of the Trumans receiving the congratulations of three thousand well-wishers on the back lawn of their Independence home.[52]

In response to an inquiry by a reporter for the *St. Louis Globe-Democrat* on his nepotism, the senator freely discussed Bess's duties (she handled some correspondence, sometimes at the office, sometimes at home, and helped him with his speeches), her compensation, and the family's financial circumstances that had made it necessary. In Washington his staff released similar information. Except for Luce's snide remark about Bess, which registered permanently in Harry Truman's mind, the matter quickly blew over and did not have any further consequences during the 1944 campaign.[53]

51. Tom L. Evans oral history, by J. R. Fuchs, 330–38, Truman Library; Ferrell, *Choosing Truman*, 61–62.

52. Ferrell, *Choosing Truman*, 59; Norma Lee Browning, *Chicago Sunday Tribune*, January 5, 1947, 13, in folder 2, 1947–July 1949, PPF, Box 31, Truman Papers, Truman Library. Both Browning and Ralph Martin, biographer and author of *Henry and Clare: An Intimate Portrait of the Luces* (New York, G. P. Putnam's Sons, 1991) have written that Clare called Mrs. Truman "Overtime Bess," while Robert Ferrell and David McCullough cite its alternative, "Payroll Bess." Ferrell, *Choosing Truman*, 59; McCullough, *Truman*, 331; *Time*, August 7, 1944, 16–17.

53. *St. Louis Globe-Democrat*, undated clipping, Clippings Concerning Mrs. HST folder, Box 1, Mary Paxton Keeley Papers, Truman Library; Ferrell, *Choosing Truman*, 57–59, 114–15, notes 43 and 44. Robert Ferrell has revealed that the president's sister, Mary Jane Truman, also was on her brother's senate and vice-presidential office payroll, but this nepotism did not become known until years after the death of the principals involved.

Happily for the nominee, his wife, and Madge Wallace, the re-disclosure of David Wallace's suicide did not occur in 1944 or even during the remainder of their lives. Yet the fear of a second public airing of the Wallace tragedy surely remained like an ominous cloud, always threatening to shatter the psychic equilibrium fashioned by Bess, her mother, and Harry. Margaret's instinctive understanding of the situation kept her from ever raising the subject with her mother.[54]

Quite unexpectedly, the favorable news coverage of Senator Truman's chairmanship of the National Defense Investigating Committee that had contributed significantly to his selection as the Democratic vice-presidential candidate turned sour as he resigned from the committee in preparation for the fall campaign. The Associated Press disclosed on August 10 that Truman had tried to prevent the publication of an article that appeared under his name in a November 1942 issue of *American Magazine*. The article, written by a member of the magazine's staff from notes provided by Truman, indirectly criticized President Roosevelt by charging that leadership was lacking in the war effort: "Leadership is what we Americans are crying for. . . . All we ask is that we be intelligently and resolutely led. We owe it to ourselves that the President act promptly to halt the selfish fights for power, the endless bickering and dissension, which have so far blocked the complete utilization of our productive energies." When Truman read the article a few days before publication, he asked that it be withdrawn on the ground that it did not reflect his views. The magazine agreed only to state in the forthcoming issue that the senator's views had changed since the article was written. Truman sought an injunction to prevent distribution, but the apparent impracticality of keeping the issue from reaching the public forced him to withdraw the complaint.

The campaign disclosure of Truman's attempt to kill the article prompted him to put the best face on the effort. He explained that he had declined to accept credit for authorship and turned the magazine's check for $750 to a discretionary fund of the Defense Investigating Committee. On the campaign trail that fall, he frequently praised the administration's conduct of the war, boasting that "this is the most efficiently conducted war in history."[55]

54. McCullough, *Truman*, 331; Margaret Truman, *Bess W. Truman*, 235.
55. Margaret Truman, *Harry S. Truman*, 161–62; *New York Times*, August 10, 1944. *Time* reporter Edward Lockett, in a review of Truman's speeches and press conferences, pointed out that the claim of the most efficiently conducted

A second article by Truman that appeared in the August 1944 issue of *Collier's* advanced his belief that the armed forces should be unified after the war, citing differences between the army and navy commanders at Pearl Harbor as a contributing cause to the success of the Japanese surprise attack on December 7, 1941. Rear Admiral Husband E. Kimmel disputed Truman's assertion that he and his counterpart in the army, Major General Walter C. Short, were not on speaking terms before the Japanese struck. Truman in this instance defended the article fully, but the explosive nature of his piece compounded Republican presidential candidate Thomas E. Dewey's quandary over making Pearl Harbor a campaign issue. Dewey, aware that a wartime airing of the matter could reveal that American intelligence had broken Japan's diplomatic codes before Pearl Harbor and its military codes after the attack, wisely allowed the opportunity to pass.[56] Truman thus escaped embarrassment over the ill-timed publication of the *Collier's* article.

Truman targeted isolationists in Congress and in the news media with all the ardor one might expect of a Wilsonian internationalist. In a charge reminiscent of the "Senate Cabal" that had blocked President Woodrow Wilson's efforts for unrestricted American entry into the League of Nations, he accused a small group of isolationist Republican senators of blackmailing the American people into electing a candidate satisfactory to them. He demanded that Dewey cut his ties to isolationists, saying, "Let us hear Mr. Dewey repudiate Billie [William Randolph Hearst] and Bertie [Robert] McCormick, both of these case-hardened isolationists . . . and ardent supporters of Mr. Dewey."[57]

The Hearst and McCormick-Patterson newspapers put Truman on the defensive during the closing days of the campaign with the charge that he had joined the Ku Klux Klan in 1922. The Klan, drawing upon anti-Negro, anti-Catholic, and anti-Jewish sentiment that flourished in the early twenties, had a sizable membership among old-stock Protestant Americans in both the cities and countryside of

---

war in history was practically the slogan of the campaign. Lockett to Eleanor Welch, October 22, 1944, Newsstories Filed *Time* folder, Box 1, Edward B. Lockett Papers, Truman Library.

56. Harry S. Truman, "Our Armed Forces Must Be Unified," *Collier's*, August 26, 1944, 16ff; *Washington Post*, August 22, 1944, Clipping File, Box 5, Democratic National Committee Records, Truman Library; Richard Norton Smith, *Thomas E. Dewey and His Times*, 425–30.

57. *Philadelphia Record*, October 24, 1944, Clipping File, Box 5, Democratic National Committee Records, Truman Library.

the Midwest and Far West. The invisible empire—its self-conferred name that exaggerated its strength—had sufficient following in Jackson County for political influence, prompting some politicians to join the order to curry favor among its membership. The Hearst press, with the assistance of a political science professor at the University of Kansas City, took the lead in securing and publishing affidavits from disaffected friends and acquaintances of Truman that he had indeed joined the Klan. Truman quickly denounced the allegation, saying, "What's the use of denying lies cooked up by Hearst and McCormick? It's just another red herring." (Later, during his presidency Truman used the same phrase to describe the tactics of the opponents of his liberal program that brought forward charges of communism in government.) Subsequent follow-up on the charge of Truman's membership in the Klan brought both retractions and reaffirmation of the original charge and new testimony from friends that Harry had never joined the hooded order. Apparently Truman had paid dues for membership in the Klan but stopped short of being initiated when he refused to promise not to hire Catholics if elected.[58]

The allegation did not hurt him in the South in 1944, where many whites were alarmed at the growing unrest and militancy of blacks during World War II. In the North, the charge gave Truman an opportunity to affirm his belief in political and economic opportunity for all Americans. The Democratic National Committee reinforced this stance by recounting "Truman's good fight for equal rights and opportunities for all; he has consistently opposed everything the Klan and the forces of intolerance represent."[59]

Truman's well-known relations with the Pendergast machine and the possibility that he might become president in the event Roosevelt should gain reelection and die during his fourth term was boldly addressed by Truman's nemesis, the *Chicago Tribune*. In its editorial of October 9, Colonel Robert McCormick's newspaper addressed the issue head-on: "Mr. Truman is running for the Vice Presidency, but his principal, Mr. Roosevelt, is not a well man and his pictures show it. . . . Mr. Truman's value is confined to his performance in his assigned role as lookout man for the city

58. Margaret Truman, *Harry S. Truman*, 187–88; McCullough, *Truman*, 164–65.

59. "The Lie about Senator Harry S. Truman," undated, Ku Klux Klan folder, Box 5, Democratic National Committee Records, Truman Library.

gangs if they ever get to pull their planned heist of the national government."[60]

Truman tried to handle questions about his qualifications for succeeding FDR in that eventuality by either brushing the question aside or by first observing that reporters were forcing him to reply: "I can only say this—you force me to make this statement. I am a modest man and I don't like to talk about myself—I was nominated by the Senate press gallery as the man who knew more about the war effort than anyone else except the president."[61]

The *Tribune* kept the matter alive, heading its editorial of late October "A Vote for FDR may be a Vote for Truman." The editorial asserted that Truman was

> the consciously forgotten man of the fourth term campaign. . . . The bosses are making their campaign on the indispensable man theory because they can't recognize the fatal weaknesses of his running mate. Mr. Truman can't make votes for himself or for anybody else and he would actively lose enormous numbers of votes if the city gangs failed to distract the attention of the electorate from the ominous fact that the Throttlebottom may well wind up in the White House.

In response to Democratic National Chairman Robert E. Hannegan's charge of a whispering campaign regarding Roosevelt's health, the *Tribune* replied: "There is no need to whisper. That is one of the principal issues of the campaign and cannot be evaded by false appeals to delicacy." The editorial concluded with a question: "Do the decent citizens want to do business with Truman?"[62]

A majority of the voters in the November election apparently dismissed the speculations over Roosevelt's declining health and Truman's ties to the Pendergast machine—now headed by Jim Pendergast, nephew of the deposed boss—by giving the Democratic team a substantial margin of victory. During the next several weeks the vice president–elect basked in the glow of the congratulations of well-wishers and favorable news comments that continued until the inaugural and for a few days thereafter.[63]

60. Editorial, *Chicago Tribune*, October 9, 1944, Clipping File, Box 5, Democratic National Committee Records, Truman Library.

61. Edward Lockett to Eleanor Welch, October 22, 1944, Newsstories Filed *Time* folder, Box 1, Lockett Papers, Truman Library.

62. Editorial, *Chicago Tribune*, October 28, 1944, Clipping File, Box 5, Democratic National Committee Records, Truman Library.

63. See correspondence and clippings in the senatorial and vice-presidential file, Truman Papers, Truman Library. For the succession of James Pendergast

Then on January 27, a week after Truman had become vice president, Tom Pendergast died. His death brought the longtime association and friendship of the two men back into view for another round of censure after Truman expressed his sorrow over his friend's passing and flew to Kansas City for the funeral mass. The *Chicago Tribune* headlined its account "Truman Bows at Bier of 'Big Tom,' His Boss" and made their connection more explicit in its description of Pendergast as an "ex-convict and one-time saloon bouncer who raised [Truman] politically from an unsuccessful haberdasher to his present pinnacle."[64]

Political loyalty and friendship of a different nature prevailed in Truman's maneuvering in behalf of former Vice President Wallace's nomination as secretary of commerce. As presiding officer of the Senate, the new vice president used his parliamentary skills to prevent a premature vote on Wallace's nomination until a compromise could be made with Southern Democrats to trim the commerce department of its power over the huge lending policies of the Reconstruction Finance Corporation. With Wallace's confirmation on March 1, Truman avoided unfavorable press treatment by liberal newspapers that would have resulted if the progressive Democrat had been rejected for the cabinet post.[65]

In Washington social affairs, Truman handled the news media with an uneven hand. What had appeared to be a routine visit to the National Press Club's Servicemen's Canteen on February 10, 1945, turned into a publicity opportunity for another guest that day, glamorous Hollywood star Lauren Bacall. After Truman had been coaxed into playing the piano, Bacall's press agent maneuvered her for a photograph with the vice president. But instead of assuming a formal and dignified pose, Bacall climbed atop the piano, draped her shapely legs over the side, and fixed an alluring gaze on Truman. As he beamed back at Bacall like a moonstruck schoolboy, an Associated Press photographer snapped the pose and the wire service transmitted the photo to its subscribers around the nation.

---

to his uncle's place at the head of a greatly weakened Kansas City machine, see Dorsett, *The Pendergast Machine,* 136–37.

64. *Chicago Tribune,* January 30, 1945; *Post-Dispatch* reporter McCulloch wrote that Truman had flown from Washington "to attend the funeral rites of the man who elevated him from an obscure county judgeship to the United States Senate." *St. Louis Post-Dispatch,* January 29, 1945; Steinberg, *The Man from Missouri,* 229.

65. Steinberg, *The Man from Missouri; New York Times,* February 12, March 2, 1945.

Margaret Truman later recalled Bess's irritation with Harry over the photograph, and Edward McKim, Truman's World War I buddy, wrote to caution Truman against being taken advantage of by others and the news media. "Remember," McKim told Truman, "you are the Vice President of the United States and that may not be all."[66]

The Trumans, as though to dispel any thoughts about the awesome responsibilities that might await them, immersed themselves in Washington social life. They received a rude reception in newspapers and magazines, however, when they were called "social butterflies" by *The Progressive* and treated as Missouri rubes out of place in Washington high society in an article written by Duke Shoop, a reporter for the *Kansas City Star*. Shoop's condescending account of the Trumans' presence as guests of honor at a party hosted by the capital's grand dame, Evalyn Walsh McLean, prompted Mary Paxton Keeley, their friend from high school days, to advise the use of a secretary to put distance between themselves and the press. In reply to Paxton, Bess called Shoop a "skunk" for his demeaning newspaper article.[67]

Yet nothing that the Trumans had experienced thus far as a political family in the public's eye could prepare them for the unrelenting attention that the news media would pay to them as the nation's first family. Harry, called to the White House to receive the fateful news of President Roosevelt's death in the late afternoon of April 12, 1945, in turn summoned Bess and Margaret for the solemn swearing-in ceremony in the Cabinet Room. There, in the presence of several members of the Roosevelt cabinet and the Chief Justice of the United States, the new president, the first lady, and their daughter began their life "in the goldfish bowl."[68]

With this final step in his rise to the presidency, Truman now entered into the historic relationship between the nation's chief

---

66. McCullough, *Truman*, 336–37; the widely circulated Associated Press photo was republished in the Truman Library Institute newsletter, *Whistle Stop* 20, no. 3 (1992): 5; Margaret Truman, *Harry S. Truman*, 244–45; McKim to Truman, February 23, 1945, McKim folder, Box 81, Senatorial File, Truman Papers, Truman Library.

67. Quoted in Alonzo L. Hamby, *Beyond the New Deal: Harry S. Truman and American Liberalism*, 50; *Kansas City Star*, February 18, 1945; Margaret Truman, *Bess W. Truman*, 244; Bess Truman to Mary Paxton Keeley, c. February 27, 1945, Letters Mrs. HST September 1944–February 1963 folder, Box 1, Mary Paxton Keeley Papers, Truman Library. Bess dated her letters with nothing more than the day of the week. Fortunately, the recipient of her letters often filed the correspondence with the postdated envelope to permit approximate dating.

68. Margaret Truman, *Harry S. Truman*, 208–12, 303.

executive and the press. The initial assessment of the Missourian and the prospect of his presidency drew many commentators, but none as interesting and as personal as the widely circulated account written by Charles Ross.

Offering "a purely personal impression of . . . the Independence, Missouri, boy whom a strange and whimsical fate has made President," Ross recounted Truman's political career: "The rise of Harry S. Truman to the Presidency is one of the amazing phenomena in American political history. Luck—or call it fate—time and again intervened to send him down the right road when another road would have stopped him at a dead end." Ross opined that an inferiority complex had once kept Truman from realizing his own worth and ability, but he missed the earnest ambition and solid achievements that kept the Missourian's name in the news and on the minds of the power brokers in the Democratic party. He also left unnoted his earlier misjudgment of the character of the man who was then seeking a seat in the U.S. Senate. Now he found in Truman's character the key to his presidency: "He is impeccably honest. He takes advice, but he can be stubborn when he makes up his mind. . . . He gets along with people. Perhaps he is too amiable; that remains to be seen."

Ross asked rhetorically if Truman would measure up: "Harry Truman has a lot of stuff—more stuff, I think, than he has generally been credited with. He has been called the average American, but he is better than average. He is no nonentity and no Harding. He may not have the makings of a great President, but he certainly has the making of a good President."[69]

Characteristically, Truman, recognizing his need for a trusted spokesman, selected his boyhood friend to become his press secretary. Ross could have asked to be excused on the grounds of ill health. He suffered from arthritis that filled his days with pain, and coronary disease sapped his energy and predestined him for a fatal heart attack more than two years before the end of the Truman presidency. But his sense of duty and a strong belief in his own capabilities, as well as his faith in Truman, compelled him to join the administration.[70] Their friendship, bent but not broken during Truman's 1934 senatorial campaign and throughout most of his first term in the Senate, had been sustained by the values of their

69. Farrar, *Reluctant Servant*, 152–54.
70. Ibid., 206–7.

formative years and now linked them in the great task of a new presidency.

It remained for others, especially the news media and the American public, to come to know Harry Truman and to find in him and his administration what pleased or displeased them. The press, as the prime source of information and interpreter of Truman and his administration, would be slow in discovering the qualities that made Truman a good man and slower still in discerning the greatness of his presidency.

2

Programs, Images, and the
Upset Election of 1948

TRUMAN'S SUDDEN ACCESSION to the presidency immediately set in motion the historic dynamics between the new chief executive and the fourth estate. He enjoyed a honeymoon with the press for the duration of the war, but the relationship soured soon after he set his postwar course. Press criticism mounted sharply during the fall of 1945 and into the spring of 1946 as the administration struggled to find solutions to labor-management strife, and surged again in the fall when Secretary of Commerce Wallace precipitated a leadership crisis by opposing the president's foreign policy. Truman regained the confidence of the public and the press after he exerted strong leadership in both domestic and foreign affairs, but his popularity and press support eroded sharply with the approach of the election of 1948. Undaunted by political foes, the opposition press, and pollsters who consigned him to defeat and oblivion, Truman took his campaign directly to the people. His victory produced the greatest miscalling of a presidential election in journalistic history.

The immediate background for Truman's exercise of presidential power rested upon the bold and vigorous leadership of Franklin D. Roosevelt in combating the economic crisis of the Great Depression of the 1930s and the national security crisis of World War II. Although Truman solemnly pledged that he would carry out President Roosevelt's policies, it remained to be seen if he would revive the prewar New Deal and embark upon an internationalist course in the postwar era.[1]

The press—chiefly newspapers and nationally circulated news-magazines and influential opinion periodicals—was not a monolith; it represented the full spectrum of political and economic interests and views. Over the past decade, however, a large majority of the nation's newspapers had been predominantly anti-Roosevelt and anti–New Deal, demonstrating these partisan views in the presidential elections of 1936, 1940, and 1944. Many newspapers made no pretext of objectivity. In 1936, for example, the anti-Roosevelt *Chicago Tribune* featured a countdown to the November election with a page-one reminder to voters of the number of days remaining "to save your country."[2]

Truman's animus toward the antiadministration press drew heavily upon its opposition to Wilsonian internationalism and Roosevelt's New Deal liberalism. From his days as a schoolboy onward, Truman had idealized Tennyson's dream of a "Parliament of Man, the Federation of the World" and championed its modern version in the League of Nations and the league's successor, the United Nations Organization. Ideologically, his democracy drew upon the egalitarian, individualistic, and economic-opportunity precepts of Jefferson and Jackson; the populist revision of late-nineteenth-century Democracy by William Jennings Bryan, updated soon after by the Midwestern brand of insurgent progressivism; and finally, the liberalism of Roosevelt's New Deal and his own Fair Deal. His blended democracy, which arrayed him against great concentrations of power—Wall Street and big labor unions, too—applied especially to publishing empires and thus assured that, as president, he would be drawn into conflict with the barons of the press.[3]

---

1. *Public Papers of the Presidents*, 1945, 2–4; hereafter cited as *Public Papers*. Specifically, Truman committed his administration to the military goal of unconditional surrender of the Axis powers, American membership in the United Nations, and the ideals of FDR.

2. Graham J. White, *FDR and the Press*, 27–46; White shows that while a definite majority of the press with the largest circulation in the nation was antiadministration, FDR's frequently asserted claim from 1936 onward that 85 percent of the press opposed his presidency is exaggerated. Ibid., 69–91; in 1932 and at the outset of his administration, FDR had the enthusiastic support of Roy Howard, Cissy [Eleanor] Patterson, and William Randolph Hearst. By 1936 Hearst and other conservative publishers opposed the president and New Deal policies. Betty Houchin Winfield, *FDR and the News Media*, 11, 23, 42, 127–30.

3. See portions of Alfred Lord Tennyson's "Locksley Hall," in McCullough, *Truman*, 64–65; Hamby, *Man of the People*, 213–17, 639. In 1946 Truman wrote

William Randolph Hearst commanded a leading position among American newspaper publishers during the first half of the twentieth century through his extensive and influential news empire. During the Truman years the Hearst daily newspapers in a dozen big cities captured 9.1 percent of the readership of the entire country; Sunday editions drew 16.1 percent of the total. Hearst's wire and news agencies International News Service and Universal News Service, the major syndicator King Features, and International News Photos extended the publisher's reach from his own press into other subscribing newspapers around the country. Thirteen magazines, eight radio stations, and two motion picture companies rounded out his media empire.[4]

The personal views of Hearst, as visible on the front page as in the editorial section of his daily newspapers, brought great power to him—corrupting, pernicious power, many believed. The Hearst press, journalism historian James L. Baughman has written, combined "provincialism and prejudice," served as forums of the publisher's "personal opinions and eccentricities," and made Hearst "the most hated figure in American journalism." Although the Hearst newspapers during Truman's presidency muted somewhat the blatant antiadministration bias they had accorded FDR, their editorials continued to hammer away at the foreign and domestic policies of Roosevelt's successor during the postwar era. Hearst and his editors also exhibited less personal enmity toward Truman than that accorded FDR, while Truman, decidedly more Victorian than Roosevelt, was repulsed by the publisher's open extramarital relationship with the movie actress Marion Davies. Hearst, he believed, was an immoral man and his press a sinister force in American life.[5]

Colonel Robert McCormick and the McCormick-Patterson press, second to the Hearst publishing empire in national circulation, outdid the larger Hearst news organization in their daily vilification of Truman and his administration. McCormick's flagship newspaper,

---

his mother and sister, "Big money has too much power and so have big unions—both are riding to a fall because I like neither." Quoted in Ferrell, *Harry S. Truman: A Life,* 230.

4. Michael Emery and Edwin Emery, *The Press and America: An Interpretive History of the Mass Media,* 305; Winfield, *FDR and the News Media,* 21.

5. James L. Baughman, *The Republic of Mass Culture: Journalism, Filmmaking, and Broadcasting in America since 1941,* 12. "The Hearst papers reflect the morals and ethics of William Randolph Hearst. He has no morals and no ethics." Quoted in Hamby, *Man of the People,* 485. For the publisher's long affair with Miss Davies, see W. A. Swanberg, *Citizen Hearst: A Biography of William Randolph Hearst* (New York: Scribner's, 1961).

the *Chicago Tribune,* thereby earned Truman's contempt implicitly as the "worst newspaper in the nation." Although the president exaggerated the national outreach of the *Tribune,* its regional influence was indisputable. The newspaper, proclaiming itself as the "World's Greatest Newspaper," reached a postwar high in circulation of more than one million, which made it the largest standard-sized American newspaper; its readership extended to a five-state area McCormick called "Chicagoland." The publisher's influence increased after he assumed control of the *New York Daily News* in 1946. His cousin, Eleanor Medill Patterson, brought the family's conservative and isolationist views to newspaper readers in the nation's capital through her ownership of the *Washington Times-Herald.* Upon Patterson's death in 1948, ownership and control of her newspaper passed to Colonel McCormick. The egocentric colonel (McCormick had attained the rank as a national guard officer in France during World War I) had a reputation, deserved or not, as a martinet, and this, too, when added to the publisher's strident nationalistic and conservative views, may have helped fuel Truman's deep-seated animosity toward him.[6]

The Scripps-Howard press, published in the East, the Midwest, and the Far West, constituted the country's third-largest newspaper alliance. Roy Howard alone of the "Big Three" publishers enjoyed an amiable relationship with Truman, but at times he, too, incurred Truman's displeasure.[7]

Initially the conservative press joined with the public in strong support for Truman's paramount objective of bringing the war to a successful end. Merrill J. Meigs, Chicago-based executive of the Hearst Corporation, prepared the way for a personal interview with Truman by sending him editorials from his newspapers lauding the

---

6. The judgment of the *Chicago Tribune* as the nation's worst newspaper is deducted from Truman's comments in 1952 wherein he identified the *Spokane-Review* as the "second worst paper in the United States" and his frequent denunciation of the *Tribune. Public Papers,* 1952–1953, 667. Truman once claimed, in a letter to Senator Burton K. Wheeler of Montana, that the newspapers of that far western state were influenced by the *Chicago Tribune.* Herbert Lee Williams, *The Newspaperman's President: Harry S. Truman,* 19. Emery and Emery, *The Press and America,* 305–11; Joseph Gies, *The Colonel of Chicago,* 232, 237, 245. Gies conceded his subject's "artless egotism" but rejected affixing to him the labels of bully and braggart. The *Tribune's* reporters understood that their stories should not contradict the views of McCormick. Baughman, *The Republic of Mass Culture,* 12.

7. Emery and Emery, *The Press and America,* 305–11; Williams, *The Newspaperman's President,* 109, 170–71.

president. Hearst newspapers also pledged to stimulate interest in the war against Japan lest armament production lag after victory in Europe. Truman, however, rejected Meig's efforts to secure a personal appointment for William Randolph Hearst, Jr., publisher of the *New York Journal-American* and, after the death of his father in 1951, his successor as head of the Hearst Corporation; he refused to see the old publisher's son until the end of the war and after public announcement of his domestic plans.[8]

The *Chicago Tribune,* like the Hearst newspapers, acknowledged that the new president needed the cooperation of the press and the American people for the successful conclusion of the war and the transition to peace. In its lead editorial on the first day of the new administration, the *Tribune* found it reassuring that Truman's former colleagues in the Senate placed "a high value on his intellect, his good sense, his industry, and his acquaintance with public affairs" and that the senators judged his qualities "fully equal to his responsibilities." Colonel McCormick instructed his Washington political correspondent, Walter Trohan, to give Truman every chance to carry on his difficult burden of bringing the war to a triumphant end.[9]

Roy Howard, chief of the Scripps-Howard publishing chain, hailed the end of the Roosevelt era as his newspaper alliance's opportunity to revise its archconservative reputation and to develop a new relationship with Truman. Howard conceded that the Scripps newspapers deserved their conservative, antiadministration reputation because of editorials "unavoidably too definitely and too continuously *agin*" FDR. "With Truman," Howard observed, "we can start . . . from scratch in our support of him so long as he continues to merit that support." Buoyed by his interview with Truman a few weeks into the new administration, Howard confided to an editor that it had "been a long time since I had run into any man who seemed more fundamentally honest, forthright, and free from political blather."[10]

8. Meigs to Truman, April 20, 1945, OF 757, Truman Papers, Truman Library; John W. McCormack to Matthew J. Connelly, April 21, 1945; Memo, Eben A. Ayers to J. Leonard Reinsch, April 14, 1945, and Reinsch's undated penciled notation that the president's calendar was too full to see Hearst; Meigs to Connelly, September 14, 1945.

9. Lloyd Wendt, *Chicago Tribune: The Rise of a Great American Newspaper,* 667–68; Walter Trohan, *Political Animals: Memoirs of a Sentimental Cynic,* 221.

10. Howard to Ludwell Denny, May 25, 1945, *Washington Daily News* folder, 1945 City File, Container 211, Roy B. Howard Papers, Manuscript Division, Library of Congress. The italics and the spelling are Howard's.

Shortly after the surrender of Nazi Germany in early May 1945, Truman took stock of the favorable treatment accorded him by newspapers. "The press has said so many nice things about me," he wrote his cousin, "I don't know how to operate. When they are jumping on me I know what to do." Truman predicted that the situation would only last a short time. "As soon as the political lines are properly drawn," he explained, "they will commence with their usual knocks, but I can take it."[11]

The honeymoon between Truman and the conservative press ended on September 6, 1945, four days after formal ceremonies in Tokyo Bay brought World War II to a close. That day Truman unveiled an ambitious twenty-one point plan of liberal legislative goals. A White House adviser had cautioned the president against presenting so many objectives at one time, but Truman had given careful thought to both the nature and timing of his postwar program. The major purpose, he later asserted, had been to inform the Hearsts and the McCormicks that he rejected the conservative course they desired.[12] Elaboration of his program during the war would have impaired the unity necessary for victory; delay of the announcement of his liberal agenda once peace was achieved invited the press to define or circumscribe the president's goals. As Truman had predicted, the announcement of a liberal course for his administration marked the end of his harmonious relationship with the newspapers. Thereafter he expected, and received, a torrent of criticism of his handling of labor and management disputes, price controls, inflation, and demobilization in general.

The domestic situation confronting the nation in the fall of 1945 and into the spring of 1946 proved to be especially challenging and vexatious for Truman. Conservative business interests, notably the National Association of Manufacturers and the United States Chamber of Commerce, hoped to rein in the power of organized labor that had flourished since passage of the Wagner National Labor Relations Act of 1935. According to Senator George Aiken, liberal Republican from Vermont, the NAM had placed two million dollars of antiunion advertising in newspapers in the month of March 1946. By 1947, Aiken charged, the NAM had spent millions of dollars

11. Truman to Mrs. Robert (Mary) Romine, May 12, 1945, Box 330, PSF, Truman Papers, Truman Library.
12. Harry S. Truman, *Memoirs of Harry S. Truman*, vol. 1, *Year of Decisions*, 481–84; Harold D. Smith to Samuel Rosenman, August 31, 1945, Message to Congress September 6, 1945 folder, Box 2, Samuel Rosenman Papers, Truman Library; *Public Papers*, 1948, 934–35.

for antiunion propaganda designed to destroy the Wagner Act. The president later expressed his belief that a "little group of politicians" and "reactionary employers" had designed a campaign "to smash, or at least to cripple, our trade union movement in a period of postwar reaction."[13]

Union labor, freed from its no-strike pledges of wartime, went on the offensive in the first months of peace. When management balked at union demands for improved benefits, numerous strikes began shortly after V-J day and continued into the spring of 1946. As the picket lines went up, unions also relied upon an educational campaign to inform the public of their side of a dispute. Corporate financial statements, union leaders maintained, demonstrated management's ability to pay higher wages.[14]

But labor lost the public relations battle. As the historian R. Alton Lee has explained, "To a public eager to shake off wartime restrictions and responsibilities," the strikes "irritated public nerves and helped to create increasing hostility toward labor. Labor's public relations were further damaged by constant reiteration of the press that wage increases were responsible for high prices and inflation."[15] Secretary of Labor Lewis Schwellenbach countered that corporate profits contributed importantly to inflation as well as wage raises. The public had a different perception, he explained, because "representatives of business, in the press and magazines, have dinned into the ears of the American people the claim that advances in prices were exclusively caused by advances in wages."

In the spring of 1946 the Truman administration's handling of the crises in coal mining and railroad transportation came to a head. The United Mine Workers of John L. Lewis and the railroad brotherhoods, particularly the locomotive engineers led by Alvanley Johnston and the firemen's union of Alexander F. Whitney, had resisted all compromise efforts. The importance of coal and rail transportation to the economy and the well-being of the general public clashed with the unions' right to strike for benefits, thus making the president's task of satisfying all parties a difficult balancing act.[16]

Growing public dissatisfaction with the administration's lack of success in mediating labor-management strife and mounting

13. R. Alton Lee, *Truman and Taft-Hartley: A Question of Mandate,* 10–11; Truman to William Green, September 13, 1952, as quoted in Lee, 15.
14. Ibid., 12–17.
15. Ibid., 17–18.
16. Ibid., 33–37.

inflation registered itself in polls showing Truman's popularity had peaked at an approval rate of 87 percent immediately after V-J Day and moved downward to a low of 32 percent in the pre-strike-settlement days in the spring of 1946.[17]

The public wanted strong presidential action, and Truman responded to the point of rashness. He ordered seizure of both the mines and the railroads and went before Congress to request legislation to draft striking miners and trainmen into the army to end the economic paralysis caused by the strikes. Unknown to the president, the railroad brotherhoods had agreed to settle their strike minutes before he entered the chamber of the House of Representatives for his nationally broadcast address. When the secretary of the senate handed Truman a note informing him of the news, he paused to announce that the strike had been settled, and then returned to his draconian proposal. A few days later John L. Lewis concluded an agreement with the government to return the miners to the pits and ultimately settled the coal strike.[18]

Although Truman's action greatly angered union labor and kept him out of its good graces until Congress incurred labor's wrath with passage—over Truman's veto—of the Taft-Hartley Act of 1947, the press, particularly conservative newspapers, praised him for ending the paralyzing strikes.[19] (A much different press reaction awaited Truman when he seized strike-bound steel mills during the Korean War.)

Truman's leadership in foreign affairs during the early postwar period, like his uneven efforts in handling labor-management strife, drew the fire of conservative and liberal critics alike. Press criticism had been ignited in the fall of 1946 when Commerce Secretary Wallace publicly challenged the administration's hard-line policy vis-a-vis the Soviet Union. The well-publicized affair, discussed later, led to Truman's dismissal of Wallace and moved his egocentric Secretary of State, James F. Byrnes, closer to his eventual resignation.[20]

Truman's standing with the press rebounded strongly in the spring of 1947 with firm direction of foreign policy by the White House and a creative state department. Secretary of State George C. Marshall

17. "The Gallup Poll," *Washington Post,* July 11, 1947.
18. Lee, *Truman and Taft-Hartley,* 35–37.
19. Ibid., 37–39, 146–54.
20. The Wallace episode is covered in chapter 4; Truman's difficulties with Byrnes are discussed in chapter 10. See also Hamby, *Beyond the New Deal,* 127–34 and Cabell Phillips, *The Truman Presidency: The History of a Triumphant Succession,* 148–55.

and a policy planning staff headed by George Kennan gave form, respectively, to the administration's programs for the economic reconstruction of war-devastated Western Europe and the containment of Soviet communism. Under Truman's leadership these policies won bipartisan support in Congress and much favorable review in the press.[21]

Truman generously acknowledged the role of newspapers in explaining and supporting his bold foreign policy initiatives. His good feelings even extended to publishers; his address to the annual convention of the American Newspaper Publishers Association and the Associated Press in April 1947 marked the first presidential visit to the publishers' group since Herbert Hoover spoke to the ANPA-AP in 1929.[22] While Truman lauded the publishers for the support given to his foreign policies, he viewed their support in the context of a free press responsible to the American public:

> Freedom, in the American tradition, is always coupled with service. The American press—a free press—must never forget its obligation to the American people. Its treatment of the recent war and its discussion of our present foreign policy are examples of the finest effort of a free, responsible press. Without abandoning constructive criticism, the press, with rare exceptions, has carried the facts fully and fairly to the American people, so that they could be the judge.

He struck the same note in his annual spring meeting at the White House with the American Society of Newspaper Editors and in the May gathering of Gridiron Club journalists.[23]

Truman's effective leadership won bipartisan support for his foreign policies and ended the crippling coal and railroad strikes, giving a generous boost to his public rating and self-esteem. The journalist Frank Gervasi took note of these changes in his article for *Collier's* in May 1947. Truman might claim that he was "the same person I always was," Gervasi wrote, "but in the eyes of ordinary

21. The *Chicago Tribune* was the major exception to newspaper support for Truman's foreign policy initiatives of 1947. The newspaper labeled the Republican support for these policies as "New Deal Republicanism" and branded the president's speech requesting aid for Greece and Turkey as a "declaration of World War III." See its editorials for March 1947.

22. *Editor and Publisher* (April 19, 1947): 9; (April 24, 1947): 10.

23. *Public Papers*, 1947, 211, 207–10; Williams, *A Newspaperman's President*, 25.

people whose mental image of the President is assembled from news stories, editorials and cartoons, he isn't. He has changed." Gervasi added: "The headlines and editorials of the past few months have praised a Truman who had the political courage to lambaste John L. Lewis, the sagacity to pick men like George Marshall for top government jobs and the farsightedness to advocate American and economic intervention where ever dollars and diplomacy can prevent the birth abroad of . . . totalitarian police states." Because of this new image, Gervasi concluded, "the people have looked more fondly on his chances for 1948."[24]

Gervasi had astutely captured the favorable situation that Truman enjoyed in the spring of 1947, but he hardly could have foreseen the nature and extent of the negative campaigning undertaken by the president's political opponents and by the press with the approach of the presidential election of 1948. Both Republicans and the antiadministration press geared for action to ensure that sixteen years of Democratic administrations would end in January 1949.

The Republican party leadership, keying on the congressional elections of 1946 as the first step to winning back the White House in 1948, portrayed Truman as an inept president. GOP campaign slogans such as "To err is Truman" and "Had Enough?" received prominent attention in the press. New slogans coined in 1948— "It's Time for a Change," and "I'm Just Mild About Harry," updated and reinforced the Republican attack.[25]

Liberal Democratic disenchantment with Truman paralleled the negative attacks of Republicans and found expression in journals such as *New Republic* and the *Nation*. These liberal journals, highly partial to Henry Wallace, attacked Truman from the left as sharply as the conservative press on the right. The *New Republic*, in fact, signed on Wallace as an editor and served, for all practical purposes, as his campaign organ after he became the presidential candidate of the Progressive Party of America. Other disenchanted liberals cast eyes toward General Dwight D. Eisenhower, Associate Justice

24. Frank Gervasi, "The President Grows Up," *Collier's* (May 4, 1947): 11, 83–85, 87.

25. Lee, *Truman and Taft-Hartley*, 47–48; in addition to the updated slogans for 1948, Truman was characterized as a "little man" and a "gone goose." Clare Boothe Luce used both terms in her address to the Republican National Convention and *Time* employed the belittling and dismissing terms frequently. See *Time* for its political coverage from June through November 1948.

William O. Douglas, and Senator Claude Pepper (D-Fla.) as potential Democratic presidential candidates.[26]

Ironically, while these liberals considered Truman's leadership inept and his domestic and foreign policies a betrayal of Franklin Roosevelt's legacy, southern white Democrats grew angry over the liberal direction of the administration. Truman's commitment to a comprehensive civil rights program for blacks and other minorities, unveiled in his February 2, 1948, message to Congress, drove southern whites into opposition. Within the month southern Democratic governors took the first steps to form a states' rights bloc intent upon defeating the Truman-led civil rights movement.[27]

In face of the apparent odds against a Truman victory in 1948, the president's White House advisers set upon a brilliant course to counter the negative assessments of the press and the political opposition. Presidential counsel Clark Clifford, drawing upon an astute memorandum drafted by Democratic strategist James H. Rowe, Jr., specifically addressed the "portrait of the president" and the need to "create in the public mind a vote-getting picture of President Truman." The memorandum noted that the current image of the president as a "sincere, courageous and able man" was a picture the American people liked.[28]

The Clifford-Rowe memorandum acknowledged the public's deeply felt belief that their chief executive must be the president of all the people; for that reason Truman could not become politically active as the nominee and leader of his party until after the party's convention in July. But to satisfy the public's "tremendous interest in its Chief Executive," the Democratic strategists suggested that candidate Truman resort to subterfuge in two principal ways. First, Truman was encouraged to invite nonpolitical celebrities to the White House for lunch or a meeting as a way of keeping the president in the news while fostering good relations with various constituencies. Secondly, the strategists urged Truman to "resort to the kind

26. Hamby, *Beyond the New Deal*, 135, 195–97; see, for example, "Truman as Leader," *New Republic* (May 17, 1948): 13–26; Irwin Ross, *The Loneliest Campaign: The Truman Victory of 1948*, 112–16, 141–62.

27. Ross, *The Loneliest Campaign*, 61–65.

28. Rowe's original document is appended to his oral history interview by Jerry N. Hess, Truman Library. Clifford left Rowe out of the picture when he presented the revised memorandum to Truman because of the president's antipathy to Rowe's law partner, Tommy Corcoran. Clark M. Clifford, with Richard Holbrooke, *Counsel to the President: A Memoir*, 189–94.

of trip which Roosevelt made famous in the 1940 campaign—the "inspection tour." "No matter how much the opposition and the press pointed out the political overtones of those trips," the memo writers concluded, "the people paid little attention because what they saw was the Head of State performing his duties."[29]

Truman rejected the idea of inviting celebrities to the White House as too contrived and unsuited to his personality and convictions. The suggestion of a "nonpolitical" train trip, however, perfectly suited his populist sentiments for carrying his program directly to the people, with and without interpretation by the news media, and he made the idea of a train tour his own when he wrote his memoirs years later.[30]

Announcement by the White House Press Office that Truman had accepted an invitation to deliver the June commencement address at the University of California at Berkeley and that he would make numerous stops en route on a train trip of several days' duration was greeted for what it was: a highly political trip designed to ensure Truman's nomination and to benefit his election in November. While the White House insisted that the western tour was "nonpolitical" because Truman would not speak under political auspices and would travel without state and national party officials, Democratic leaders conceded that the trip was designed to "sell" the president. Carroll Reece, chairman of the Republican National Committee, quipped that the trip was about as "nonpolitical as the Pendergast machine."[31]

The press entourage for the trip broke all records for travel with a presidential party. Fifty-eight reporters for newspapers and magazines, six radio correspondents, four newsreel cameramen, four television reporters, four still photographers, and one cartoonist— David Low of the *London Evening Standard*, working on special assignment for *Life*—signed up for the tour at a cost of approximately one thousand dollars per person. The press coverage, an editorial in the *New York Herald Tribune* noted, made it clear that President Truman "intends to appropriate the headlines for the next

29. Ibid.
30. Ross, *The Loneliest Campaign*, 26–27; Harry S. Truman, *Memoirs by Harry S. Truman*, vol. 2, *Years of Trial and Hope*, 178.
31. *Public Papers*, 1948, 227–28; *Washington Post*, June 3, 1948; Editorial Comment on Western Trip folder, Box 3, Records of the Democratic National Committee, Truman Library.

two weeks . . . on one of the most important and hopeful journeys of Mr. Truman's career."[32]

Extreme pessimism about the president's chances of winning a full term prevailed in the press corps. Doris Fleeson reported on the first day of the tour that the ordinarily lighthearted journalists "are feeling slightly ghoulish as they settle down to work" because all shared "the uncompromising verdict of 50 leading Washington correspondents [polled by] *Newsweek*" that Truman would not be elected. Conservative columnist David Lawrence reported that "talk among Washington observers has been that the President's stock had fallen so low, not only within his own party but with the country as a whole, that he couldn't possibly make things worse for himself and might even make them better if he did a bit of personal campaigning."[33]

While the president's venture into the Midwest and the Far West allowed him to make the case for his nomination and election directly to the people, it also afforded the antiadministration press its opportunity to portray his efforts in a bad light. The biases of publishers and editors of nationally circulated newspapers and magazines thus loomed as the major obstacle to the president's effort to cast himself as the champion of the people and the architect of a successful foreign policy.

From the outset to the end of the campaign, the publications of Henry R. Luce, publisher and editor-in-chief of *Time, Life,* and *Fortune,* played the most important role in the antiadministration press's opposition to Truman's election bid. Each of the Luce publications had mastered the art of promoting the publisher's views. *Time,* cofounded by Luce in 1923, had limited its objectivity from its beginning to reporting on both sides of a question but clearly indicating "which side it believes to have the stronger position." A few years after Luce launched *Life* in 1936, the highly successful

32. *Washington Post,* June 3, 1948; Marquis Childs, "Washington Calling," *Washington Post,* June 5, 1948; Alice A. Dunnigan, *A Black Woman's Experience: From Schoolhouse to White House,* 228; *New York Herald Tribune,* June 4, 1948, in Editorial Comment on Western Trip folder, Box 33, Records of the Democratic National Committee, Truman Library.

33. *Washington Star,* June 4 and 7, 1948, in Editorial Comment on Western Trip folder, Box 33, Records of the Democratic National Committee, Truman Library; *Newsweek* (June 7, 1948): 9, 14. The newsmagazine polled the nation's leading political writers throughout the campaign. For the first time in the ten-year history of the poll, the writers were unanimous in their presidential forecast and predicted a victory for Thomas E. Dewey. *Newsweek* (October 11 and November 1, 1948): 15, 20.

photo weekly added an editorial page to make the publisher's position on issues and presidential candidates even more explicit than its articles and photo essays. *Fortune,* founded in 1930, unabashedly championed capitalism and the American way of life as envisioned by its publisher.[34]

The Luce publications enjoyed a large and significant readership in all parts of the nation. In 1948 *Time's* circulation exceeded three million per week while *Life's* weekly subscribers totaled 5.2 million. Both magazines were standard reading fare in the barber shops and beauty salons of America, and the waiting customers, in addition to library patrons who thumbed through current and well-worn back issues, contributed to *Life's* estimated pass-on reading audience of sixty million over a six-week period. *Time's* readership among Washington reporters added greatly to its influence, too. *Fortune* exerted influence as an interpreter of free enterprise for its business-minded readers and as a source of information for radio commentators and newspaper columnists. The magazine also published the *Fortune* poll conducted by Elmo Roper's organization, which prided itself on correctly predicting the winning margin of the victor in the presidential elections of 1936, 1940, and 1944.[35]

During Truman's presidency, the readership, revenues, and influence of the Luce publications thus justified the characterization of Henry Luce as the reigning press baron in the United States. His singular influence rivaled that of newspaper publishers Hearst, McCormick, and Howard combined because the views expressed in the Luce publications were deliberately shaped to project a national consensus on vital issues. Thus the weekly installments of the Luce-directed consensus that portrayed an inept chief executive engaged in a hopeless presidential campaign weighed as heavily with readers as the daily biased accounts of antiadministration newspapers.[36]

34. James L. Baughman, *Henry R. Luce and the Rise of the American News Media,* 31–32, 63–73, 89–102, 142. *Life* began an editorial page in March 1943.
35. Ibid., 2, 73, 165; *Time* reported on its circulation in "A Letter from the Publisher" ([August 9, 1948]: 10).
36. Ibid., 2, 5–7. James L. Baughman has convincingly argued that while more Americans were more likely to read a daily newspaper or listen to a radio newscast than to examine an issue of *Life,* "rival mass communicators had come to accept the fundamental premises of [Luce's] 'American Century.'" Moreover, *Life* and *Time,* Baughman has explained, offered their readers—and the newspapers that Luce's editors gleaned for information—a "directed synthesis" aimed at achieving a national consensus on issues of greatest importance to Luce. The account of *Time* and *Life* and *Fortune* coverage of Truman's election

Luce's disaffection with President Truman represented a significant shift from his earlier favorable opinion of Senator Truman as chairman of the important wartime national defense investigating committee. Luce believed that Truman as president had moved too slowly in meeting the challenge of the Soviet Union. As a lifelong friend of Nationalist China—Luce's parents were Presbyterian missionaries in China, and he spent the first fourteen years of his life there—he was displeased, too, that the administration had refused to lobby Congress for large-scale military and economic aid to the nationalists in their civil war with communist forces. The publisher disliked Truman's domestic program as well, and he judged the Missourian as being too little for the big job of president. These convictions also rested on Luce's belief that the two-party system and American democracy required that a Republican capture the White House after sixteen years of Democratic control.[37]

The bias of the Luce publications against Truman's 1948 campaign became apparent at the beginning of the president's Midwest and western tour. *Life* published an assortment of uninspiring photographs to document its claim that Truman's trip to garner grassroots support had been a fiasco. In its issue of June 21, 1948, the magazine featured a half-page photo of the "acres of empty seats" in the ten-thousand-seat Ak-sar-ben auditorium in Omaha, where Truman delivered a Saturday night radio address on farm policy before an in-house audience of about two thousand. The caption for the lead photo reported that the widespread reproduction of the picture in newspapers had "dealt a serious blow" to Truman's campaign. The story about "a badly stumbling Truman" was enhanced with a photo of a solitary soldier posted along a parade route without viewers in Cheyenne. Another picture showed the hapless president posing with a dog collared with a sign welcoming him to Sun Valley; yet another photograph revealed Truman sitting alone in a ski lift chair high above the ground with no one in sight. A final shot in the *Life* photo essay featuring the president and his World War I buddies marching in downtown Omaha obscured the fact that the greatest crowd of spectators in the city's history—an estimated 160,000 persons—had lined the parade route standing eight and ten deep on the sidewalks on the morning of his auditorium address.

---

bid in this chapter is an illustration of this highly influential, but in this case unsuccessful, technique.

37. Ibid., 8, 148–50, 152–57.

The clever photo essay conveyed the clear message of a national consensus opposed to a full term for Harry Truman.[38]

Time contributed to the anti-Truman treatment with a picture of the sparse Omaha audience in the Ak-sar-ben auditorium accompanied by the story of an embarrassing miscue by the president at the dedication of an airport in Carey, Idaho, a few days later. Truman had been handed the name of the person for whom the airport was being dedicated in handwriting at the last minute for the unscheduled dedication. The assemblage of veterans in uniforms and American flags led him to believe that the honoree was a World War II airman named William Smith instead of a local civilian girl, Wilma Smith. When he made two mistakes in the dedication and received correction from the deceased girl's mother, *Time* and the press in general reported the mishap as evidence of poor planning and execution by the presidential party.[39]

Although *Time* and *Life* continued to slight and downplay Truman's western tour, other press coverage changed for the better. Anthony Leviero's account of the Truman appearances ten days into the tour for the *New York Times* received a positive headline: "Campaigner Truman Makes Some Headway. Personal Approach Is Winning Friends and Influencing People in the West." Leviero found the upturn in three themes hammered home by the president:

> (1) Get to know your President. They say a lot of things about me that are not true. Here I am. Look me over and decide for yourself.... (2) The present Congress (dominated by the Republicans) is not working for the greatest number. (3) You in the audience are to blame for having an unsatisfactory Congress. Two thirds of you stayed home in 1946.... Now if you will all go out and vote in November and support me, we will have prosperity, we will keep our country stable and thus assure the peace of the world.[40]

While Leviero tempered his report by stating that it was too early to know if Truman's "great effort will have a decisive influence, either at the Democratic National Convention in July or at the polls in November,"[41] Robert L. Riggs, reporter for the *Louisville Courier-Journal*, asserted that Democrats who expected Truman to step aside for another nominee would be disappointed. Within a

38. "The Truman Train Stumbles Badly," *Life* (June 21, 1948): 43–45.
39. *Time* (June 21, 1948): 23–24.
40. *New York Times*, June 13, 1948.
41. Ibid.

little more than a week, Riggs wrote from San Francisco, Truman had performed

> what must be accounted almost a political miracle: He has transformed for the people of the United States their mental picture of their President. Gone from their minds is the image of a fumbling, bumbling, almost inarticulate Chief Executive, who, despite a world of good intentions, scarcely comprehended the scope of the duties which fall to any occupant of the White House.
>
> In the place of that conception is a new mental picture of a first-class fighting man, a scrappy party leader who has a definite political philosophy, and who is determined to lead his party and his nation along the road of that philosophy.[42]

Riggs concluded that "there is . . . no such thing as the 'new Truman,' concerning whom so much has been made. It is the same old Truman . . . [in] a new role in which the people are seeing him for the first time."[43]

Richard Strout, correspondent of the *Christian Science Monitor* and "TRB" columnist for the *New Republic,* reported on the same phenomenon. Earlier, in April 1948, when liberals were heavily influencing the public's image of a miscast Truman in the role as the nation's chief executive, Strout had offered his own contribution:

> I defy anyone, any reasonable person to meet Harry Truman and not like him. I have attended many press conferences, frequently disagreed with him, but he always seemed direct, friendly and disarmingly unassuming. He is the kind of man who would make the ideal next-door neighbor—he would respect your rights, make allowance for your dog in his petunia bed, do thoughtful things for the family and shovel more than his share of the snow. These are reasonable and important virtues.[44]

But, Strout concluded, in three years at the White House, "Truman has never raised enough fanatical warmth to boil an egg."[45]

Now the president's cross-country trip allowed Strout to reassess Truman's ability to communicate with the people and to generate

42. Robert L. Riggs, "The Worm Has Turned," *Louisville Courier-Journal,* June 12, 1948, Editorial Comment Western Trip folder number two, Box 34, Records of the Democratic National Committee, Truman Library.

43. Ibid.

44. Richard L. Strout, "Candidate in the White House," *New Republic* (April 5, 1948): 11.

45. Ibid.

warmth among his listeners: "Most reporters on board feel this warmth has increased as the journey progressed," he wrote. "Just why is a matter of speculation, but it may be that word has gone around that a scrappy fighter is making an uphill fight."[46]

The president's ability to scrap effectively with the dissidents in his own party and with the Republican opposition gained further credence following his appearance and speech in Los Angeles in the closing days of his tour. Truman entered Los Angeles in top form, fresh from the campus of the University of California at Berkeley, where a record commencement crowd of sixty thousand witnessed the conferring of an honorary Doctor of Law degree upon the president. (The *Chicago Tribune* slanted the facts by taking note of the forty thousand vacant seats in the coliseum.) Close to one million Los Angelenos lined the streets to catch a glimpse of the president riding in an open convertible from Union Station to the Ambassador Hotel on Wilshire Boulevard. The size of the crowd served as a rebuke to James Roosevelt, the late president's son and a leader of California Democrats in open rebellion against the presidential nomination of Truman.[47]

In his address at the Greater Los Angeles Press Club on June 14, Truman dispelled the lingering notion that he had been greeted with apathy in Nebraska and in his swing through the Far West. He remarked that the mayor of Omaha had told him that "the greatest crowd that has ever been on the streets of Omaha was there to see me." Similar turnouts had been accorded him at Butte, Montana, where more people showed up at the arena than the number of residents in the city. He measured the size of his early morning crowd in Spokane at "about two acres of people," while Seattle and San Francisco had accorded him the greatest reception given to a guest, topped only by Los Angeles. To the delight of his audience, he explained: "It was said over the radio the other night by a Member of the Senate [Robert A. Taft of Ohio] that I was stopping at the whistlestops, misinforming the people about the situation. Los Angeles is the biggest whistlestop." The audience whistled, shouted, and clapped in approval of Truman's setting the record straight.[48]

46. Quoted in Ross, *The Loneliest Campaign*, 88.
47. Ibid., 88–89; Robert Donovan later cited the obvious bias of the *Chicago Tribune* as an example of reportage that angered Truman. See his retrospective interview in Kenneth W. Thompson, ed., *Ten Presidents and the Press*, 40.
48. Ibid.; *Public Papers*, 1948, 348–49.

Both reporters and the president found the western tour enlightening in different ways. Joseph Driscoll, national correspondent for the *St. Louis Post-Dispatch,* noted that the disclosure of the president's folksy, hearty, and homespun nature "has been a revelation even to correspondents who covered Truman at the White House." Truman thought that the trip outside the nation's capital had been beneficial to the reporters for what it revealed about the land and national resources. As he explained to one crowd early in his tour, "I brought a lot of reporters with me on this trip, and I venture to say there isn't half of them ever saw anything west of the Appalachian mountains. Now they are going to find out where the country lies and where the resources of the country come from." He added, "And I hope they will tell their eastern readers and constituents just exactly what they have seen."[49]

Newsman Strout made his contribution to objective journalism by wiring a protest to *Life* for its reportage of Truman's western trip. Apparently seeing for the first time the now-dated issue of *Life* and its distorted characterization of Truman's tour as a fiasco, he offered a correction: "I was one of the 40 or 50 Washington correspondents on the two-week Truman trip and must protest the article in the June 21 issue of *Life.* Your declaration that Truman's crowds were small just isn't so. I am no Truman enthusiast; I am just disheartened by irresponsible and snide journalism."[50]

Life published Strout's telegram in its "Letters to the Editor" section of the magazine's issue for July 12 and offered a weak explanation: "*Life* went to press before President Truman had completed half of his trip, thereby reporting only the early mistakes and mixups." The magazine acknowledged that by the end of the journey Truman had "thoroughly recouped his false start." In light of the magazine's lack of coverage of the highly successful Far West portion of the tour, its expression of regret "that the time element caused a one-sided picture of the tour as a whole" had a ring of insincerity.[51]

Reporter Leviero's assessment of Truman's direct campaigning efforts, published in the *New York Times,* captured the political significance of the tour for the president and his party. President

49. *St. Louis Post-Dispatch,* June 15, 1948, Editorial Comment on Western folder number two, Box 34, Records of the Democratic National Committee, Truman Library; *Public Papers,* 1948, 311–12.

50. "Letters to the Editors," *Life* (July 12, 1948): 2.

51. Ibid.

Truman, he wrote, "is returning to the capital with the conviction that he has decidedly improved the Democratic party's position through the West and with high hopes of election." Sources close to the president, Leviero wrote, were gratified with the results of the preconvention tour. "They concede he is in a tough fight but they give him a chance of winning, where they despaired a month ago."[52]

Time, however, undercut this guarded optimism by assigning respective "destined to win" and "sure to lose" labels to the national conventions of the Republicans and Democrats meeting in Philadelphia in mid-June and mid-July respectively. The newsweekly led the bandwagon parade for Thomas E. Dewey by featuring the Republican presidential nominee on the cover of its July 5 issue. The accompanying stories gave a glowing treatment of Dewey and his running mate, Governor Earl Warren of California, while consigning Truman to the dustbin of history. Clare Boothe Luce, the publisher's wife and featured speaker at the Republican convention, dismissed Truman with finality, telling the cheering delegates that he was a "gone goose."[53]

Two weeks later *Time*, in reporting Mrs. Luce's own retirement from politics to devote her time to writing, added her prediction that the Dewey-Warren ticket was "sure to win." In the same issue *Time* claimed that the nomination of Warren as vice president had forced Democratic strategists to give up "any remaining hope of carrying California." According to *Time*, "White House visitors whistled to keep up their courage."[54]

Time's gloomy account of the Democratic National Convention reinforced its earlier effort to declare a national consensus behind the Republican presidential candidate. "Most Democrats, large and small," the newsmagazine reported, "had given up hope of Truman's election in November." Consequently, *Time* concluded, the Democratic convention would "only be a mournful wake before the funeral in bleak November."[55]

While *Time* devoted extensive coverage to the "dump Truman" effort among dissident Democrats, it did not get egg on its face by predicting that the president would not be nominated. The magazine only went as far as to report that four of the six previous presidents

52. *New York Times*, June 17, 1948, Editorial Comment on Western Trip folder number 2, Box 34, Records of the Democratic National Committee, Truman Library.
53. *Time* (June 28, 1948): 10.
54. *Time* (July 12, 1948): 11.
55. Ibid.

elevated to their position following the death of a president had been unceremoniously denied their party's nomination.[56]

Meanwhile, Truman continued to show the public and the news media his determination to lead the Democratic ticket to victory. As he predicted, the efforts to dump him had failed (with an assist from General Eisenhower, the leading choice of the dissidents, who refused to allow his name to go forward). In his rousing acceptance speech to weary convention delegates, Truman promised that he and his running mate, Senator Alben Barkley of Kentucky, "will win this election and make these Republicans like it—don't you forget that!" His recitation of his efforts to combat inflation, provide public housing for slum dwellers, obtain a national health insurance program, expand social security coverage, and raise the minimum wage were all predictable, but he dropped a bombshell with his announcement that the Republican-controlled Eightieth Congress would be recalled to enact the program promised in the GOP platform.[57]

The recall of Congress into special session that July heightened the significance of the president's campaign strategy to blame Congress for the nation's domestic difficulties. During his preconvention western tour he had labeled the Congress the "worst" in history. After its two-week special session produced few results, he heartily agreed with a reporter's characterization of the Eightieth Congress as a "do-nothing" Congress. Journalist Irwin Ross, writing in his splendid history of the 1948 campaign, summed up the situation after the special session by observing that Truman "now had another useful epithet with which to belabor the 'worst' Congress. The special session had been a great success."[58]

The fall campaign opened with traditional Labor Day speeches by both major candidates, who then began train tours, complete with a large press entourage; ultimately Truman traveled through thirty-four states for a total of twenty-two thousand miles, and Dewey's "Victory Special" covered about the same territory and distance. *Time* reported in September that Truman, the "dogged little man who (the polls said) couldn't win," was attracting large crowds. Yet the president sounded "frantic—and just a little ludicrous. The performance was interesting; but since Mr. Truman has never shown much capacity for leadership," *Time* concluded, "it promised little

56. Ibid.
57. Ross, *The Loneliest Campaign*, 129, 133–36.
58. Ibid., 139.

of accomplishment." *Life* minimized the turnout of eighty thousand Iowa farmers for Truman's speech at the national plowing contest on September 12 by featuring a photograph of about twenty farmers listening intently to the president. Both publications reflected the conviction of editor Luce: "After 16 years of one party, it was time to clean house." *Life*, in its editorial for the October 18 issue, endorsed Dewey.[59]

Truman met the antiadministration press and radio head-on. He frequently pointed out to his audiences that *Time-Life*, metropolitan newspapers, and various radio commentators were part of the special interests opposed to his program for the people. In New York City on October 28, he stated that he had visited nearly all the great cities of the nation "to tell the people what the issues are. They couldn't find out otherwise because 90 percent of the press is against us—90 percent of the radio commentators are against us; and the only way you can find out the truth is for me to come out and tell you what the truth is." Truman's slightly faulty arithmetic on his newspaper opposition, derived from a recent survey published in *Editor and Publisher*, apparently had been deducted from the trade journal's report that only 16 percent of newspapers in its national press survey had endorsed the president's election.[60]

He concluded on this theme on October 29 in St. Louis, the last stop on his cross-country tour before returning home to Independence. He recalled that the conservative press had started "the smear campaign on your President . . . in all its vile and untruthfully slanted headlines, columns, and editorials" immediately after he had unveiled his liberal program in September 1945. "Hearst's character assassins, McCormick-Patterson saboteurs all began firing at me, as did the conservative columnists and radio commentators," he declared. When he started the campaign for election, he continued, "the song was you can't win . . . Ninety percent of the press is against us, but that didn't discourage me one little bit. You know, I had four campaigns here in the great State of Missouri, and I have

59. *Public Papers*, 1948, 935; Smith, *Thomas E. Dewey and His Times*, 519–38; *Time* (September 27, 1948): 19; *Life* (October 4, 1948): 42; Editorial, *Life* (October 18, 1948): 44.

60. *Public Papers*, 1948, 904–5; *Editor and Publisher*, September 11, 1948, 11. Sixty-eight of the newspapers surveyed, which accounted for 70 percent of national circulation, backed Dewey. J. Strom Thurmond, candidate of the States' Rights Democratic Party, received support of 3.87 percent of the papers while Wallace had less than 1 percent.

never had a metropolitan paper for me that whole time. And I licked them every time!"[61]

The press, so confident that Governor Dewey would be elected president on November 2, began to publish special reports, magazine articles, columns, editorials, and front-page news stories on the anticipated Republican administration. *Life* captioned a full-page picture of Dewey in its November 1 issue "The Next President"; *Time*, equally confident of a Dewey victory, published an advertisement for the November issue of the *Kiplinger Washington Letter* devoted to how the Dewey administration would perform. The October 30 issue of the *Kiplinger Magazine* "elected" Dewey not only in 1948 but also in 1952 with its feature story that asserted "Dewey will be in for eight years." *Fortune*, drawing upon the polling service of Elmo Roper and proud of its record of having predicted with close precision the outcome of the three previous presidential elections, joined its sister publications in projecting Dewey the winner. Nationally syndicated columnists, writing columns for postelection publication, dealt with various aspects of a Dewey administration. Drew Pearson identified the most likely candidates for Dewey's cabinet, while the syndicated columnists Joseph and Stewart Alsop and Walter Lippmann worried about how the government would function until the inauguration of President-elect Dewey.[62]

The *Chicago Tribune*'s early edition headlined "Dewey Defeats Truman" won the dubious distinction of the most famous and lasting record of a miscalled presidential election. Truman ensured that the erroneous headline would be immortalized by posing for photographers with a copy of the newspaper as the Washington-bound train stopped in St. Louis. The photograph's circulation exceeded the *Tribune*'s limited, recalled edition by several million.[63]

61. *Public Papers*, 1948, 935, 938; *St. Louis Post-Dispatch*, October 31, 1948.

62. "Our Next President Travels by Ferry Boat over the Broad Waters of San Francisco Bay," *Life* (November 1, 1948): 37; *Time* (November 1, 1948): 21 and (November 15, 1948): 63; "The Fortune Survey," *Fortune* (October 1948): 29–32.

63. McCullough, *Truman*, 718. Newspapers around the nation used the photo taken by Associated Press photographer Byron H. Rollins; *Time* and *Newsweek* printed the photo of Frank Cancellare, photographer for Acme. *Chicago Tribune* executives in 1972, in commemoration of the newspaper's 125th anniversary and in newfound admiration and affection for the former president, presented a bronze plaque of the famous front page for display at the Truman Library. Truman died before the presentation could be made, but his family and close associates expressed their belief that he would have been highly pleased to receive the plaque and the sentiment that prompted the gift. Wendt, *Chicago Tribune*, 683–84.

While political analysts began to identify the factors for Truman's victory, newspapers and newsmagazines began to acknowledge their unprecedented failure in predicting the outcome of the election. The *Washington Post* resorted to humor in a telegram sent to the president:

> YOU ARE HEREBY INVITED TO A 'CROW BANQUET' TO WHICH THIS NEWSPAPER PROPOSES TO INVITE NEWSPA-PER EDITORIAL WRITERS, POLITICAL REPORTERS AND EDITORS, INCLUDING OUR OWN, ALONG WITH POLL-STERS, RADIO COMMENTATORS AND COLUMNISTS. . . . MAIN COURSE WILL CONSIST OF BREAST OF TOUGH OLD CROW EN GLACE. (YOU WILL EAT TURKEY). . . . DRESS FOR GUEST OF HONOR WHITE TIE. FOR OTHER—SACK CLOTH. . . .

(Truman declined, and turned the invitation to a reiteration of his campaign promise to maintain prosperity and abundance: "We should all get together now and make a country in which everybody can eat turkey whenever he pleases.")[64]

Despite evidence of grassroots support for Truman on the pre-convention trip and the fall campaign tour, few reporters overcame the feeling that a game but inadequate president was headed for certain defeat. Reporter Leviero, convinced by what he had seen in small-town and big-city support for Truman during both the June and fall train tours, was one of the few journalists who believed that Truman would win. Other reporters had observed the same favorable, even enthusiastic response to Truman's campaigning but could not interpret the response correctly. Robert Donovan, who covered the campaign train of Truman for the *New York Herald Tribune*, dismissed the size of the turnout for the president because he assumed Dewey attracted similar numbers. The reporters, broad-casters, and cameramen covering Truman's fall campaign got the president's attacks upon the Republican presidential candidate and the "do-nothing Republican 80th Congress" on the front page, on the airwaves, and on newsreel and television screens, yet looked and found a fly in the ointment: Truman, while waging an effec-tive campaign, could not win. Richard Rovere, writing in the *New Yorker*, observed that "Traveling with the president, you get the feeling that the American people . . . would . . . give him just about anything he wants except the presidency." For these reporters it was

64. *Time* (November 15, 1948): 63.

a case of Truman is on the attack, winning friends and influencing voters, but he could not win. Other correspondents simply could not revise their initial assessment. Illustrative of the latter was Frank Kingdom, who harkened back to the preconvention trip in his erroneous postelection column written for the liberal *New York Post* before the results were in: "People had decided last June that Truman was not big enough for the job."[65]

Some reporters attributed their misjudgment of the election outcome to the national public opinion polls that declared Dewey the winner by virtue of his seemingly unsurmountable lead. Still, as Edwin C. Heinke, assistant managing editor of the *Indianapolis Times* conceded, the polls, while as wrong as the political pundits of press and radio, were not to blame for the almost universal miscalling of the election results: "The returns made me realize how good, old-fashioned legwork—the kind I hadn't done—was still the most important part of our press structure. I think that a good deal of our press reporting has strictly gone to hell." The Indiana journalist concluded that the election "has been a wonderful lesson to those newspapermen who still have enough sense left to know that they got a lesson the hard way, and that they'd better brush up again on the fundamentals."[66]

Heinke's astute analysis failed, however, to account for the deliberate bias of publishers and editors against Truman. Luce and his editorial team assessed this factor in the individual and collective shortcomings of *Time, Life,* and *Fortune* in reporting on the 1948 presidential campaign. The publisher himself accepted responsibility for the calls in reportage and editorial work, while Joe Thorndike, managing editor of *Life,* wrote Luce to account for the blame: "I do think that we . . . were misled by our bias. . . . We were too ready to accept the evidence of pictures like the [near] empty auditorium at Omaha and to ignore the later crowds." In a line that would have pleased Harry Truman very much, Thorndike called for "a very sober rededication to the principles of honest journalism." And a few years later, Hedley Donovan of *Time,* although no supporter of Truman, demurred on Luce's offer to make him editor-in-chief until he received assurances from Luce that he would not be asked

65. George Tames oral history, by Benedict K. Zobrist, 65. Truman Library. Donovan is quoted in Thompson, ed., *Ten Presidents and the Press,* 32. Richard H. Rovere is quoted in *Time* (November 15, 1948): 63.

66. "The Press," *Time* (November 15, 1948): 65–66.

to slant the news as the Luce publications had done against Truman in 1948.[67]

The "accidental" presidency of Harry Truman, expected by so many to end in January 1949, received the approval of a plurality of voters to continue for a full term. The voters who supported Truman and elected him president in his own right thereby conferred upon him one of the greatest honors that can come to a chief executive elevated to the office upon the death of the president. The mantle of leadership, by necessity shared in part with the late president during the first three-plus years of the Truman administration, now rested solely upon his shoulders. It remained to be seen if Truman would be magnanimous in victory to his Republican opposition, to the breakaway southern states' rights adherents, to left-wing Democrats that had supported Henry Wallace, and to the press and radio that had either opposed his election or who had written him off as an accidental president.

67. Robert T. Elson, *The World of Time Inc.*, vol. 2, *The Intimate History of a Publishing Enterprise, 1941–1960*, 235–36; Curtis Prendergast with Geoffrey Colvin, *The World of Time Inc.*, vol. 3, *The Intimate History of a Changing Enterprise, 1961–1980*, 164. See also Baughman, *Henry R. Luce*, 172–75.

3

Presidential Power and the Power of the Press, 1949–1953

PRESIDENT TRUMAN'S RELATIONSHIP with the press became increasingly complex and contentious during his full term, 1949–1953. At the outset he cast himself as the people's advocate opposed by special interests and, by implication, their handmaiden, the "kept" press. He also struck the pose of a confident, decisive, and honest president determined to achieve enactment of a domestic Fair Deal without burdening taxpayers with costly defense expenditures. The nation's security needs and military capability in the Cold War and the Korean War, however, reordered Truman's priorities. In the process, numerous opportunities arose for conflict with the news media over presidential authority in foreign and military affairs, censorship, and ultimately, freedom of the press.

Truman's upset victory invited, even demanded, a generous response from the news media. Roscoe Drummond of the *Christian Science Monitor* described Truman's first news conference following the election as "an easy, comfortable press conference, because embarrassing issues had not yet arisen and embarrassing questions thus were not on the agenda. Nobody had a chip on his shoulder—the President least of all." The Truman on display, Drummond noted, was not a "new Truman;" rather he was "the same Truman with new confidence, new poise and decisiveness, new determination to stand on his own convictions and his own judgments."[1]

Truman's apparent good humor over the miscalled election delighted Democrats at the inaugural-eve dinner in January. In an able mimicking of the precise, clipped voice of radio newsman H. V. Kaltenborn, the president repeated the distinguished broadcaster's election-night prediction that "While Mr. Truman is a million votes ahead of the popular vote, when the country vote comes in, Mr. Truman will be defeated by an overwhelming majority." The audience howled with laughter.[2]

Initially, though, Truman had wanted to lash out at the press for writing him off in the recent election. In an unused portion of the State of the Union message of January 5, his simmering resentment inspired an unconvincing disclaimer: "Now, I have no bitterness in my heart against anyone, not even the bitter opposition press and its henchmen, the paid columnists and managing editors and the bought and paid for commentators." Ostensibly a lack of time for his radio address had kept the contentious remarks unread, but it is likely that his speechwriters and advisers argued strongly against quarreling with the news media at the outset of his full term.[3]

As delivered, the president's State of the Union message forcefully affirmed his philosophy of democratic liberalism balanced with an appeal for cooperation and harmony:

> We have rejected the discredited theory that the fortunes of the Nation should be in the hands of a privileged few. We have abandoned the 'trickle down' concept of national prosperity. Instead, we believe that our economic system should rest on a democratic foundation and that wealth should be created for the benefit of all.
>
> The recent election shows that the people of the United States are in favor of this kind of society and want to go on improving it.[4]

1. Roscoe Drummond, "State of the Nation," *Christian Science Monitor*, December 1, 1948, Ethel and Nellie Noland folder, Box 320, PSF, Truman Papers, Truman Library.

2. *Public Papers*, 1949, 110; *New York Times*, January 20, 1949.

3. The unread draft is printed in Hillman, *Mr. President*, 148–49, along with Truman's view that the statement belonged in his private papers. If, however, Truman's speechwriters argued him out of his contentious remarks, I did not find any evidence to support my supposition on the position of his aides in their papers on deposit in the Truman Library. In any event, the remarks were not delivered.

4. *Public Papers*, 1949, 1–2.

His legislative objectives, ranging from public housing to national health insurance to civil rights, he asserted, were the foundation of the nation's foreign policy. He acknowledged that the task of achieving his liberal goals would not be easy because of the strong opposition of selfish interests. He asked for, and pledged himself to, cooperation with Congress, farmers, labor, and business. "Every segment of our population and every individual," he declared, "have a right to expect from our government a fair deal."[5]

Legislative action on the Fair Deal agenda, however, received a setback at the outset of the Eighty-first Congress despite the sizable Democratic majorities in both the Senate and the House. Southern Democrats in the Senate successfully held the line on Rule XXII, which required a two-thirds vote of those present for cloture—the ending of debate to permit a vote on an issue such as civil rights. A bipartisan coalition even strengthened Rule XXII by requiring a "constitutional" two-thirds majority to invoke cloture. Senate approval of the tougher requirement on March 17 by a vote of 63 to 23 effectively ended any chance for civil rights legislation for the remainder of Truman's term.[6]

News coverage of this inauspicious beginning provoked Truman to charge the press with impeding his efforts to cooperate with Congress for the enactment of his legislative program. Departing from a prepared speech to the National Conference of Mayors on March 19, two days after the strict revision of Senate Rule XXII, he now spoke his mind about his detractors in the news media:

> I have been much interested in the attempts of the usual trouble-makers to make it appear that there is bad feeling between the Eighty-first Congress and the President of the United States. It seems that whenever I make a recommendation to the Congress, many newspapers and columnists set up a howl about the President trying to dictate to the Congress. And then if the Congress makes any decision that varies at all from my recommendations, these same troublemakers start a gleeful chorus about how the Congress has thrown the whole Democratic program overboard.[7]

5. Ibid., 1–7, 114–16. The offer of technical assistance to developing nations, only hinted at in the State of the Union message, was boldly pronounced as Point IV of the president's inaugural address.

6. Ross, *The Loneliest Campaign,* 265; Donald R. McCoy and Richard T. Ruetten, *Quest and Response: Minority Rights and the Truman Administration,* 171–77.

7. *Public Papers,* 1949, 174.

The president's broadside at the press did not go unchallenged. Robert U. Brown, columnist for the important trade journal *Editor and Publisher,* cited a lack of specificity in Truman's reference to "many newspapers and columnists." The columnist also objected to the characterization of the press as "the usual troublemakers." Looking to the past for a pattern, Brown asserted that

> It's been "open season" on newspapers for more than 10 years now. It's the popular thing to do. It's bound to get a laugh at any public gathering. That's no reason for the President of the United States to smear an entire press as "troublemakers" when the vast majority of the newspapers and the men on them are merely trying to tell the public what is going on in Washington. It's a difficult enough job to do without the President throwing obstacles in the way, casting aspersions on the integrity and reliability of all the press, good and bad.[8]

Truman took direct aim at the publishers of metropolitan newspapers at a Democratic gathering in July 1949. He reminded the audience that these publishers "were of the opinion that a certain country boy from Missouri didn't have a Chinaman's chance to win the election and be president." He reiterated his charge that the metropolitan press had never supported him in any of his political campaigns. "I have no respect for any of their political prognostication or influence," he said.[9]

Columnist Brown, in response, now saw in Truman's comments about the press a partisan purpose designed to "discredit all newspapers for political reasons." The president, he charged, "wants a Congress that will spend and spend. If he can convince the U.S. public by next election time that our newspapers are talking through their hats (and most of them favor government economy) then he will be a long way along the road to helping the Democratic party elect those Congressmen and Senators who will do his bidding." Brown wondered aloud: "Why do newspaper editors take his criticisms of the press lying down? Why don't they speak up and point out his political reasons for making these statements?"[10]

8. Robert U. Brown, "Shop Talk at Thirty," *Editor and Publisher* (March 26, 1949): 56.

9. Indirectly, Truman rebuked Jacob M. Arvey, chairman of the Cook County Democratic Committee and host of the reception for the president on July 19, 1949. The text of the president's informal remarks was not released by the White House and was not included in the published papers of the president. *Editor and Publisher* (July 23, 1949): 64.

10. Ibid.

Editor and Publisher took the columnist's advice that September. In a review of Truman's relations with the press since the upset election, an editorial writer opined that at first the president was "playing the record strictly for laughs;" but since his [mid-July] statement in Chicago, "he has given up clowning about how he beat the newspapers in the last election and he has become seriously intent on destroying public confidence in them."

As evidence for this serious allegation, the trade journal editor cited two recent speeches of the president. In Philadelphia, in an address to the national convention of the American Legion, Truman had charged that "there is a good deal of misunderstanding and misinformation about our international economic policy . . . deliberately stirred up by certain newspapers and politicians for political reasons." In a Labor Day speech to workers in Pittsburgh, he linked the press to "spokesmen and lobbyists for organized special interests" opposed to the president's program. The editorial concluded that while it might be good politics for Truman to take to the road to build public support for his legislative program, it was not "good strategy, good taste, or good sense for a President of the United States in the name of political expediency to continually attack our free and independent newspapers." Truman's "unwarranted slurs and insinuations are unsupported generalizations designed to degrade the nation's foremost medium of communication whose record of honesty, integrity and truthfulness is second to none."[11]

The developing fray between the president and the press attracted some support for the president's right to criticize antiadministration newspapers. The editor of the *San Diego Journal* argued that press criticism of Truman's "choice of intimates, most of his political views, his use of the English language, his economic theories and his farm-boy sense of humor," entitled the president to have the same freedom in his relations with newspapers.[12]

Editor and Publisher, while conceding the president's right to criticize the press, charged that his technique of attacking all newspapers for the alleged sins of a few were "designed with one purpose in mind—to associate all newspapers with so-called 'organized special interests.'" Moreover, Truman's assertions about misunderstanding and misinformation deliberately stirred up by certain newspapers

11. Editorial, *Editor and Publisher* (September 10, 1949): 32.
12. Ibid.

amounted to a generalization aimed at ruining the reputation of all newspapers for accuracy and reliability.[13]

Truman took note of the ongoing controversy in private correspondence with Arthur Krock of the *New York Times* that fall:

> *Editor and Publisher* and one or two of the sabotage sheets controlled by Hearst and McCormick take the attitude that I have a bitter and resentful attitude toward the press. That isn't true at all. Nobody, as you are well aware, has had to take it or been more able to take unjust criticism than I have. But that is a two-way street, particularly when I am President of the United States and can get a hearing on what I have to say.[14]

This disclaimer, excepting his attitude toward the newspapers of Hearst and McCormick, had the ring of truth. Yet Truman's combative personality and his eagerness to defend and advance his policies guaranteed conflict with the antiadministration press. Moreover, his inability to gain congressional approval of his major Fair Deal proposals made matters worse. Southern Democrats relied upon the filibuster to defeat his civil rights proposals, and conservatives in both parties blocked adoption of his national health insurance program with claims that the plan would "socialize medicine." Only his housing program, in a much scaled-down version, passed Congress in 1949—the one major exception to an otherwise thin domestic legislative record.[15]

Meanwhile, both the president and the press continued to feel their way into the new state of affairs regarding national security in the developing Cold War. Military technology for intelligence-gathering during World War II and its aftermath had vastly increased the storehouse of information that could not be disclosed to the public without informing the nation's enemies. To safeguard this information, the government created new weapons of news management: the top secret stamp and security regulations that attempted to govern what could or could not be released.[16] Truman, for the most part, still strongly believed that the press, through old-fashioned patriotism, should be self-regulating in determining

13. Ibid., 54.
14. Truman to Krock, October 10, 1949, quoted in Williams, *The Newspaperman's President*, 194.
15. Donald R. McCoy, *The Presidency of Harry S. Truman*, 163–90.
16. Stewart Alsop, *The Center: People and Power in Political Washington*, 193.

what news should be withheld from publication. To a significant extent the press shared this notion, too; during World War II it had voluntarily submitted to the suppression of news that could have been potentially damaging to the nation.

But self-regulation had limits. Truman could never forgive the *Chicago Tribune* for its 1942 publication of intelligence-sensitive information pertaining to the American naval victory at Midway over the Japanese navy. Unbeknown to the Japanese, U.S. cryptographers had broken Japan's military codes, which gave the American fleet a strategic edge over the enemy. In Truman's view, the *Tribune*, in publishing the names of Japanese ships involved in the Battle of Midway, had jeopardized the continued use of the code-breaking techniques. The *Tribune*, he believed, earned his contempt as a "sabotage sheet"; Colonel McCormick, he wrote privately to his daughter, deserved to be shot as a traitor.[17]

Truman stayed out of the quarrel among influential columnists that developed in the fall of 1948 after Joseph and Stewart Alsop published an article entitled "If War Comes" in the September 11, 1948, issue of *Saturday Evening Post*. The Alsops, writing a few months after the Soviet blockade of land access to Berlin, had suggested that war might break out between the Soviet Union and the United States over the future of Germany. They described how in that event the United States would wage war. Arthur Krock, feeling that voluntary self-censorship and national security had been violated by the Alsops and by government officials who had supplied them top-secret information, complained at length to Secretary of Defense James V. Forrestal. According to Krock, the article informed the possible and named enemy [the USSR] "where and how our airplanes will strike, and with what types of airplanes; where they will be based if we can arrange it; what are the Russian targets in those areas known in detail to our intelligence groups; what are some of the Russian counterweapons (submarines) known to us and what types they are." Krock concluded, "We lost lives in getting

17. For different interpretations of the *Tribune's* account of the Midway battle, see Dina Goren, "Communication Intelligence and the Freedom of the Press: The *Chicago Tribune's* Battle of Midway Dispatch and the Breaking of the Japanese Naval Code," *Journal of Contemporary History* 16 (October 1981): 663–90. For a discussion of Truman's general and specific designation of newspapers as the "sabotage press," see Williams, *The Newspaperman's President*, chapter 14; Margaret Truman, ed., *Letters from Father: The Truman Family's Personal Correspondence*, 98–99.

these facts, and now they can be bought for ten cents" (the price of a single issue of the *Saturday Evening Post*).[18]

Later, the publication of more security information leaked from the Air Force and the Atomic Energy Commission angered Truman and members of Congress. When *Fortune* identified atomic energy installations throughout the United States in its March 1949 issue, Representative George H. Mahon (D-Tex.) called the disclosure a "bombardier's map" for the enemy. A concurrent United Press story revealed that secret discussions had been held before the military Joint Chiefs of Staff pinpointing seventy vital Russian targets. In an effort to plug leaks and still congressional and presidential criticism, Forrestal consolidated all military information functions effective March 31, 1949.[19]

The administration's announcement of September 23, 1949, that the Soviet Union had detonated an atomic device may have been taken by Truman as much to preempt its surprise disclosure by the Soviet government as by American news media unfriendly to the administration. Although the president lent authority to the ominous news by issuing the announcement through Press Secretary Ross, skeptics in Congress and in the Pentagon, including Louis Johnson, successor to Forrestal as secretary of defense, privately disbelieved the Soviet accomplishment. (The distinction Truman made between an atomic device and a workable atomic bomb is recounted in the epilogue.) Consequently, the Alsops decided to determine if the Russian test was a fake or the real thing.[20]

The columnists first attempted to gain information from government sources. When that effort proved unsuccessful, Stewart Alsop turned to a physicist at Georgetown University and asked how evidence could be obtained to verify an atomic explosion. The professor, without any knowledge of the specific scientific evidence collected by the United States, provided an answer: "split nuclei in air samples, seismographic confirmation, and so on."[21]

18. Joseph and Steward Alsop, "If War Comes," *Saturday Evening Post* 221 (September 11, 1948): 15, 17ff; Arthur Krock, *Memoirs: Sixty Years on the Firing Line*, 457–58.

19. *Editor and Publisher* (March 26, 1949): 21.

20. Arthur Krock, "Truman Chose Timing of Bomb Announcement," *New York Times*, October 2, 1949. See also David Halberstam, *The Fifties* (New York: Villard Books, 1993), 25–26. *New York Times*, September 24, 1949; Alsop, *The Center*, 194–95.

21. Alsop, *The Center*, 194; apparently neither Truman nor the Alsops took note of an article in *Newsweek* (October 3, 1949) that cited, in a manner

Publication of this information led Truman to conclude, erroneously, that the Alsops had tapped into his top-secret document, and he ordered the FBI to determine the source of the alleged leak. The FBI, finding government sources secure, sent two agents to interrogate the columnists. Stewart Alsop later explained: "We did not tell them about the physics professor, and they left convinced, no doubt, that we had some still-open pipeline into the 'secret places of the most high.' "[22] A wiser course for the columnists would have been to disclose that many scientists could have supplied the information they had published and that Truman erred in believing that the information could only have come from government sources.

The outbreak of hostilities in Korea on June 25, 1950, and the president's commitment of U.S. armed forces there gave rise to several new areas of conflict between him and the news media. The use of American combat forces in Korea without a congressional declaration of war, the potential use of atomic weapons, the firing of a popular supreme military commander, the decision to fight a limited war in Korea while maintaining a "Europe First" policy, and the authority to command private property for military production, all issues generated by the Korean War, involved presidential power to a maximum degree. Ultimately, the protracted, acrimonious conflict between the president and the press over these matters came to be perceived by the press as a challenge to its own freedom.

Initially, Truman's decisive action to employ American armed forces in the Korean conflict did not crystallize strong opposition or public discontent. Six months into the war, Arthur Robb, erstwhile columnist of *Editor and Publisher*, observed, "In all the hindsight lamentations over our Korean misfortunes, I haven't seen any that go to the root of the trouble—the Administration's disregard last June for the Constitution's provision that vests the right to declare war in Congress." Robb added that while the fighting in Korea was not officially a war but a police action ordered by the United

---

similar to their account published that December in the *Washington Post*, how seismographs and radiation counters could detect a distant atomic explosion.

22. Joseph and Stewart Alsop, "How Red A-Blast Was Detected," *Washington Post*, December 31, 1950, NSC–Atomic Energy Russia folder, Box 201, PSF, Truman Papers, Truman Library; Truman to the Attorney General [J. Howard McGrath], January 7, 1951, NSC–Atomic Energy Russia folder; Alsop, *The Center*, 195.

Nations, "in fact it is the toughest war that Americans have waged, with the exception of the Civil War and the World Wars."[23]

Interestingly, in questioning the constitutional right of the president to commit the nation to war without an act of Congress, Robb accepted the terminology "police action." This term originated at the president's news conference of June 29, 1950, following the outbreak of the hostilities in Korea a few days earlier.

"Are we or are we not at war?" a reporter asked.

Truman had not yet ordered ground troops into the fray—he would issue that order later in the day—and he answered with a simple declaration: "We are not at war."

"Would it be correct," another reporter asked the president, "against your explanation, to call this a police action under the United Nations?"

"Yes," Truman replied. "That is exactly what it amounts to." Thus the term gained currency at a time when the character of the war and American involvement remained in a formative stage.

Later in the conference, Truman elaborated on the involvement of the United Nations and the United States in Korea. Describing the attack as the work "of a bunch of bandits which are neighbors of North Korea"—a reference to the Soviet Union—he explained that the members of the United Nations "are going to the relief of the Korean Republic."[24]

Two weeks later, at the president's July 13 news conference, a reporter asked: "Do you still call this a police action?" Truman replied in the affirmative, but transformed the word "action" to "reaction": "Yes," he said, "it is still a police reaction."[25]

The president did not address Congress and the American people on the course of the war until July 19. In his message he praised the legislators for their strong, bipartisan support of the steps he had taken in Korea. "The expressions of support which have been forthcoming from the leaders of both political parties for the action of our Government and of the United Nations in dealing with the present crisis," he declared, "have buttressed the firm morale of the entire free world in the face of this challenge."[26]

---

23. The initial endorsements of Truman's decision to intervene in Korea and the six-month "honeymoon" with Congress are discussed in McCoy, *The Presidency of Harry S. Truman*, 224, 248; *Editor and Publisher* (December 16, 1950): 64.

24. *Editor and Publisher* (December 16, 1950): 64; *Public Papers*, 1950, 504.

25. *Public Papers*, 1950, 522.

26. Ibid., 536.

A White House survey of press reaction to the president's radio and television address revealed that a large majority of metropolitan newspapers had praised the president's policy of taking vigorous action against Communist aggression abroad; a few newspapers argued that he should have called for price and wage controls, rent controls, and rationing power, too. In pointing out that the president's speech had met with "unusually strong, unified press support," the survey also commented favorably upon the president's use of television to inform the American people.[27]

The *Chicago Tribune* characteristically stood in a distinct minority with its wholesale disapproval of the president's speech, charging that Truman intended "to use the war in Korea to win even larger opportunities for [government] graft. His intent, claimed the *Tribune*, was "to break down our form of government."[28] No wonder Truman considered the *Tribune* the worst newspaper in the country.

The most contentious issue of the Korean War centered around the conflicting military objectives of the president and his Far Eastern commander, Douglas MacArthur. Both men had considerable difficulty with press coverage of the war and with the news media's interpretation of their numerous differences. Consequently, each resorted to various strategies designed to advance their respective positions with the news media. In the end the president prevailed, but at considerable cost to his popularity and in his ability to govern during the last years of his administration.

Although the press had numerous reporters in Japan and Korea to cover MacArthur's activities, reporters chafed under "military security" rules enforced by the general's public information office. As early as February 1948 both the Tokyo Correspondents Association and the American War Correspondents Association had expressed dissatisfaction with restrictions on the press to General MacArthur, Secretary of Defense Forrestal, and Secretary of the Army Kenneth Royall.[29] Thus, when the Korean War began, MacArthur's control over the news remained a bone of contention between him and journalists.

27. "Analysis of President Truman's Speech on the Korean Crisis, July 19, 1950," General Politics Letters/Documents folder 2, 1949–50, Part III, Box 8, David Niles Papers, Truman Library.

28. Editorial, *Chicago Tribune*, July 20, 1950, General Politics Letters/Documents folder 2, 1949–50, Part III, Box 8, David Niles Papers, Truman Library.

29. Report, Tokyo Correspondents Club, February 18, 1948, MacArthur folder number two, Box 237, Drew Pearson Papers, Lyndon B. Johnson Library, University of Texas, Austin.

News reporters assigned to MacArthur's headquarters and the general got off to a shaky but good start as they accompanied him on his flight to the Korean war zone on June 29. MacArthur had warned the reporters that he was unsure that fighter cover would be given to their unarmed transport plane, nor was he certain where the plane would land. "If you are not at the airport," he quipped, "I will know you have other commitments." When a correspondent assured MacArthur that the reporters would be there, he grinned and acknowledged their courage.[30]

The swift dispatch of American correspondents to South Korea exposed them at once to the dangers of battle. Reporters covering the retreat of Republic of Korea soldiers on June 28, including Marguerite Higgins, Tokyo correspondent of the *New York Herald Tribune,* and Keyes Beech, newsman for the *Chicago Daily News,* narrowly escaped injury when explosives prematurely destroyed a bridge on the Han River, killing hundreds of South Korean soldiers. Within weeks of the first press reportage on the war, Ray Richards of International News Service and Corporal Ernie Peeler of the Army newspaper, *Pacific–Stars and Stripes,* were killed while covering front-line fighting. In less than a month, the press casualties in the Korean War exceeded the number during the first year of World War II.[31]

Censorship came to the fore at the outset of the war. Colonel M. P. Echols, MacArthur's public information officer, stated that while there was no plan to apply censorship to reporters in connection with war coverage, he asked correspondents to cooperate to prevent disclosure of "strategic or helpful information." Echols's statement asserted, "The word censorship is abhorrent to General MacArthur, as it is to all who believe in freedom of the news and a true democratic society," but "inaccurate and irresponsible reporting endangers our interests and the lives of our soldiers, sailors and airmen engaged in combat with a sinister aggressor."[32]

Throughout July and August, as the invading North Koreans forced South Korean and U.S. troops to retreat to a defensive perimeter at Pusan, Army information officers cracked down on reporters whose stories criticized military decisions and the conduct of soldiers. Despite a reassurance from Eighth Army public information

---

30. *Editor and Publisher* (July 1, 1950): 11.
31. *Editor and Publisher* (July 1, 1950): 11; (July 15, 1950): 7; (August 5, 1950): 9.
32. *Editor and Publisher* (July 8, 1950): 7.

officer Lt. Colonel R. L. Thompson that there would be no ban on "fair and honest criticism," his earlier order that "criticism of command decisions or of the conduct of Allied soldiers on the battlefield will not be tolerated" raised doubts in the minds of reporters. Thompson's revision of the statement to add the qualifying word "unwarranted" was also unreassuring in light of his explanation that the army would be the "sole judge and jury on whether criticism is unwarranted or not." Colonel Echols reiterated his request for compliance with the voluntary censorship code as a substitute for formal press controls. Echols charged that interviews with wounded or shell-shocked soldiers demoralized and frightened "[Korean] men who might otherwise fight on the democratic side." Correspondent Ray Erwin reported that two newsmen sent to Japan for "reorientation" had apparently broken the voluntary censorship code that forbade mentioning unit affiliation, specific locations, and troop movements.[33]

The censorship issue became linked to the White House in late August when President Truman countermanded a call by General MacArthur for use of Chinese nationalist troops in Korea. In this well-known controversy MacArthur had advanced his proposal in a speech prepared for delivery at the Veterans of Foreign Wars annual encampment. Truman, fearful that deployment of Chinese nationalist troops could bring Communist China and the Soviet Union into the fighting and thus precipitate a third world war, ordered the speech withdrawn. MacArthur's original address nevertheless was published in the press and in the *Congressional Record. Editor and Publisher* reported that news correspondents looked for "censorship at the source" to increase in the wake of the president's displeasure over recent public utterances on military and diplomatic policy.[34]

Fundamental policy differences between the president and the general, seemingly resolved in their well-publicized meeting at Wake Island in mid-October, took on a larger significance after a massive Chinese intervention had sent MacArthur's troops reeling backward from advanced positions in North Korea. The urgency MacArthur attached to expanding the war to China itself through the use of American air and sea power with the support of nationalist Chinese forces became a common topic of conversation in Washington.[35]

---

33. *Editor and Publisher* (July 8, 1950): 7; (August 5, 1950): 9.
34. *Editor and Publisher* (August 5, 1950): 9.
35. McCoy, *The Presidency of Harry S. Truman,* 244–45, 261.

Truman took note of the reports about his and MacArthur's divergent views in a press conference November 30. With a sharpness that increasingly characterized his meetings with reporters, Truman rebuked the correspondents for suggesting that the general had exceeded his authority. Stunned by Truman's comment that MacArthur had done "nothing of the kind," the reporters remained silent.

"Well," Truman asked, "what is the matter?"

The reporters retraced the differences between the two men as evidence of the general's insubordination.[36]

The contentious press conference took an even more unexpected turn when a reporter asked Truman a follow-up question to the president's remark that "we will take whatever steps are necessary to meet the military situation, just as we always have."

"Will that include the atomic bomb?" the reporter asked.

"That includes every weapon we have," the president replied. The ensuing questions led Truman to make a number of provocative statements, including his explanation that "the military commander in the field will have charge of the use of the weapon, as he always has."[37]

In the closing moments of the conference, Truman angrily lashed out at reporters for stories he characterized as "attacks and speculations and lies that have been told on the members of this Government." He added, "I am getting tired of all this foolishness, and I'm going to 'bust loose' on you one of these days."[38]

While the reporters laughed at Truman's parting shot, Press Secretary Ross acted quickly to defuse Truman's explosive comments on the use of the atomic bomb. In a press release that afternoon, Ross put the best face on the president's remarks. The release confirmed that "Naturally, there has been consideration of this subject [the use of the atomic bomb] since the outbreak of the hostilities in Korea, just as there is consideration of the use of all military weapons whenever our forces are in combat." The statement offered further explanation:

> Consideration of the use of any weapon is always implicit in the very possession of that weapon. However, it should be emphasized, that, by law, only the President can authorize the use of the atom bomb, and no such authorization has been given. If

36. *Public Papers,* 1950, 725–26.
37. Ibid., 727.
38. Ibid., 728.

and when such authorization should be given, the military commander in the field would have charge of the tactical delivery
of the weapon.

The release concluded: "In brief, the replies to the question at today's
press conference do not represent any change in this situation."[39]

While Truman's remarks on the possible use of the atomic bomb
provoked banner headlines in the world press and brought British
Prime Minister Clement Attlee scurrying to Washington for consul-
tation, the communiqué released at the end of the prime minister's
meeting with the president did not change the explanation provided
by Truman in his press conference and the clarifying statement
issued by Secretary Ross.[40]

Sadly, Charles Ross's handling of the uproar over the president's
exchange with reporters on the possible use of atomic bombs in the
Korean conflict was his final act. As the sixty-five-year-old press
secretary prepared to give Frank Bourgholtzer of NBC a recorded
account of the Truman-Attlee meeting for broadcast, he slumped to
his desk, dying instantly of a heart attack. His death on December
5 removed from Truman's inner circle a close friend and valuable
adviser, as well as a loyal and hard-working press secretary.[41]

Respectful coverage of Ross's death and his service as the president's spokesman filled the front pages and editorial sections of the
nation's newspapers for the next few days,[42] providing a break in the
tension-laden exchanges between Truman and reporters. Of all the
journalistic tributes to Ross, the *Wall Street Journal* most percep-
tively noted that two loyalties had commanded the president's press
secretary:

> One was to his old friend, schoolmate and President. The other
> was to the business of telling the public what goes on in the
> world and, if possible, why. Sometimes the two inevitably con-
> flicted, and the remarkable thing is that no one ever questioned
> his loyalty to the other.
> For that, Harry Truman is deeply in Charlie Ross's debt. And
> the rest of us are, too.[43]

39. Ibid., note 3, 727.
40. Farrar, *Reluctant Servant*, 220–21.
41. Ibid., 225–26.
42. Ibid., 227–29.
43. Quoted in Farrar, *Reluctant Servant*, 228.

Truman penned his own tribute to Ross, echoing many of the journalistic salutes to an outstanding member of the guild. He found the larger contribution of Ross to his presidency in his lifelong friend's counsel on questions of "high public policy which he could give out of the wealth of his learning, his wisdom and his far-flung experience. Patriotism and integrity, honor and honesty, lofty ideals and nobility of intent were his guides and ordered his life from boyhood onward."

The president, meeting with reporters in the press room where Ross had conducted twice-daily news briefings for more than five years, started to read his tribute. But his voice broke before he could complete the first sentence. A long period of silence followed until Truman regained his composure; still he could not complete his statement.

"Aw, hell! I can't read this thing. You fellows know how I feel, anyway."

He laid the text on a table, and he left the room, tears streaming down his face.[44]

The following month the matter of presidential authority to send troops to Europe and a rehash of the potential use of atomic weapons in the Korean War resurfaced at the president's news conference. Truman, prepared for a question on his authority to send troops abroad, read from a statement that cited his constitutional power as commander in chief of the armed forces to send troops anywhere in the world. That power, he added, had been recognized repeatedly by the Congress and the courts. For the next several minutes reporters asked questions to elucidate the matter, specifically on whether he would consult with Congress before sending more troops to Europe. The fury of questions on when and under what circumstances the president would consult with Congress produced as much confusion as clarity, but the stories published from the exchange reported that Truman said that he would consult with Congress on the matter.[45]

The subject came up again at the news conference of January 18 as reporters engaged Truman in semantics over his constitutional authority and the need to consult Congress on the sending of troops abroad. Probably feeling badgered by the line of questioning at two previous news conferences and perhaps confused himself by now on

44. Ibid., 229–31. The tribute is printed in *Public Papers, 1950,* 737.
45. *Public Papers, 1951,* 4, 18–23.

what had been reported in the press, Truman blamed the reporters for the confusion:

> You know, it's a peculiar situation, sometimes, that arises here. Last week, I made it perfectly plain exactly what I would do with the legislative branch . . . and the statement that I made about consultation [with the Congress] was not quoted in a single paper in the United States. . . . At the same time, two or three weeks ago, there was a question came up here about atomic energy and its use for national defense. It was rather badly garbled and created an argument that was entirely unnecessary.

He would appreciate it, Truman said, if the reporters would state the facts "as I state them to you."[46]

The correspondents quickly challenged Truman on his command of the facts. They had indeed reported that he planned to consult with Congress and their editors had printed the story accurately. The exchange ended in a standoff, with Truman insisting that the reporters would understand his point by reading the news conference transcript. The reporters stuck by their guns, and properly so. What about the comment on the atomic bomb, one reporter asked? Read the *New Yorker*, Truman advised, a reference to writer John Hersey's recent article that used "an exact and complete transcript of what was said and what was meant."[47]

In fact, Hersey's article, written with the cooperation of the White House Press Office, provided an account of the controversy over the possible use of the atomic bomb along the same lines expressed in the press secretary's news release. Robert Brown suggested in his weekly column in *Editor and Publisher* that Truman had purposely created a row with the press as a means of taking some of the heat off him in the Senate debate over presidential authority. "It is known that President Truman and others before him," Brown contended, "have been clever enough to use an occasional blast at the press as a smoke screen for some other more dangerous or ticklish subject that might arise at the press conference." Truman's criticism of the press for its treatment of his remarks on the atomic bomb, Brown averred, was an attempt to "get off the hook" even at this late date.[48]

---

46. Ibid., 112–14.
47. Ibid., 113–14.
48. John Hersey, *Aspects of the Presidency*, 3–8, 59–66; Robert U. Brown, "Shop Talk at Thirty," *Editor and Publisher* (January 27, 1951): 64.

Years later *New York Herald Tribune* reporter Robert Donovan returned to this controversy in his history of the Truman admin- istration. Donovan suspected that Truman had deliberately manip- ulated reporters on the possible use of tactical atomic bombs in the Korean War, ostensibly as a stratagem of war. But finding no evidence in Truman's papers to support this suspicion, he concluded that the remarks on the subject should be regarded as an "unwise provocation by the president." However, in light of the use of atomic diplomacy employed by the Eisenhower administration to obtain an armistice in Korea in July 1953, some value may have attached to Truman's words, intended or not.[49]

Significantly, Truman had both practical and moral grounds for not using atomic weapons in Korea. Subsequently declassified pa- pers revealed that the president feared that an unexploded warhead could fall into the enemy's hands and be used to its advantage. He had stated the moral reason for not using atomic weapons in his November 30 press conference when the subject first arose. He told reporters, "It is a terrible weapon. And it should not be used on innocent men, women, and children who have nothing whatever to do with this military aggression. That happens when it is used."[50]

Still, the administration went forward with a multibillion-dollar request for nuclear and conventional weapons appropriations from Congress on the day following his controversial remarks. The pres- ident's request—the front-page story of the *New York Times* and other newspapers for December 2, 1950—asked that Congress sup- ply slightly more than a billion dollars in a total defense request of $16.5 billion to expand the nation's existing stockpile of atomic weapons.[51]

49. Donovan's quote is in Thompson, ed., *Ten Presidents and the Press*, 41– 44; see Roger Dingman, "Atomic Diplomacy during the Korean War," in Sean M. Lynn-Jones, Steven E. Miller, and Stephen Van Evera, *Nuclear Diplomacy and Crisis Management*, 114–55.

50. A newspaper account of the technical security reasons for not using atomic weapons in Korea was published in the *New York Post*, December 31, 1950. See "HST File, Atom Policy," Box 12, Democratic National Commit- tee Clipping File, Truman Library. In 1977 documents of the Senate Foreign Relations Committee made public the fact that the Joint Chiefs of Staff had considered recommending the use of atomic bombs during the Korean War but did not find any strategic targets worthwhile. *Los Angeles Times*, March 7, 1977. *Public Papers*, 1950, 727; 1952–1953, 1200–1201. Truman expanded upon his point about using nuclear weapons in his farewell address.

51. *New York Times*, December 2, 1950.

If this turn of events worked to the advantage of the president, the editorial writer of *Editor and Publisher* thought otherwise. The editorial stated that Truman's criticism of newspapers in reporting on the contemplated use of atomic weapons in Korea and the dispatch of troops to Europe "was not only unjustified but tended to undermine public confidence in the press just at a time when he, of all people, should be interested in promoting public confidence in that press." The president would be the loser, the editorial concluded, for "the press is his primary medium for informing the public also. If he convinces the people they can't trust what they read in the papers about comments of other people—then how long are they going to trust what the newspapers report him as saying?"[52]

Abundantly clear at the time was the reversal suffered by the United Nations forces commanded by General MacArthur following the massive intervention of Chinese "volunteers" in the Korean War in late November. The intervention left the president angry and the public confused, and completely blew away MacArthur's prediction to Truman at Wake Island that the fighting would be substantially over by Thanksgiving.[53]

Now MacArthur interpreted the situation as "a whole new war with a new enemy," and the headstrong commander refused to settle for a cease-fire and limited objectives in Korea as advocated by the Truman administration to preserve its "Europe First" policy. When MacArthur allowed his opposing views to be aired by Truman's Republican opposition, the die was cast. The president recalled the general on April 11, 1951.[54]

Although Truman seemed to be resigned to the initially strong public censure for firing MacArthur, White House aides were unwilling to wait for the storm of criticism to subside. Presidential aide George Elsey took the lead in building a case in the press for the president's action. At the direction of the president, Elsey supplied *New York Times* correspondent Anthony Leviero with a transcript of the Wake Island conference. Leviero's news story of April 21, 1950, clearly established MacArthur's faulty judgment on the prospect of Chinese intervention and helped to relieve adverse criticism of the president. A second effort by Elsey lined up *Saturday Evening Post* writer Beverly Smith for a series of articles that summer. When Elsey asked Truman to read Smith's first article in draft form, the

52. Editorial, *Editor and Publisher* (December 9, 1950): 42.
53. Phillips, *The Truman Presidency*, 320–21.
54. McCoy, *The Presidency of Harry S. Truman*, 239–48, 261–62.

president commented, "It seems to me to be factually correct, so I guess you can okay it." Truman added that he did not think the *Post* would publish the piece because it seemed "friendly and favorable to the Administration." That was the objective, of course. When Elsey informed Truman that *Post* editor Ben Hibbs had already approved the article and was eager for the remainder of the series, Truman remarked that he found that scenario hard to believe.[55]

Ironically, the general reportedly shared Truman's belief that the press had been a divisive force in their relationship and did not properly convey the facts of their dispute to the public. The source of this interpretation, Major General Charles A. Willoughby, chief of intelligence to MacArthur, advanced this view in a December 1951 *Cosmopolitan* article entitled "The Truth about Korea." Willoughby leveled a withering blast at several newsmen, charging them with "inaccurate, biased, and petulant" reporting of the fighting in Korea and "giving aid and comfort to the enemy." Excepting a few newspapers—the Scripps-Howard chain and the Hearst press— Willoughby aimed his fire at seven "journalistic soothsayers": Hanson W. Baldwin, military correspondent for the *New York Times;* Homer Bigart and Frank Kelley, *New York Herald Tribune;* Hal Boyle and Relman Morin of the Associated Press; columnist Joseph Alsop; and radio commentator and newspaper columnist Drew Pearson. He charged all with "irresponsible reporting." "The typewriter attack from the rear," Willoughby observed, "can sometimes be worse than the enemy." He concluded, "I am convinced the nuance of defeat created an atmosphere of tension, uneasiness, and distrust between Tokyo [MacArthur's headquarters] and Washington. This is believed to have been the major cause of the MacArthur-Truman split."[56]

Several newsmen targeted by Willoughby quickly offered rebuttals, citing Willoughby's underestimating the number of Chinese troops that had infiltrated into Korea as evidence of his inability to get the facts straight. Baldwin replied in the *New York Times* that the general's account was "as misleading and inaccurate as some of his intelligence reports." Boyle acidly commented that "Generalities

55. George M. Elsey oral history, by Jerry N. Hess, vol. 2, 280–85; Elsey to author, June 14, 1995. Leviero, for his part, said that he got the Wake Island transcript by being "the right person at the right time." His article received a Pulitzer Prize for 1951. See his account in *Editor and Publisher* (May 26, 1951): 14. The memoranda on Smith's article are in Korea: B. Smith's Article SEP 11/10/51 folder, Box 76, George M. Elsey Papers, Truman Library.

56. Willoughby's major charges are quoted in *Editor and Publisher* (December 1, 1951): 10.

about 'bias and prejudice' cannot outweigh the hard facts of defeat and the cold statistics of losses. It was not 'bias and prejudice' that rolled the Army back across thousands of square miles of lost ground."[57]

Meanwhile, Truman's desire to prevent the publication of security information that could benefit the nation's enemies prompted the issuance of an Executive Order on September 24, 1951, prescribing regulations for classifying and protecting security information. The order specified four classifications of security information—top secret, secret, confidential, and restricted—and designated the National Security Council as a review agency to ensure uniform compliance "both as to safeguarding security information and to prevent the classification procedure from being used to withhold information which can be divulged without harm to the national security."[58]

Although Truman had recognized that "improper application of the classification powers is repulsive to our democratic form of Government," the press quickly denounced his executive order. *Editor and Publisher,* despite the fact that the nation was at war, charged that the president had established an "unparalleled peacetime censorship" that was "unnecessary and dangerous." Members of the Associated Press Managing Editors Association, meeting in convention shortly after the president issued his order, ventured into name-calling, with one editor asserting that Truman should be called a liar for declaring there was no censorship, "either directly or implied" in the executive order. In an open letter to the president, the association expressed its opposition to his order "as a dangerous instrument of news suppression." The letter also took issue with Truman's assertion that the new regulations would actually make more information available to the public rather than less. The National Editorial Association, while adopting a resolution in which they viewed the presidential order with "the gravest apprehension," acknowledged both their and the president's responsibilities to safeguard and protect the security of the nation.[59]

The editors of *Editor and Publisher* argued further that "Presidential strategy in defense of the Executive Order establishing security regulations in all departments is to convince the public it is the fault

---

57. Ibid., 10–11.
58. *Public Papers,* 1951, 536–37.
59. Ibid., 537; *Editor and Publisher* (September 29, 1951): 38; (October 6, 1951): 38; (October 6, 1951): 12; (October 20, 1951): 7.

of the press that secret information has gotten into the hands of the enemy." In its editorial of October 13, 1951, the journal resented the implication that the loyalty and patriotism of newspapers and magazines were suspect. Moreover, its editorial charged that the president ignored the fact that newspapers and magazines followed the accepted practice of clearing beforehand doubtful information with the appropriate government departments and agencies.[60]

Truman had opened himself to such criticisms in comments made in defense of his security information order at his news conference on October 4, 1951. He cited as "an outstanding example . . . the publication in *Fortune* magazine of all the locations and the maps of our atomic energy plants." Moreover, Truman added, newspapers had published air maps of the nation's major cities with arrows pointing to the key points in those towns. The following dialogue ensued:

> Q. I think that information was given out by the departments—
> The President. Well, I don't care who gave it out. The publishers had no business to use it, if they had the welfare of the United States at heart.
> Q. I don't know if the military or atomic energy—
> The President. I don't care who gave it out. The publisher should be just as patriotic as I am, and I wouldn't give it out.
> Q. The story was . . . attributed to a military agency—
> The President. Yes, and if the military agency gives you that, and an atomic bomb falls on you on account of that, at the right place, who is to blame?[61]

Later in the conference, a reporter asked if the executive order was related to the White House announcement of the previous day of another atomic explosion in the Soviet Union. Truman denied that there was any connection, stating that he had issued the order before the explosion had occurred.

Reporters, still troubled that Truman had blamed the press for publishing sensitive information, continued the exchange:

> Q. Well, my experience has been that the editors did not make up these maps—
> The President. They did, in *Fortune* magazine.
> Q. I mean the civil defense map—

60. *Editor and Publisher* (October 13, 1951): 38.
61. *Public Papers*, 1951, 554–56.

The President. Well, they were air pictures of the great cities. And it's terrible. I wish I had them of Russia and their manufacturing plants. I could use them.[62]

May Craig brought the discussion over censorship and freedom of the press to a head with a pointed question: "Mr. President, have you weighed the importance of the free press in relation to military security?" Yes, Truman replied, and if it was dangerous to give civilian agencies the power to determine what should be given to the people, then he would change the regulation.[63]

Despite continued heated exchanges between Truman and news reporters over national security needs and freedom of the press, in practice the information policies of government agencies and the publication of security-related articles in the press changed very little. Two months after the issuance of the regulation, a *Washington Post* survey of several agencies revealed few had actually used the "security information" stamp. The press continued to print security information that by previous standards would have angered Truman, as in the disclosure of detailed construction plans regarding the hydrogen bomb facilities at Aiken, South Carolina, and in the article written by Stewart Alsop and Ralph Lapp for an October 1952 issue of the *Saturday Evening Post* that provided a graphic account of how a hydrogen bomb worked. The president's aides, anticipating that he would explode over the detailed account of a hydrogen bomb's awesome destructive power, advised him to offer no public comment on the piece in order to attract no further attention to it.[64] Probably only the lack of time, however, kept Truman from rebuking the press for publishing information he deemed vital to the security of the nation.

In the spring of 1952 Truman and the press held one final grand encounter over presidential power, national security, and freedom of the press. The clash resulted from press reaction to the president's order for the seizure of strike-bound steel mills that threatened, in Truman's view, to deprive the military fighting in Korea of essential war materials. The president's action provoked strong editorial

62. Ibid., 556.
63. Ibid., 556–57.
64. *Editor and Publisher* (January 26, 1952): 8; (December 13, 1952): 8; Stewart Alsop and Ralph Lapp, "The Inside Story of Our First Hydrogen Bomb," *Saturday Evening Post* 225 (October 25, 1952): 29ff; see also folder NSC, Atomic Bomb, Alsop article, Box 199, PSF, Truman Papers, Truman Library.

opposition on constitutional merits alone; only the pro-labor *New York Post* among major newspapers supported the seizure.[65]

Initially, the public debate over Truman's actions centered on the question of the authority conferred upon the president through the implied powers of Article II of the Constitution. The press kept its focus on the central issue until the president's joint news conference for the Washington news corps and members of the American Society of Newspaper Editors on April 17, 1952. At the conference an unidentified person arose to ask the provocative question:

"Mr. President, if you can seize the steel mills under your inherent powers, can you, in your opinion, also seize the newspapers and/or the radio stations?"

Truman replied: "Under similar circumstances the President of the United States has to act for whatever is for the best of the country. That's the answer to your question."[66]

This all-encompassing response to a hypothetical question drew both angry and measured response from publishers and editors. The American Publishers Association, meeting in annual convention a few days later after the news conference, passed a resolution strongly denouncing the president for implying that he might have the power to seize the press. The editors of the American Society of Newspaper Editors, reflecting the view of many that the president had been unfairly asked to comment on a hypothetical question as a means of drawing him into a controversy, tabled a motion of censure. H. V. Kaltenborn, president of the Radio News Analysts Association, agreed with the editors that Truman had been drawn unfairly into a dispute.[67]

Truman greeted the furor over his latest encounter with the news media by characterizing it as "a lot of hooey" and by reiterating what he had stated at a previous news conference: "The President of the United States has very great inherent powers to meet great national emergencies. Until those emergencies arise a President cannot say specifically what he would do or would not do." Truman added, "I can say this, that the thought of seizing press and radio has never occurred to me."[68]

---

65. Maeva Marcus, *Truman and the Steel Seizure Case: The Limits of Presidential Power*, 89.
66. *Public Papers, 1952–1953*, 272–73.
67. *Editor and Publisher* (April 26, 1952): 11, 122.
68. *Public Papers, 1952–1953*, 290–91.

While reporters seemed satisfied with Truman's explanation, some editors kept him on the hook. *Editor and Publisher* excoriated him for refusing to make a complete renunciation of his "implied powers" position. In the opinion of the trade journal, Truman "blithely and unconcernedly declares 'I am the law,' as have dictators in the past, arrogating to himself power and authority never intended to be in his hands, usurping the fundamental right of the people specifically guaranteed in the Constitution."[69]

Later, the perceived challenge to the freedom of the press by presidential action found resolution indirectly in the courts. On June 2, 1952, the United States Supreme Court, in a 6 to 3 decision in *Youngstown Sheet and Tube v. Sawyer*, affirmed a lower-court order invalidating the government's steel-seizure order by rejecting the "inherent power" argument of the president.

Widespread and happy agreement in the news media greeted the Supreme Court's redressing of executive power. The *New York Times* went to the core of the issue with its jubilant editorial: "We have, in the opinion delivered by Justice [Hugo] Black yesterday and sustained by five other justices, a redefinition of the powers of the President. Under this opinion the trend toward an indefinite expansion of the Chief Executive's authority is deliberately checked."[70]

In this indirect manner, the press in general and the antiadministration press in particular finally chalked up a victory over presidential power. Moreover, the victory had been won through the judiciary in the framework of the Constitution with the assistance of a vigilant and militant press.

Lost from sight, however, was the democratic spirit that had guided Truman in his war of words with the news media over such matters as censorship, presidential authority in foreign and military affairs, and freedom of the press. Indeed, the occasion for many of the contentious exchanges between Truman and reporters was the president's frequent, regularized news conference that he called "the greatest show in town."[71] But it was democracy's show, too, and it was one of the strong pillars of Truman's democratic faith in the people's right to know about their government through a free press.

69. *Editor and Publisher* (April 26, 1952): 80.

70. Marcus, *Truman and the Steel Seizure Case*, 212.

71. Truman described his meetings with press and radio as "the greatest show in Washington" for the benefit of visiting foreign journalists at his news conference of September 22, 1950. *Public Papers, 1950*, 645.

4

The President's News Conference

IT WOULD BE DIFFICULT to conceive of the Truman administration without the news conferences, for they embody and display so much of the president's philosophy of government, his personality, and his relationship with the men and women of the Washington news corps. And from the broadened perspective of recent years, with the drastic reduction in the number of news conferences held by his successors, Truman's regular and frequent meetings with the press constitute a worthy legacy.[1]

At the outset of his administration, Truman adopted his predecessor's rules governing news conferences. Some news would be "off the record," with the information to be kept secret; "background information" could be used, but not with attribution to the president; other information from the president could be attributed to him, but not quoted directly. The president could be quoted directly only with permission. Explaining that his demanding schedule ruled out

---

1. The presidential news conference became a rare event during the Nixon administration, especially after the Watergate break-in and coverup became news. Presidents Ford, Carter, and Bush met with the press on a scaled-back but still regularized basis. Ronald Reagan reverted to the infrequent and irregular news conference schedule of Nixon. The average number of news conferences of each president from Truman to Reagan is given in Emery and Emery, *The Press and America*, 303. Truman news conferences include his annual meetings with the press to go over the federal budget. See, for example, *Public Papers*, 1946, 374–84.

the twice-weekly meetings favored by Franklin Roosevelt, Truman stated that he would hold one news conference a week, alternating between a morning and afternoon session to give equal treatment to early and late newspaper editions. Except for trips abroad and election-year campaigning in 1948 and 1952, he adhered closely to his objective of holding weekly press meetings.[2]

On April 17, 1945, five days into his administration, Truman held his first news conference for press and radio in the president's office of the White House. The record turnout of 348 correspondents exceeded the capacity of the room, forcing many reporters onto an outside terrace. Standing erect behind his desk, Truman fielded questions in a direct, straightforward manner. At the end of the conference the reporters gave him an encouraging round of applause. His confident performance, Arthur Krock noted, corrected the initial impression of the news media and the nation of a man almost overwhelmed by his great responsibilities.[3]

The only discordant note after Truman's initial news conference came in response to his announcement that J. Leonard Reinsch of Cox Broadcasting would assist him "with press and radio affairs." Newspapermen, unhappy with the prospect of getting daily briefings from a radio man, quickly made their dissatisfaction known to the president's inner circle. Truman convened a second news conference three days later to announce that Charlie Ross would serve as press secretary. He may have had his boyhood friend in mind all along and intended for Reinsch to assist him primarily in his radio addresses. He had tried to recruit Ross for the 1944 campaign, but Joseph Pulitzer II, apparently without consulting Ross, sent back word that the *Post-Dispatch* could not spare him during the summer vacation season. A presidential request, however, was of a different order, and Ross took a leave of absence to sign on as press secretary. Truman handled the awkward situation by explaining that he had acquiesced in the request of James Cox, Reinsch's employer, to release Reinsch from full-time duty at the White House. It seemed to Reinsch and broadcast journalists that he had acquiesced as well in the preferred arrangement of newspaper reporters.[4]

2. James E. Pollard, *The Presidents and the Press: From Truman to Johnson,* 27.

3. Robert H. Ferrell, ed., *Truman in the White House: The Diary of Eben A. Ayers,* 11, 8–13; *New York Times,* April 18, 1945.

4. *Public Papers,* 1945, 8–9; 16–19, 166–67; Pulitzer to Ross, August 15, 1944, Microfilm Reel 96, Joseph Pulitzer II Papers, Library of Congress. The request

Invariably Truman and his news conferences invited immediate and frequent comparison with the conferences of FDR. James J. Butler, covering the new president's first conference for *Editor and Publisher*, expressed relief that one annoying aspect engendered by twelve years of meetings with Roosevelt—the "giggle chorus"— would probably cease to exist. The "chorus," he explained, comprised about a dozen reporters who gathered around Roosevelt's desk and laughed at the "slightest sign of humor on FDR's countenance."[5] Butler clearly belonged to the group of reporters who disliked Roosevelt.

FDR, in turn, had mixed feelings about the Washington news corps. At times he could charm and compliment the reporters, but he resorted to ridicule and humiliation if a journalist incurred his displeasure, going so far on one occasion as to award, in absentia, an Iron Cross to John O'Donnell of the *New York Daily News* for writing articles that Roosevelt believed violated voluntary wartime censorship outlining war plans for the European theater.[6]

Truman's decision to reduce presidential news conferences to one meeting per week drew a complaint from some reporters that the flow of news from the White House would be greatly reduced. In response, Press Secretary Ross declared that "Truman gives out more news at one press conference than Roosevelt customarily gave out at ten." Ross noted, too, that FDR held few press conferences during the last six months of his life. Moreover, wartime secrecy had kept many of Roosevelt's conferences "off the record," whereas under Truman climactic events such as the surrender of Nazi Germany, the use of the atomic bomb against Japan, the Soviet declaration of war against Japan, and the Japanese surrender were all announced by the White House and, at times, by the president himself. In addition, the change in presidential administrations provided a flood of information on departures and new appointees.[7]

---

for Ross had come from Robert E. Hannegan, Chairman of the Democratic National Committee, and a native of St. Louis; Farrar, *Reluctant Servant*, 155–58, 205–6, 154–55, 159–60.

5. *Editor and Publisher* (April 21, 1945): 9.

6. White, *FDR and the Press*, 44–45; Winfield, *FDR and the News Media*, 67–68.

7. Ross's comments appear in Ross to C. E. Kane, September 21, 1945, as quoted in Farrar, *Reluctant Servant*, 176. For news stemming from the change in administrations, see for example the presidential news conferences for April through August 1945 in *Public Papers*, 1945, passim.

These prime news announcements and informative news conferences helped to promote a long honeymoon between the press and the president.

Beyond the factual content of the Truman news conferences, some reporters believed that the president failed to provide necessary background information. Truman's style of giving short, direct answers to questions contrasted greatly with the discursive manner of Franklin Roosevelt. Felix Belair, Jr., reporter for the *New York Times*, described the Roosevelt conferences as being like "the opening night of the Ziegfeld Follies while President Truman's are like amateur night." For Belair, the differences of the conferences could be explained by the personalities of the two men: "President Roosevelt was a tremendously accomplished actor in dealing with the press and would elucidate his point by parable, by history, by calculus, if necessary." By contrast, "President Truman will simply say 'No,' or 'It's not time to talk about that yet' or 'Yes, and for the following reasons—one, two, three—and goodbye.' "[8]

Newsweek's Ernest Lindley acknowledged that the expansive style of FDR had produced valuable conferences, permitting both reporters and the public to gain insights into Roosevelt's mind and objectives. Truman did not use his conferences for that purpose, Lindley speculated, because "his mind doesn't work that way. Unlike Roosevelt, he is not an originator and he doesn't have the habit of thinking aloud."[9]

Yet Truman could be expansive, too, as he demonstrated in background, off-the-record meetings with editors, publishers, and radio journalists. Apparently he and his press secretaries and advisers never entertained the thought of transforming the conferences from a rapid give-and-take questioning session to a slower-paced, discursive and reflective treatment of the issues by the president. By not taking this approach, Truman drew criticism from reporters at the time, and from scholars since, for missing opportunities afforded by press conferences to provide leadership for his program and policies.[10]

8. As quoted in *Editor and Publisher* (March 16, 1946): 58.

9. Ernest Lindley, "Washington Tides," *Newsweek* 28 (October 28, 1946): 30.

10. See, for example, Truman's meeting with newspaper editors in April 1946. The president employed the same expansive style in a meeting with radio analysts on May 13, 1947. *Public Papers*, 1946, 206–14, and 1947, 238–41. Elmer E. Cornwell, Jr., *Presidential Leadership of Public Opinion*, 161–65; Monte M. Poen, *Harry S. Truman versus the Medical Lobby*, 74–75.

By the fall of 1946 press criticism of the Truman news conferences had grown from a trickle to a torrent, in response to the confusion generated by the president's mixed signals on the foreign policy views advanced by Secretary of Commerce Wallace. This well-known story finds Wallace, in a visit with Truman on September 10, informing the president that he was going to speak on U.S.-Soviet relations in an address in New York City on September 12. Truman looked over a portion of the speech, and when Wallace supplied an advance copy to reporters, he stated that the president had read the address and approved it.

At the president's news conference on the day of Wallace's address, William H. Mylander, a reporter for the *Minneapolis Star Journal and Tribune* (and later publicity director of the Republican National Committee) queried Truman on the speech and thus set in motion what became one of the president's biggest blunders in his meetings with reporters. Mylander had read the talk and understood that Wallace's advocacy of a "go slow" approach ran counter to the administration's hard-line policy toward the Soviets. Did Truman approve the speech, he asked? At first Truman wisely replied that he couldn't answer questions on a speech that had not yet been given. Mylander pressed on, and Truman blundered by saying that he approved Wallace's speech in its entirety.[11]

Wallace's address made headline news and caused a crisis in the administration. Truman had either shifted to a softening of his tough Soviet policy or he did not realize what he had done. Consequently, all hell broke lose. Secretary of State Byrnes cabled the president from Paris, where he was attending a meeting of foreign ministers, that he must have the president's support or he would resign.[12]

Charlie Ross took the lead in crafting a press release that stated that the president had not approved a new line of departure in American-Soviet relations; rather, he had only approved Wallace's right to make the speech. This explanation fell short of the mark, however, and *Time* flatly branded it a "clumsy lie."[13]

In the end Truman convened a special news conference on September 20 to clarify the nation's foreign policy and the new protocol

11. Pollard, *The President and the Press*, 29–30; *Public Papers*, 1946, 426–28; Phillips, *The Truman Presidency*, 130. Robert Ferrell has shown that Wallace made some changes in the speech looked over by Truman that favored the Soviets (*Harry S. Truman: A Life*, 424, note 19).

12. *New York Times*, September 12, 1946; Robert J. Donovan, *Conflict and Crisis: The Presidency of Harry S. Truman, 1945–1948*, 222–28.

13. *Public Papers*, 1946, 427; *Time* 50 (September 23, 1946): 22.

for clearance of views expressed by members of the executive branch of government. His statement covered the initial faux pas of his previous press conference, the feeble follow-up explanation, and the resolution of the conflict between Wallace, Byrnes, and himself. First, he declared that the nation had only one foreign policy; second, he had requested the resignation of Wallace, whose advocacy of policy vis-a-vis the Soviet Union ran counter to the policy guiding Secretary Byrnes; third, in the future members of the executive branch would be required to clear foreign policy statements with the department of state; fourth, internal dissension over the administration's foreign policy would be referred to the president. He cleared the air with the secretary of state by adding that Byrnes "consults with me often, and the policies which guide him and his delegation [in the ongoing Paris Conference] have my full endorsement." Reporters, informed in advance that the president would take no questions, left after Truman's dismissing words: "That's all gentlemen."[14]

Not unexpectedly, the Wallace affair and the way it was handled by Truman and his press secretary prompted some presidential watchers to question the appropriateness of holding press conferences. *U.S. News*, in a profile of Ross in its issue of September 27, 1946, reported that the task of correcting the president had become burdensome to his press secretary; and because many of the presidential statements requiring correction or modification had occurred at press conferences, there was talk of discontinuing them. *Labor*, the newspaper of several railroad unions, offered its blunt opinion that "the press conference as conducted in Washington is a foolish performance which does infinitely more harm than good. No man living can face a battery of newspaper men once a week, respond to any questions they fling at him, and hope to escape serious damage." The newspaper advised Truman to "not only tighten up on his press conference, he should abolish the institution."[15]

Journalists at both ends of the political spectrum were quick to defend the presidential news conferences. Liberal columnist Lindley, writing in his *Newsweek* column "Washington Tides," granted that "an unorganized rapid-fire barrage of questions from 50 to 200 correspondents" was not an efficient way to elicit information. "Orderly exploration of an important topic is seldom possible," he explained, in part because many questions pertained to matters of

14. *Public Papers, 1946*, 431.
15. *U.S. News* 21 (September 27, 1946): 59–64; the quote from *Labor* is as it appears in *Editor and Publisher* (November 2, 1946): 9.

local rather than national interest. Mistakes had happened, Lindley conceded; still, overall Truman had made very few slips, his average as good as Roosevelt's. He concluded that despite limitations and imperfections, the conferences "yield a net increment of information which the public would not otherwise receive." The conservative *Editor and Publisher* concurred with Lindley's analysis, adding, "We hope that [Truman] will continue to see the press regularly and that he does not consider proposals for altering a procedure that worked to the advantage of his predecessor and can work equally well for him."[16]

Several months later the newsworthiness and significance of the press conferences came under renewed attack from Roscoe Drummond in an article published in the February 3, 1948, issue of *Look*. Drummond, who covered the White House for the *Christian Science Monitor*, asserted that the Truman press conferences had "reached about the same state of responsiveness as a dead telephone with its wires cut and the receiver off the hook." Truman had become uncommunicative, he said, by dodging the searching questions of reporters with replies such as "No. Figures not yet ready. . . . I can't answer that. I have no information on that. I will announce that when it is ready" and "No comment." Moreover, the newsman charged, Truman had reduced meetings with the press to "a little more than one press conference a month, spaced to avoid times when 'hot' news might bring embarrassing questions from the reporters." Truman's evasive answers and his heavy reliance on mimeographed statements, the reporter concluded, had greatly diluted the value of the press conference.[17]

Some journalists agreed with Drummond's negative assessment of the newsworthiness of the presidential news conferences. Felix Jager of *Look* complained privately to a fellow journalist that the conferences of 1948 were "dull and uninformative." Columnist Stewart Alsop rarely attended the news conferences, and when he did, his purpose was to not to gather information, but to see the president in the flesh in order to judge his physical and psychological state.[18]

16. Ernest Lindley, "Washington Tides," *Newsweek* (October 28, 1946): 39; *Editor and Publisher* (November 2, 1946): 9.

17. Roscoe Drummond, "No News from the White House," *Look* 13 (February 3, 1948): 92.

18. Jager to May Craig, January 15, 1948, Scrapbook 17, Elizabeth May Craig Papers, Library of Congress; Alsop to Martin Sommers, March 1, [no year, filed with 1949 letters], Container 26, Joseph Alsop Papers, Library of Congress.

Ross offered a rebuttal to Drummond's charges, not in an influential magazine where his defense could have reached an audience similar to the readership of *Look*, but in private correspondence. The presidential news conferences, he asserted, provided a regular flow of information from the White House. The charge that Truman had held little more than one press conference a month was simply incorrect. "The truth," Ross wrote, "is that the President, during the six months from July, 1947 to January, 1948, held 17 'regular' press and radio conferences and four special press conferences—a total of 21 meetings with the press."[19]

No journalist offered a more thoughtful analysis of the significance of frequent and regular presidential news conferences than Anthony Leviero in an article for the August 21, 1949, issue of the *New York Times Magazine.* The conference, he wrote, had become "a factor in our checks-and-balances system of government. Nothing anywhere else in the world compares with it." At a recent meeting with reporters, he noted, Truman subjected himself to "free-hand, no-holds-barred questioning," fielding "forty-two questions covering sixteen topics in a twenty-minute mass interview." Comparisons of the presidential news conference with the question period in the British House of Commons were often made, Leviero acknowledged, "but how can a formal Parliamentary proceeding be compared with this free-wheeling affair of the press and the President?" "Where," he asked, "is the resemblance when it is neither the press that asks nor the head of the nation that answers?"

Leviero noted, too, the democratic character of the press conference as evidenced by the absence of rank among the questioners: "Joe Beagle of The Podunk Bugle has as much standing with his question on an irrigation project in his district as Mr. Pundit of the big newspaper chain, who is eager to know . . . whether the next Big Four conference may be expected to bring a German settlement." The conference, Leviero concluded, was "an exercise in democracy as well as a prime source of news."[20]

Truman vacillated in his feelings about his weekly meetings with journalists. Privately, he may have worried that he might disclose information that should be kept under wraps. A reporter for Tass, the official Soviet news agency, was accredited to the White House, as

19. Ross to Belair, Jr., January 14, 1948, Roscoe Drummond folder, Box 2, Charles G. Ross Papers, Truman Library.

20. Anthony Leviero, "The Presidential News Conference," *New York Times Magazine* (August 21, 1949): 10, 51–52.

were representatives of the press from other foreign countries. The Soviet reporter apparently did not query the president at any conference, following the practice of other foreign correspondents to hear answers rather than ask questions of the president. Interestingly, too, when *Editor and Publisher* took up the matter of representation of Soviet journalists throughout official Washington, it defended their accreditation on the grounds of freedom of the press.[21]

Truman had mixed feelings, too, about the protocol of the news conference. In January 1946 he confided to Harold Smith, director of the Bureau of the Budget, that at times the reporters' questions seemed to be impertinent, bordering on disrespect of the presidency.[22] He could be caught off guard, too, as when May Craig, taking her cue from Truman's observation at his news conference of March 26, 1947, that the meeting marked his one-hundredth meeting with reporters, asked him for an assessment of the news correspondents.

"Well, you really put me on the spot, Miss May," he responded, "but I enjoy these press conferences immensely. . . . I think you have been eminently fair to me ever since we started. . . . I have no quarrel with you at all." Major quarrels and impertinent questioning at future conferences, as we shall soon see, required a much different assessment.[23]

The preconference banter that took place between the president and wire service reporters and front-row regulars provides additional insight into the president's prevailing mood and the advantage these reporters enjoyed in being the first to enter the room when the meetings were held in the White House. The exchange of August 25, 1949, recorded by presidential stenographer Jack Romagna for the

---

21. James Reston of the *New York Times* cited the fear of Truman administration officials of disclosing sensitive information in the presence of Tass correspondents as one of the factors for the withholding of information. *Time* (February 20, 1950): 75. A rare exception to the practice of foreign correspondents to leave the questioning to American reporters occurred at the president's news conference of August 16, 1945, when a reporter for the French News Agency queried Truman about zones of occupation in Japan. *Public Papers, 1945*, 226. Franklin D. Roosevelt's press secretary, Steve Early, had informed members of the Foreign Press Association in 1945 that "there was no rule, written or otherwise, that would prevent a resident foreign correspondent from asking questions at Mr. Roosevelt's press conferences." Jonathan Daniels to Robert de Saint Jean, March 5, 1945, General File–Press folder, Box 10, Eben A. Ayers Papers, Truman Library. *Editor and Publisher* (October 6, 1951): 38.

22. Harold D. Smith, diary, January 31, 1946, Truman Library, copy of original on deposit in the Franklin D. Roosevelt Library, Hyde Park, New York.

23. *Public Papers, 1947*, 184–85.

complete record but not for the transcript published in the official *Public Papers*, revealed Truman's good humor that day:[25]

> The President: What do you say, gentlemen?
> Q. Not too much.
> Q. Let's make this short and sweet.
> The President: I am always in favor of that. That is up to Smitty (Merriman Smith). (laughter). . . .
> Merriman Smith: We've been "had." [Here Smith referred to the customary high prices charged reporters by hotel owner Barney Allison of Kansas City when they covered the president during his visits to the area.]
> The President: I am certainly sorry . . . I'm pretty near crying now. (much laughter).
> Q. Anything to keep Barney's morale up.
> Q. Don't you think that Barney is an optimist?
> The President: Well, now, you know what an optimist is, don't you? A pessimist is a man who wears belt and suspenders, but an optimist wears neither. (laughter). . . .
> Q. Mr. President, may I borrow one of your pencils temporarily, I have only a little one? (laughter).
> The President: I will let you have it.
> Q. Where did you get that little one?
> The President: I'm sure he borrowed it, and from the White House, too. (more laughter).

The press conference went well that day.[24]

Truman's unfortunate choice of words at some news conferences could produce politically damaging results as they did in his meeting with correspondents on August 5, 1948. Truman came to the conference with prepared statements bearing on actions of the Republican-controlled Congress and executive branch policy on control of its documents. In one statement he lambasted the Congress, called into special session as a part of the president's election strategy, for planning to adjourn without dealing with inflation. The ensuing questions of correspondents attempted to draw out the president on rising living costs and his fall campaign plans until Harold Stacy, a reporter for the *Columbus* (Ohio) *Dispatch*, suggested a connection between the failure of Congress to deal with inflation and the ongoing hearings of the House Committee on Un-American Activities on spy rings and communist influence in government.[25]

24. For the pre–news conference banter at the conference of August 25, 1949, and on other occasions, see the Press Conference Files, Box 63, PSF, Truman Library.

25. Edward Folliard to Truman, October 21, 1953, Box 72, PPF, Truman Papers, Truman Library.

Stacy's question, though unplanned, was prompted by the explosive testimony given by Whittaker Chambers two days earlier in his appearance before the House committee. Chambers, a former communist and currently a senior editor of *Time*, testified that an elite group of communists and fellow travelers had entered government service during the New Deal and rose to trusted positions in the Roosevelt and Truman administrations. Among those named by Chambers as a part of a communist apparatus in the federal government was Alger Hiss, functionary to President Roosevelt at the Yalta Conference and secretary of the United Nations Organizing Conference during the Truman administration. On the same day that Truman met with the press, Hiss appeared before the House committee to deny categorically Chambers's charges, thus setting in motion a centerpiece of the Cold War anticommunist crusade on matters of loyalty and disloyalty to the nation.[26]

"Mr. President," reporter Stacy asked, "do you think that the Capitol Hill spy scare is a 'red herring' to divert public attention from inflation?"

"Yes, I do," Truman responded, "and I will read you another statement on that, since you brought it up."[27]

Truman's carefully worded statement addressed the policy of the executive branch on written requests from congressional groups for information relating to individuals employed by the federal government. While unclassified employment records could be made available to congressional committees, Truman stated, "No information of any sort relating to the employee's loyalty, and no investigative data of any type . . . shall be included in the material submitted to a congressional committee." Hewing to the line of presidential power and the independence of the executive from the legislative branch, Truman declared that the White House alone would determine whether a certain document or a group of documents should be supplied to Congress. Satisfied with the investigation by the FBI and federal grand juries on the matter of communist infiltration of government, the president condemned the current congressional inquiries. "The public hearings now under way are serving no useful purpose," he said. "On the contrary, they are doing irreparable harm to certain people, seriously impairing the morale of Federal employees, and undermining public confidence in the Government." The

26. Ibid.; Alan D. Harper, *The Politics of Loyalty: The White House and the Communist Issue, 1946–52*, 71, 119–21.
27. *Public Papers*, 1948, 432–33.

hearings, Truman added, using the phrase supplied by Stacy, "are simply a 'red herring' to keep [the Republican-controlled special session of Congress] from doing what [it] ought to do."[28]

The following day Truman's characterization of the HUAC hearings as a "red herring" made the front pages of newspapers across the nation. Republicans, seizing on the opportunity Truman's remark offered to illustrate its charge that the president and liberal Democrats were "soft on communism," ensured that the phrase and the issue of communists in government would have a long life in the developing Cold War.

Significant, too, but almost lost from sight, was the president's declaration on maintaining executive control of its documents pertaining to federal employees. Senator Homer Ferguson (R-Mich.), in a Senate speech on August 7, denounced the president for his position. Ferguson, expressing his views as a newspaper publisher as well as a member of Congress, charged that the issue of secrecy in government and the accretion of presidential power was more serious than the issue of communism.[29]

Truman, increasingly concerned that the Republican-biased press was not getting his side of the national security debate into the newspapers, decided in mid-February 1950 to grant an exclusive interview to Arthur Krock. He had extended the invitation to Krock at Washington's exclusive F Street Club, where he and Mrs. Truman had gone for an evening social event, and the interview itself took place in the president's office. The topics covered in his conversation with the columnist, as revealed in the subsequent news story Krock wrote for the *New York Times*, gave the president's perspective on the course of the Cold War and the prospects for peace and domestic tranquillity in light of the mounting tide of anticommunist hysteria. His comments, outlining the steps he had taken to combat disloyalty, countered the recent demagogic charge of Senator Joseph R. McCarthy that "205 known communists were working in the United States Department of State."[30]

The attention of the Washington news corps, however, was drawn not to the substance of his interview—which appropriately appeared on the front page of the *Times*—but to the means Truman had

28. Ibid.
29. *New York Times*, August 8, 1948.
30. Ken Hechler, *Working with Truman: A Personal Memoir of the White House Years*, 220; Williams, *The Newspaperman's President*, 75–76; *New York Times*, February 15, 1950.

employed to impart it.[31] For reporters, the president's reliance upon a single messenger was more significant than the message. Consequently, an angry press corps squared off with Truman at his next news conference on February 17. After an initial line of questioning confirmed that the president had authorized the interview, a reporter, mindful of Truman's previous snips at columnists, asked, "Does that represent a softening of your attitude toward columnists, and vice versa?" Truman replied, "No, it does not."

At this point, as the miffed reporters fell silent, Truman lectured them on civility and his presidential prerogatives: "May I say to you gentlemen [and ladies—for he had lapsed into his old habit of inappropriate address] right now—you seem to be in a kind of disgruntled mood this morning—that the President is his own free agent. He will see whom he pleases, when he pleases, and say what he pleases to anybody that he pleases. And he is not censored by you, or anybody else." He had tried his best to be courteous and expected to continue to be that, Truman added, "but I don't like your attitude this morning, so just cool off."[32]

While these feisty remarks elicited some laughter, the prevailing sentiment among reporters was anger. Radio commentator Earl Godwin attempted to mediate.

"Mr. President, inasmuch as I am not disgruntled . . . —I might say to you, sir, as I used to work in the newspaper game—[laughter] that particular type of thing [the exclusive interview] these fellows feel, I think . . . is a reflection on every bureau chief and reporter in the White House."

"It is nothing of the kind," Truman interjected.

"That is their attitude," Godwin replied, "and I hope that you will pardon me if I bring that to your attention?"

"That's all right, but it's nothing of the kind," Truman repeated. "But I don't stand for anybody to edit my actions. I am a free agent, even if I am the President of the United States."[33]

Truman's effort to get the conference on track with other questions failed when Craig and Doris Fleeson, perhaps in part to remind him and the newsmen that newswomen were present, too, pursued the matter. Craig acknowledged the president's right to do as he pleased, but asked if others might also obtain exclusive and private interviews.

31. *New York Times*, February 15, 1950.
32. *Public Papers*, 1950, 159.
33. Ibid.

"That remains to be seen," Truman replied. "I will cross that bridge when I get to it."

Fleeson, pressing for an answer now, engaged the president in a spirited exchange:

> Q. We were under the impression that there was a rule which had—custom, at least, which had the binding force of a rule?
> The President. It is a custom. I will continue that custom—
> Q. But you will—
> The President: but I will do as I please with regard to breaking it. [Laughter].
> Q. Yes sir. That is the information I want.
> The President: That is the answer. You have the information. And I am not disgruntled in the slightest. [More laughter].
> Q. Why should you be?
> The President: I am in as good a humor as I can possibly be, but I would like to answer some questions that have a bearing on the present situation.
> Q. I will give you one, Mr.President.
> Q. You think our business is quite important, do you?
> The President: Sometimes I am not so sure.[34]

Truman had had sharp exchanges with reporters before, but the issue of exclusive interviews involved the principle of equal access to the president. The imbroglio put the press on guard against future instances of favoritism and, by extension, to Truman's exercise of presidential power. Measured against other decisions of his presidency, Truman's privileging Krock with an exclusive interview was seemingly unimportant, but in terms of its significance for his relations with the White House correspondents, the interview marked a turning point by ushering in a prolonged period of tension and troubled relations in press conferences and beyond.

The news conference blow-up over Krock's exclusive interview and the impertinent line of questioning that ensued won for Truman the unexpected support of David Lawrence, the staunch conservative editor of the influential weekly newsmagazine, *U.S. News and World Report*. "There is no reason, in my judgment," Lawrence wrote Truman a day after the stormy news conference, "why a President should be subjected to impertinent questioning of any kind. Trick questions and questions designed to embarrass a President have been spurned from time to time but, even in laughing them off

34. Ibid., 160.

or frowning upon them, undue significance is sometimes given to the fact that such questions were actually asked."

The solution to impertinent questioning, Lawrence advised, lay in the submission of questions in writing at least two hours before the conference begins. The president should have the right to select the questions he desired to answer. Once the president decided to answer a particular question, it would be opened to the usual repartee. This arrangement, Lawrence argued, would permit an opportunity for further information to be supplied by the president's colleagues in government departments prior to the conference. The net result, Lawrence believed, would be a more informative news conference.

Lawrence's other suggestions involved a change in the traditional meeting site and the use of new technology. He urged that the conferences be moved from the president's office, where crowding and poor acoustics prevented some correspondents from hearing the questions and the answers, to an auditorium in the old State Department building. He asked that the news conferences be recorded "using some of the new mechanical recording devices which would enable two stenographers later to transcribe very rapidly what was said at the conferences for reference use only."[35]

While Truman rejected Lawrence's suggestion for requiring written questions in advance of the news conference and delayed the recording of the conferences until 1951, he acted quickly to relocate the conferences from the White House. Five years of meeting the reporters in the Oval Office (the term came into limited journalistic usage in 1951) was enough for Truman. Reporters had used the ashtray on his desk to dispose of their cigarettes and spilled ink from their fountain pens on the carpet. When reporters filled the room to capacity, some stood on chairs. Truman could not see reporters in the back and those in the rear of the room often could not see or hear him. Clearly a room change was in order.[36]

---

35. Lawrence to Truman, February 17, 1950, January–November 1950 folder, OF 36, Truman Papers, Truman Library.

36. The writer John Hersey referred to the president's office as the oval office (uncapitalized) in his series of essays on Truman and the White House. See "Forty-Eight Hours," *The New Yorker* (April 21, 1951): 40. But see also the entry for "Oval Office" in William Safire, *Political Dictionary: The New and Enlarged Edition* (New York: Random House, 1993), 499–500. Ferrell, ed., *Truman in the White House*, 346–47. Presidential aide Ken Hechler has written that some reporters ground out their cigarettes on the carpet *(Working with*

On April 27, 1950, the president inaugurated his first news conference in the Indian Treaty Room of the old State Department building. Now Truman went to the reporters instead of vice-versa, with the correspondents seated and rising when the president entered. The new protocol called for the reporters to state their name and affiliation before asking questions. The president stood behind a small desk to take the reporters' questions. Later, microphones were installed at his desk and throughout the room.[37]

While the expansive Indian Treaty Room solved the problems of overcrowding and hearing and seeing on the part of all, the arrangement also placed both physical and psychological distance between the president and the correspondents. The new quarters lacked the mystique of the Oval Office and imposed a formality of their own, especially in the seating arrangement and the identification and affiliation procedure. The assembling of reporters before the arrival of the president precluded the customary banter exchanged between Truman and the front-row regulars as others filed into his White House office.

Krock, perhaps motivated by the indirect criticism he received from the White House correspondents after Truman had favored him with an interview, devoted a column applauding the new arrangements. He noted that the "vested interests"—reporters assigned to the White House—showed their dissatisfaction by maintaining "unusual reticence." "In this baroque hall," Krock wrote, "with everyone seated except the President, the psychology by which they dominated his crowded office seemed to have vanished." Moreover, Krock observed, "no more could anyone in the rear rank, if so minded, throw a 'curved ball' question at the President and remain unidentified except by a few in the near vicinity." The change of location also pleased the president.[38]

By the end of the year, with the death of Charlie Ross in December, an era of managing the press conferences came to a close as well. Ross could be succeeded but not replaced. His personal relationship with Truman permitted him to speak frankly with the president on all subjects, and he functioned as one of his closest

---

Truman, 217). When a reporter once used the ashtray on the president's desk for disposing his cigarette, a colleague remarked, "Is nothing sacred?" Press Conference Number 45, January 24, 1946, Press Conference Files, Box 62, PSF, Truman Library.

37. Ferrell, ed., *Truman in the White House,* 219; *Public Papers,* 1950, 284.
38. Arthur Krock, "In the Nation," *New York Times,* April 28, 1950.

advisers. He prepared Truman for press conferences by asking questions as impertinent as some posed by reporters. In one preparatory meeting, his sharp questioning of Truman elicited an angry reply. Ross roared with laughter, making his point that Truman must be on guard for a similar inquiry in the conference and would need a civil answer.[39]

With Ross gone, the task of preparing the president for his news conferences fell to the new press secretary, Joseph Short, Jr. Short came to his position with extensive firsthand experience on the other side of the desk as White House correspondent for the *Baltimore Sun*. One of four reporters who had traveled with Truman during the 1944 vice-presidential campaign and privileged with the president's friendship, he reportedly was Truman's choice for press secretary if Ross had declined the offer in 1945. Short had also felt the president's sting in one press conference when he asked Truman to name the special interests to which he had referred several times. Truman replied that while he did not think that would be difficult, it would not be necessary for him to name them for a reporter of the *Baltimore Sun*. The *Sun* people, Truman declared, knew the special interests and supported them all the time. In selecting Short to be his spokesman, Truman made his usual distinction between working reporters whom he personally liked and respected and the newspaper for which they wrote. Short's qualifications outweighed those of other candidates, including the perennial press assistant Eben A. Ayers, whose long tenure in the White House Press Office came to an end when Short reorganized his staff by adding two new assistants.[40]

Short, like Ross, experienced considerable difficulty in serving as the president's spokesman. He lost his temper with the reporters occasionally, but kept in the good graces of newspaper correspondents by maintaining their privileged position over their colleagues in radio and television news. He permitted sound recordings of the news conferences to allow radio broadcasters to reproduce portions of the news conferences with approval of the White House Press Office, but maintained the ban on live radio broadcast. He also rejected the request of Telenews, a producer of newsreels for television, to bring

---

39. See chapter 3 for an account of Ross's death and the editorial comment on his life and career. The story of Ross's impertinent questioning is related in Elsey oral history, by Hess, 77–79.

40. James J. Butler, "Joe Short, White House Press Secretary, Dies," *Editor and Publisher* (September 27, 1952): 8; *Public Papers*, 1949, 157; Ferrell, ed., *Truman in the White House*, 386–88; Hechler, *Working with Truman*, 216.

its cameras into the press conference to obtain a visual record for distribution. Short's brief tenure as press secretary ended with his unexpected death at his home on September 18, 1952.[41]

With his administration now in its final months, Truman turned to the late secretary's assistants, Roger Tubby and Irving Perlmeter, for handling the press office for the duration of his term. Tubby, given the primary position as press secretary, had been an upstate New York newspaper reporter before joining the government as a public affairs specialist. Short had recruited him from the state department, where he compiled a set of possible questions and answers for the press conferences of the secretary of state. He brought this technique to the White House, where it represented a written format similar to the oral briefings and reviews pioneered by Ross. Perlmeter, also a career government public affairs officer, served as Tubby's assistant with responsibility for coordinating the small but expanding television appearances of the president. The Tubby-Perlmeter team did not alter the nature and function of the press conferences. They acquiesced in the earlier decisions of Ross and Short to bar television and newsreel coverage of the conferences, permitting only wire and disc recordings and U.S. Army Signal Corps motion picture camera filming for background and historical purposes. Live visual transmission of presidential news conferences awaited the presidencies of Eisenhower and Kennedy. Thus the president's meetings with the news media remained largely unchanged throughout the Truman presidency.[42]

Truman appropriately used the occasion of his final news conference to emphasize its importance as a forum of communication between the president and the public. Concerned over a subsequently published report that incoming President Eisenhower might discontinue the news conferences, Truman read into the record his strong hope that they would be continued. "This kind of news conference

41. Hechler, *Working with Truman*, 216–19; Irving Perlmeter to Joseph Short, Jr., May 10, 1951, and Short's unsigned and undated attached note, August 1950–May 1951 folder, OF 73, Truman Papers, Truman Library; James Butler, "Joe Short, White House Press Secretary, Dies," 8.

42. Roger Tubby oral history, by J. R. Fuchs, passim, Truman Library; Irving Perlmeter oral history, by Charles T. Morrissey, passim, Truman Library. The U.S. Army Signal Corps, newsreel operators, and television cameras were allowed to film Truman's news conference of December 11, 1952, for historical and delayed use. *New York Times*, December 12, 1952; Hechler, *Working with Truman*, 218–19. J. Leonard Reinsch, *Getting Elected: From Radio to Roosevelt to Television to Reagan*, 104–5; Emery and Emery, *The Press and America*, 396.

where reporters can ask any question they can dream up—directly of the President of the United States—illustrates how strong and vital our democracy is." He added, "There is no other country in the world where the chief of state submits to such unlimited questioning." In spite of the differences that existed between himself and newspapers, he said, "I think it is important for our democratic system of government that every medium of communication between the citizens and their Government, particularly the President, be kept open as far as possible."[43]

In the ensuing exchange with correspondents, Truman defended his performance in fielding questions and the few changes he had introduced in the press conferences. He endorsed the move of the meeting site from the White House to the old State Department building. He stressed his belief that the press conferences should be held with regularity, explaining, "I think it adds to the information of the public as to what goes on, and I think they are entitled to know what is in the President's mind." He ruled out the practice of having written questions submitted in advance, preferring instead "the rough and tumble press conference we have right here. If I can't take care of myself," he said, "that's my fault."[44]

Edward T. Folliard of the *New York Times* good-naturedly pressed Truman on this point:

> Mr. President, it has been said that you made some mistakes or had some embarrassing experiences in press conferences. Granting that, if you will—[laughter]—The President. But I don't, Eddie—but go ahead.
> [More laughter]
> Well, do you think the advantages all around outweigh the risks or the embarrassments?
> The President. Oh, yes, I think so. . . . in 324 press conferences I imagine I have had all the experiences that a man can possibly have at a press conference, and I have never felt that I would want to discontinue them. And I have never felt that I have been unfairly treated.[45]

Sentimentality prevailed as Merriman Smith, rising to bring the final news conference to a close, reversed the traditional phrasing

43. *New York Times*, January 18, 1953; *Public Papers,* 1952–1953, 1189.
44. *Public Papers,* 1952–1953, 1191.
45. Ibid.

from "Thank you, Mr. President" to "Mr. President, Thank you!" His colleagues responded with warm and sustained applause.[46]
    Truman left the room teary-eyed and smiling.
    The curtain had rung down on "the greatest show in town."[47]

46. Ibid., 1196.
47. *New York Times*, January 16, 1953.

Truman, in the presence of Bess and Margaret, takes the presidential oath on April 12, 1945. (Abbie Rowe, National Park Service, Courtesy of Harry S. Truman Library)

The new president holds his first news conference in the Oval Office of the White House, April 17, 1945. (George Skadding, Life Picture Services)

The president's news conferences became more formal in April 1950 when the meetings were moved from the president's office in the White House to the Indian Treaty Room in the old State Department building. (INS photo, Corbis-Bettmann Archives)

"Acres of Empty Seats" is how *Life* described Truman's June 1948 appearance at Omaha's Ak-sar-ben auditorium, obscuring the fact that a record crowd had seen the president in a downtown parade earlier that day. (AP/Wide World Photos)

"Acres of People" was Truman's apt description for the large crowds that turned out to see him during his June 1948 preconvention tour and the fall campaign. Here the president addresses midwesterners at the National Plowing Match, Dexter, Iowa, September 18, 1948. (Courtesy Harry S. Truman Library)

Television joined the crowd at the railroad station for the medium's first-time-ever coverage of the president's late September campaign visit to Fort Worth, Texas. (Fort Worth *Star-Telegram*, Courtesy of Photograph Collection, Special Collections Division, The University Texas at Arlington Libraries)

On this occasion Truman exchanged roles with the White House news photographers. He inscribed the photograph, "I take pictures of the 'One More Club.' HST." (INS photo, Corbis-Bettmann Archives)

A relaxing meeting of the president with reporters at his vacation retreat on the U.S. Naval Base, Key West, Florida. Press Secretary Charles G. Ross is standing in the extreme right, second row. (Paul Bagley, U.S. Navy Photo, Courtesy Harry S. Truman Library)

Doris Fleeson (left) and May Craig, celebrated columnists and regulars at the president's news conferences, on a Honolulu stop-over at the Air Force's 1949 round-the-world flight. (U.S. Air Force Photo, Courtesy Kenneth Spencer Research Library, University of Kansas)

Alice A. Dunnigan, Washington chief of the Associated Negro Press Association, at the beginning of her coverage of the capitol and the White House in 1947. (Courtesy of Robert W. Dunnigan)

Marguerite Higgins, *New York Herald Tribune* correspondent, in Korea for coverage of the war in 1950 and 1951. (Carl Mydans, Life Picture Services)

The scene at the Blair House, temporary living quarters of the Trumans, diagrammed to tell a photo story of the attempt on the life of President Truman on November 1, 1950. (INS, Corbis-Bettmann Archives)

Harry and Bess in retirement at their home in Independence. The TV camera was present to tape a March 1955 telecast for Edward R. Murrow's "Person-to-Person" show. (Reprinted by Permission of the *Kansas City Star*)

5

Gentlemen of the Press

MANY TIMES DURING HIS presidency Harry Truman addressed the reporters at his news conference as "Gentlemen" despite the visible presence and participation of several female reporters.[1] Truman's greeting showed his preference for men in his inner circle and reflected the dominant and separate sphere of males in American society at midcentury. The news profession in turn mirrored America's patriarchal social order. Men dominated journalism as reporters, columnists, newscasters, editors, publishers, and owners, and they enjoyed a preferred relationship with the president.

Long before Truman became president, his predecessors had made themselves and the White House accessible to the men of the press. Theodore Roosevelt produced two important innovations: he met with the press regularly and provided two wire service reporters a small room in the new wing of the White House. During the presidency of Franklin D. Roosevelt, the press room was relocated across the corridor from the Oval Office to accommodate nearly a

---

1. Truman also referred to the front-row regulars as "boys" and the White House photographers as the "picture boys." See the news conference for May 8, 1952, *Public Papers*, 1952–1953, 323. His salutation to the "gentlemen" became infrequent after the news conferences were moved from the White House to the Indian Treaty Room of the old State Department building. The first words from the president there were usually "Please be seated," although on occasion he still failed to include the women in his greetings. See *Public Papers*, 1950, 284.

dozen full-time reporters stationed at the White House.[2] The White House press corps, with credentials supplied by the press office, could enter the Executive Office building with the ease of eminent government officials and the president's staff. But women were not admitted to the press room because they represented none of the major news media that maintained daily coverage of the president's activities.

In Truman's time the eighteen-by-forty press room, crowded with a dozen desks and forty telephones, served the reporters as an office, waiting area, and conference site for twice-daily briefings from the president's press secretary. A single couch permitted a fortunate reporter a place for an after-lunch nap. An errand runner, engaged exclusively by the correspondents, fetched coffee for the group in the morning and liquor and beer for late-afternoon refreshment. The reporters literally made themselves at home in the White House press room.[3]

Understandably, in an era when the American public still preferred the newspaper for news information, the White House wire service reporters who wrote for the three major press associations enjoyed a privileged status. The writers for United Press, Associated Press, and International News Service were the first reporters to be assigned daily at the White House, and their agencies supplied most of the nation's daily newspapers and radio stations with news via teletype.[4]

The White House wire service reporters were also accorded rank and privilege by the president and by their colleagues. Merriman Smith of United Press, whose White House assignment began in 1941, was senior to colleagues Ernest B. (Tony) Vacarro of Associated Press and Robert G. Nixon of International News Service. Consequently, he held the informal title of press corps "dean." The trio, by tradition, led other reporters into the president's office for news conferences, where they could always get the attention of

2. Pollard, *The Presidents and the Press*, 569–70, 574. But see Stephen Ponder, "The President Makes News: William McKinley and the First Presidential Press Corps, 1897–1901." *Presidential Studies Quarterly* 24 (fall 1994): 823–36. George Tames oral history, 23–24.

3. Merriman Smith, *Thank You, Mr. President*, 3–4, 10–11. It was still a custom in the mid-fifties for a new correspondent assigned to the White House to take a bottle each of scotch and bourbon to the press room when first reporting to work. Robert Pierpoint, *At the White House: Assignment to Six Presidents* (New York: G. P. Putnam's Sons, 1981), 27.

4. Smith, *Thank You, Mr. President*, 2.

the president from their front-row position. Senior member Smith determined when the news conference had exhausted the topics, if not the president, and ended it with the customary "Thank you, Mr. President."[5]

Other regulars assigned to the Truman White House represented metropolitan newspapers: Anthony Leviero for the *New York Times;* Bert Andrews, Dave McConnell, and Robert Donovan at various times for the *New York Herald Tribune;* Jack Doherty for the *New York Daily News;* Edward T. Folliard, *Washington Post;* Joseph A. Fox, *Washington Star;* Carleton Kent, *Chicago Sun-Times;* Philip L. Warden, *Chicago Tribune;* Joseph Short, Jr., and, following his appointment as press secretary in 1950, Robert Ruth, for the *Baltimore Sun. Time* assigned Edward Lockett to the White House in 1945, and a few years later he was succeeded by Win Booth.[6]

By 1950 broadcast journalists had received assignments from their news organizations to the White House. Bryson Rash of the American Broadcasting Company, Frank Bourgholtzer of the National Broadcasting Company, and Ed Darby of Transradio, a news service serving a group of radio stations, were the first radio newsmen to report regularly full-time from the executive mansion. Charles Collingwood of the Columbia Broadcasting System divided his time between New York and Washington. (CBS reporter Robert Pierpoint, the first reporter employed exclusively by television to receive a regular assignment to the White House, did not arrive until 1957.)[7] The proximity of these newsmen to the president and the power of their news organizations conferred upon them influence and celebrity; they, along with the wire service reporters, stood at the apex of the Washington news corps pyramid.

A few members of the Washington press corps who wrote columns for major newspapers or news syndicates, or both, and columnists for nationally circulated newsmagazines enjoyed top

5. Ibid., 209–10. Smith's technique of questioning at a presidential news conference is described in Pierpoint, *At the White House,* 27. How Smith came to assume the role of ending the news conferences is described in the Robert Nixon oral history, by Jerry N. Hess, 399–401.

6. "Famed Byline" newspaper article, Folder 1, Box 10, Ayers Papers, Truman Library; Official log, White House Key West Vacations, Truman Library.

7. Ibid.; Pierpoint, *At the White House,* 27. Pierpoint received a rough reception from the "dean" of the correspondents, Merriman Smith. "Why," Smith asked, "did CBS think a punk like you could cover the White House?" It helped the then thirty-two-year-old Pierpoint to realize later that Smith was not sober when he asked the question (28–29).

status as well. Columnists Lippmann of the *New York Herald Tribune*, Krock and James Reston of the *New York Times*, Lawrence of *U.S. News and World Report*, Frank Kent of the *Baltimore Sun*, Strout of the *Christian Science Monitor*, the Alsops of the New York Herald Tribune Syndicate, and Marquis Childs of the *Washington Post* were widely read in syndication.

Stewart Alsop believed that the Washington press corps, insofar as it wielded influence, was enhanced by a characteristic shared with the upper bureaucracy of the permanent government establishment: "It survives elections."

> Presidents may come and Presidents may go but a James Reston or a Marquis Childs goes on forever. The simple fact of having been a part—an influential part—of Political Washington while four or five Presidents have come and gone (or, as in the case of David Lawrence eleven Presidents have come and gone) imparts to a successful political reporter a certain status and authority— and on occasion, to tell the truth, a certain pomposity as well.[8]

Joseph Alsop, the senior, longer-established columnist of the Alsop brothers writing team, understood, too, that his prestige and influence derived from membership in a patrician family as well as his political acumen. As a self-described "very minor member" of the "WASP Ascendancy"—he was a grandnephew of Theodore Roosevelt and a cousin of Franklin and Eleanor Roosevelt—Alsop spoke with a cultured New England/New York accent, and dressed in London-tailored suits with shirts, shoes, ties, and hats from Brooks Brothers. Educated at Groton and Harvard, Alsop, while not wealthy, moved comfortably and confidently in the company of the elite of American society. His friends included Wall Street investment bankers and well-connected lawyers, some of whom— James V. Forrestal, Robert Lovett, and Dean Acheson—became powerful members of the Truman administration; old politicians such as James F. Byrnes and a rising political star, Congressman John F. Kennedy, and intellectuals such as George Kennan were also a part of Alsop's social set. Many of these men were frequent dinner guests at Alsop's house in fashionable Georgetown and valuable conduits of information, on and off the record.[9]

8. Alsop, *The Center*, 171–72.
9. Joseph W. Alsop, with Adam Platt, *I've Seen the Best of It: Memoirs*, chap. 1, 274–75, 388–89, 405–7, 419–22, 433–35.

According to one apocryphal story, a visitor to the Alsop house (not "home," Alsop would insist), struck with the beauty of the heirloom furniture that appointed several rooms, asked Alsop where he had bought the antiques. Alsop replied stiffly: "One does not buy antiques, one inherits them."[10] The story sums up the world of the Alsops and the WASP Ascendancy that gave these privileged gentlemen an advantage in collecting, analyzing, and interpreting the news of the president and the powerful of Washington.

The Washington press corps pyramid had as its base several hundred reporters sent to the capital at the war's end to cover national approaches to ordinary affairs such as food and housing shortages. The primary beat for most reporters in Washington was not the White House; rather, they covered developments in the departments, agencies, and bureaus of the federal government. General assignment reporters such as Richard Cull, Jr., Washington bureau representative of the *Dayton* (Ohio) *Daily News*, who worked hard to collect stories from the lower echelons of government, did not stand in awe of the White House regulars. According to Cull, many reporters "had the idea the White House regulars were 'potted plants' just sitting comfortably in the press room waiting to be called to the twice-a-day briefings by the White House press secretary."[11]

But not all Washington reporters were as conscientious as Cull. Joan Marble of United Press Radio, writing anonymously in *Harper's* in February 1949, took the capital press corps to task for a myriad of sins, including laziness, ignorance, and submission of public information handouts to their newspapers under their own byline.[12]

While proximity to the president and the influence of their news organizations conferred greatest authority and prestige to the White House correspondents and a few columnists, gender and racial biases in Washington worked to the advantage of all male white reporters. Discrimination based on sex, race, and social class prevailed in three of the most influential Washington press corps gathering places: the National Press Club, the Metropolitan Club, and the Cosmos Club.

In many ways the history of the National Press Club paralleled the growth of the Washington press. Founded in 1908, the organization made a shrewd move in 1925 when it acquired title to a lot at the

10. Ibid., 22. The gist of the story, in fact, was told by Joseph Alsop about his brother Stewart (263).

11. Richard Cull, Jr., oral history, by Niel M. Johnson, 9–10, 43, 83.

12. Ibid.; "Washington's Armchair Correspondents by One of Them," 49–52. Marble was identified as the author of the story in *Newsweek* 36 (December 25, 1950): 40.

corner of Fourteenth and F Street, a scant three blocks from the White House and in the heart of the city's news center, hotel, restaurant, theater, and shopping district. A corporation was formed to construct a modern office building to house press club members and other tenants, and in 1926 President Calvin Coolidge presided over ceremonies for the laying of the building's cornerstone. Congress made its contribution to the fourteen-story structure by exempting it from the eleven-story height limitation of the district. When the building opened in 1928, the reporters in Washington required only a fraction of the office space in the club, so space was rented to insurance companies, banks, lawyers, and newspaper reporters turned public relations agents. In the 1930s, the growth of the federal government under the Roosevelt New Deal brought many additional reporters to Washington and swelled their number to approximately 360 by 1934.[13]

The tremendous growth in the capital press corps after World War II led to the opening of Washington offices in the National Press Club by many of the nation's largest newspapers. The *New York Herald Tribune, Philadelphia Evening Bulletin, Wall Street Journal, Christian Science Monitor,* and *Cincinnati Enquirer,* among others, assigned reporters to cover the Washington scene, making the National Press Club the "journalistic crossroads of the nation."[14] (Other major newspapers, including the *New York Times,* maintained offices in the Albee Building.)

While female reporters could rent space in the National Press Club Building—Craig and Fleeson shared an office there—they, and all blacks, were barred from the dining room, the press club bar, and the auditorium where news makers spoke from time to time. Occasionally the women could prevail upon the men to change the site of a famous visitor's speech, as they did in 1952 in moving Winston Churchill's talk to the Mayflower Hotel. The women also persuaded Perle Mesta, minister to Luxembourg, to speak to the National Women's Press Club a day before her talk to the male reporters at the National Press Club; otherwise women and blacks were excluded from the headline-making appearances of prominent guests who, by tradition, made their first speech in Washington at

---

13. Winfield, *FDR and the News Media,* 56. But see also Frank Gervasi, "Headline Heaven," *Collier's* 122 (October 16, 1948): 16–17, 64; Scott Hart, "From Such a Bond," in Cabell Phillips et al., eds., *Dateline: Washington: The Story of National Affairs Journalism in the Life and Times of the National Press Club,* 26–37.

14. Gervasi, "Headline Heaven."

the club. The white newsmen could also exchange gossip over lunch or a drink during the cocktail hour, thus contributing an important part to the "old boys' network" that originated in the White House press room and emanated to all parts of the city and beyond. By 1949 the club had made a few concessions to white female journalists by constructing a separate lounge and dining area for their daily use and by opening its main dining room to the wives of male white journalists on Sundays and weekday evenings.[15]

The exclusive Metropolitan Club extended membership to only a few select male white journalists. Krock of the *New York Times* lunched there regularly. His guest on one occasion was Senator Harry Truman; Krock collected background information on the committee the Missourian chaired for investigation of the national defense program. Walter Lippmann, one of the few Jews admitted to membership, also dined at the Metropolitan Club. Merriman Smith, a nonmember, described the club as "a midday status symbol, a luncheon haven for thought-makers, White Division." The patrician Alsop brothers were members of the Metropolitan Club and its snootier cousin, the Cosmos Club. Steward Alsop admitted that club membership conferred advantages to the news reporters who dined with the rising and ascendant power brokers of Washington. The disadvantage of gathering a news story at the club, he explained, came through the observation of others who noted his guest as the likely source of a forthcoming column. Alsop thought that the exclusive club setting was greatly overrated as a means of gathering news, but women, black reporters, and nonmember male white journalists had their doubts.[16]

15. May Craig, "Inside in Washington," *Portland* [Maine] *Press-Herald,* September 17, 1949, Entry of Gannett Publications for the Raymond Clapper Award folder, Container 2, Elizabeth May Craig Papers, Library of Congress; Frederick C. Othman, "Every Day is Election Day," in Phillips et al., *Dateline: Washington,* 255–56; Gervasi, "Headline Heaven," 64; *Editor and Publisher* (January 12, 1952): 12. Reporter Richard Cull, Jr., took note of the change in the press club from a social club, "with emphasis on the boys getting together after work over a drink or a game of cards to talk over the news of the day," to a professional club, "with more rooms for news meetings and seminars. . . . Harry Truman, like the rest of us old timers, probably would prefer the Club the way it was." Undated statement in Richard Cull, Jr., folder, Box 1, Richard Cull, Jr., Papers, Truman Library.

16. Krock, *Memoirs,* 220. Ronald Steel, *Walter Lippmann and the American Century,* 195–96, 112, 551. Lippmann belonged to the Cosmos Club as well. Merriman Smith, *The Good New Days,* 76–77. Alsop, *The Center,* 25, 174, 185–86.

The Cosmos Club, founded shortly after the Civil War by men of science, still retained that orientation in the Truman years, but over time it had elected a few nonscientists to membership. Sponsored membership was always limited because of the cap set at two thousand; when a member died, the membership committee could draw from a list of prospective members compiled years before. Only three of Truman's predecessors—William Howard Taft, Woodrow Wilson, and Herbert Hoover—were deemed worthy of membership before or during their presidencies, while the more plebeian National Press Club had made associate members of Truman and his predecessors back to William Howard Taft. Until the Cosmos Club moved to the Sumner Welles mansion on Massachusetts Avenue in 1951, it occupied an ornate Victorian building adjacent to Lafayette Park across from the White House. The only concession the exclusive gentlemen's club made to women was the addition of a ladies' quarters, but female guests were never allowed in the main building. Harvey Washington Wiley, sponsor of the Pure Food and Drug Act of 1906 and a resident member, found the arrangement quite satisfactory. "I was so satisfied with this club that I didn't take time to get married until I was sixty-seven years old," he once boasted. On a given day the scientists lunching there might have as partners newsmen Childs, Elmer Davis, Lippmann, and Drew Pearson.[17]

In the opinion of United Press reporter Smith, whose reporting for the wire service did not require the cultivation of Washington power brokers except the president and the press secretary, the most exclusive club of all was the president's yacht, the *Williamsburg*. Occasionally Truman invited a few reporters whose company he enjoyed for a weekend cruise. Smith, who rubbed Truman the wrong way on several occasions, was never invited.[18]

17. Milton Lehman, "America's Choosiest Club," *Saturday Evening Post* 223 (January 13, 1951): 34–35, 108–10. Truman, proposed for membership in the Cosmos Club after he left the White House, solicited the advice of his former aides Charles Murphy and William Hassett on the matter. Hassett, believing that the invitation should have been extended during Truman's presidency, advised against the application, whereupon the former president stopped the membership proposal. Murphy to Hassett, October 29, 1958, and Hassett to Murphy, November 7, 1950, Charles Murphy folder, Box 1, William D. Hassett Papers, Truman Library. The Cosmos Club extended an invitation to President John F. Kennedy but he declined on the ground that the exclusive club had no black members and was, at the time, rejecting the nomination for membership of journalist Carl Rowan. Carl Rowan, *Breaking Barriers: A Memoir*, 202–6.

18. Smith, *The Good New Days*, 10.

Nor was Smith a member of the Hard Rock Club, formed by Truman on a whim for the handful of newsmen who had accompanied him into a silver mine in Montana during his 1944 vice-presidential campaign. He expanded the social club's membership to include the three pool reporters who accompanied him to Potsdam in the summer of 1945. When these newsmen sported a small pin designating themselves as members of the exclusive club, a few of their disgruntled colleagues started a "The Association of Men Who Are Not Close to Truman" club.[19]

The occasional gatherings of the Hard Rock Club continued until the summer of 1946, when *Time* reporter Edward Lockett, one of the privileged members, sent background materials to his magazine on a dinner and poker session with the president at a Washington hotel while Bess and Margaret Truman were in Independence. *Time's* report of the boys' night out greatly angered Press Secretary Ross, but seemed to have left the president more remorseful and disappointed than angry. He decided to let the Hard Rock Club fold and thereafter turned a cold shoulder to Lockett.[20]

Truman continued to socialize with a few reporters throughout his presidency, but he kept newspaper columnists outside his social circle. Columnists, as interpreters of the news, opinion makers, and the purveyors of gossip and news leaks, wielded too much unrestrained power to be liked by Truman. In private correspondence, he categorized the lot into two broad categories: the "gutter columnists," who included Westbrook Pegler, Walter Winchell, and Pearson, and the "ivory tower" columnists such as Lippmann, Krock, and the Alsops. He considered the former the bane of a free and responsible press and took the "ivory tower" columnists to task for attributing to him positions that he had never advocated or even contemplated. He referred to the Alsop brothers as the "All Slops" and wrote angry but unsent letters to Lippmann and Krock.[21]

19. Smith, *Thank You, Mr. President,* 37.

20. *Time* 23 (June 26, 1946): 19–20; Thomas F. Reynolds, "What a President Does on His Night Off as Guest of Capital Correspondents' Group," *Chicago Sun,* June 23, 1946, "Hard Rock Club" folder, Box 3, Records of the Democratic National Committee, Truman Library; Louis Liebovich, *The Press and the Origins of the Cold War, 1944–1947,* 141.

21. Williams, *The Newspaperman's President,* 176, 179; Truman's angry letters to Lippmann and Krock are published in Monte M. Poen, ed., *Strictly Personal and Confidential: The Letters Harry Truman Never Mailed,* 27–28, 57–58. The unsent letter to Lippmann is discussed in Ferrell, ed., *Truman in the White House,* 315. The reference to the Alsop brothers is in Hechler, *Working with Truman,* 108.

Truman elaborated, in an unpublished piece that he kept filed in his desk drawer, his views on columnists, publishers, and editors:

> The men who write columns for the classified press sell their writing ability just as . . . lose [sic] ladies sell their bodies to the madam of a bawdy house. They write columns on policy in domestic affairs and on foreign affairs from the rumor source and as long as the "madam"—the publisher will pay them for this sort of [lewd] thing that's what they want.
>
> In many cases the publisher only wants talent to present his distorted view point. Hearst, Pulitzer, Scripps-Howard, Gannett, Bertie McCormick and the Patterson chain are shining examples. Many a great and talented scribbler has sold his soul to these purveyors of 'Character Assassination.' The old Moslem assinsins [sic] of Mesopotamia have a much better chance of a considered judgement in the end than have these paid mental whores of the controlers [sic] of our so called "free press."
>
> This so-called "free press" is about as free as Stalin's press. The only difference is that Stalin frankly controlled his and the publishers and owners of our press are always yapping about the Constitution and suppressing a free press.[22]

The president's diatribe continued: "News should never be edited. Editorials should be frankly the opinions of the owners & publishers and should be so stated. But news should be reported as it has happened." He closed his fulmination by observing that he knew of only one paper with a national circulation—an indirect but clear reference to the *New York Times*—that printed the news and confined editorial opinion to the editorial page. "The Hearst, Knight, Pulitzer, McCormick-Patterson, L. A. *Times*, Dallas *News*, and the New Orleans *Times Picayune*," he concluded, "are the worst news editors in the business—but I'm happy to say their thinking readers are aware of their mishandling of the facts and their political influence is not what they'd like to have it."[23]

Columnist Frank Kent sufficiently provoked Truman on two occasions to cause the president to write him abusive letters. A letter in 1951 that accused Kent of being a "prostitute of the mind" was never sent,[24] but the president mailed his letter of February 12, 1949, that assigned Kent, along with Lawrence, Pegler, Pearson, and

---

22. Undated commentary, "The Columnist & the Publisher," Desk File, Personal Notes Set II, Box 3, PPF, Truman Papers, Truman Library.
23. Ibid.
24. Truman to Kent, September 2, 1951, in Poen, ed., *Strictly Personal and Confidential*, 24.

Winchell, to a class of intellectually dishonest journalists. Truman had been angered by Kent's column devoted to a discussion of a bill providing for increased government compensation for the president and others in the executive branch.

Kent wrote the president to explain his position on the proposed measure (he wanted accountability for expense accounts rather than opposing the increase per se); he demurred as well from the accusation that he was intellectually dishonest. His gracious reply prompted Truman to pen a letter of apology, along with an explanation that the stress of his duties after four years was perhaps causing him to develop "a set of nerves." "Burn the letter," Truman requested, "and forget it was ever mailed!" When Kent returned the letter, uncopied, to the White House, Truman wrote once again to the columnist to express his regrets and to thank him for being "a gentleman and . . . scholar."[25]

Truman's occasional vacations in Key West provided respite from the daily pressures in Washington for himself, his aides, and the reporters who accompanied him there. These infrequent vacations turned into all-male affairs when Bess and Margaret were not present. As a result, some of the men reporters let their penchant for schoolboy pranks and imbibing transgress on their professionalism and appropriate decorum for a presidential party. Truman helped to set the stage for the reporters' antics with a stunt of his own. After his plane landed ahead of the plane carrying the press corps, he posed with pencil and pad at the bottom of the stairs when the reporters deplaned. Then he proceeded to pepper wire service reporter Robert Nixon, president of the White House Correspondents Association, with timely questions. As a photographer snapped the scene, they all had a good laugh.[26]

The next laugh was on Truman as a few reporters hatched a plan to sneak a small burro onto the naval base where the presidential party was housed. The taxi bearing the reporters and the burro got past the marine guard and headed for the president's detached bath pavilion to board the animal for the night. The next morning, when Truman went for his shower, he found the donkey had relieved itself during the evening. Reporter Leviero alluded to the affair by noting

25. Truman to Kent, February 12, 1949; Kent to Truman, February 14, 1949; Truman to Kent, February 17, 1949; Truman to Kent, February 22, 1949; all in Harry S. Truman folder, Box 9, Frank R. Kent Papers, Maryland Historical Society, Baltimore, Maryland.
26. *New York Times*, March 7, 1949.

in his story for the *New York Times* that the burro was a "small, gentle animal, almost completely inoffensive." Truman laughed off the prank, but the Secret Service and the navy were not amused. The *Times* buried the story deep inside section one and Truman ended the affair by calling off an investigation into the breach of security.[27]

The reporters let their hair down in other ways, too. One reporter who drank too much was incapable of turning out a story of a presidential news conference for his newspaper. Three reporters, each one unaware that the other two were covering for their incapacitated colleague, filed carbons of their story with their wayward friend's editor, who sent word back that he preferred the second version of the three accounts.[28]

On one occasion Joseph Fox found himself locked out of the presidential compound without press credentials. A marine guard telephoned the press office to ascertain if the *Washington Star* reporter was in fact on the official press list. The reporter who took the call responded: "Is Fox inside or outside the base? If he is inside, keep him in; if he is outside, keep him out." Locals, assuming that the distinguished-looking Fox was a very important person, snapped his photograph.[29]

Joe Short, then reporting for the *Baltimore Sun*, was privileged to join the presidential party for poker but lost twenty-five dollars in the game. When the *Sun* refused to pay the charge, he responded, "Okay, if you don't want me to play poker with the president of the United States, I won't."[30]

Reporters who socialized with members of the White House staff at Key West continued to ferret out potential news stories. Bill Lawrence of the *New York Times*, who shared a cottage with White House Correspondence Secretary William Hassett, learned from Hassett during Truman's visit there in December 1951 that the president had decided against seeking reelection in 1952. Lawrence received confirmation of Truman's retirement plans in a mid-February private interview with the president; he was sure he had a Pulitzer Prize–winning story but Truman decided against giving permission to Lawrence to publish it.[31]

27. *New York Times*, December 12, 13, 1949; George Tames, *Eye on Washington: The Presidents Who've Known Me*, 34–35.

28. Stephen Hess, *The Washington Reporters*, 22.

29. Tames oral history, 42–43.

30. Frank Holman story, undated, President Truman and Press Secretaries folder, Box 1, Cull Papers, Truman Library.

31. Bill Lawrence, *Six Presidents, Too Many Wars*, 183–88.

Another off-the-record story of the president was related to the guests at the fortieth anniversary dinner of the National Press Club on March 29, 1948. With no women present—women could not belong to the club—Truman told the journalists about William Howard Taft when the former president was Secretary of War and the honoree of a dinner roast. As the president related the story, the toastmaster at the earlier affair, Chauncey Depew, stated that while Taft was the speaker of the evening, he doubted very much whether the corpulent gentleman could speak because he appeared to be pregnant. "Mr. Taft got up and made the statement," Truman said, "that he might be pregnant, and if it was a girl he would name it after Mrs. Taft, and if it was a boy he would call it William Howard, Jr., but if it was wind, and that is what he thought it was, he would call it Chauncey Depew."[32]

Newsmen were discreet, too, about the president's infrequent use of demeaning terms for blacks. Marquis Childs recounted years after the Truman presidency one conversation that revealed the president's ingrained views on race and feminism. Childs had been dispatched to the White House in 1947 by Agnes Meyer, wife of the publisher of the *Washington Post* and a journalist in her own right, to ask Truman to address an interracial group gathered for the presentation of the Wendell L. Willkie awards for black journalists. The *Post* had created the awards in an effort to improve black journalism and to further relations between the white and black press. Truman bluntly expressed his feelings for Meyer. "Well," he told Childs, "it's a good thing she sent you instead of coming herself. . . . Hardly a day goes by that I don't get a letter from that woman or from Eleanor Roosevelt telling me how to handle this job." Regarding blacks, Truman informed Childs, "I get along pretty well with the burr heads, . . . until sooner or later I say n——r." But he could see no reason why he should not confer the awards, and he made the presentations to the delight of all the guests.[33]

It irritated Truman to receive initial unfavorable comparisons with President Roosevelt on civil rights when, in fact, his record outpaced his predecessor. At Truman's first presidential news conference on April 17, 1945, Harry McAlpin asked Truman to comment on how he felt about many of the things President Roosevelt did for Negroes, especially his interest in the Fair Employment Practices

32. Remarks of the President at the National Press Club, March 29, 1948, Box 62, PSF Historical File, Truman Papers, Truman Library.
33. Marquis Childs, *Witness to Power,* 93.

Commission and the fight to eliminate the poll tax. "I'll give you some advice," Truman replied. "All you need to do is to read the Senate record of Mr. Harry S. Truman on that."[34] Truman's record was exemplary on FEPC, elimination of the poll tax, and a federal antilynching law, but his curt response to the black newsman shed little light on his past and future action in the area of civil rights.

A few days later Truman met privately with black newspaper editors to learn of their concerns and hopes for the new administration. The meeting went smoothly until one of the editors pressed Truman for appointment of a black as a presidential assistant. Truman bridled at the suggestion and brusquely replied that he alone decided who would work for him.[35]

Despite these contretemps, black reporters of both genders broke old barriers and gained new ground during the Truman years, due in large part to Truman himself. Following his lead, the White House Press Office accredited additional black reporters during his presidency and contributed to the modification of exclusionary rules for black journalists who sought admission to the press galleries of the House and the Senate. And in March 1947 the exclusion of black reporters from the travel roster of presidential trips abroad ended when Lemuel E. Graves, Jr., of the *Pittsburgh Courier*, P. Bernard Young, Jr., of the *Norfolk Journal and Guide*, and Llewelyn A. Coles, editor of the *Columbus* [Ohio] *State News* traveled with the presidential party to the Virgin Islands. In 1948 John D. Young III of the *Chicago Defender* and Stanley Roberts of the *Pittsburgh Courier*, along with Alice Dunnigan of the Associated Negro Press, represented their news organizations on the Truman western "nonpolitical" tour to break the final barrier in access to the president both in Washington and on his travels around the country.[36]

Truman's overall good relationship with black reporters and their publishers occurred within the context of his advocacy of a comprehensive civil rights program. He showed the direction of his administration in the spring of 1945 by urging congressional action to make the wartime Fair Employment Practices Commission

34. White, *FDR and the Press*, 18–19; *Public Papers*, 1945, 10–11; McCoy and Reutten, *Quest and Response*, 19.

35. Ferrell, ed., *Truman in the White House*, 29.

36. Press Secretary Ross readily approved Alice Dunnigan's request to travel with the presidential party on its western tour and on one occasion during the trip he included the newswoman in his social circle. Dunnigan, *A Black Woman's Experience*, 241–42. *Editor and Publisher* (February 21, 1948): 68. *New York Herald Tribune*, May 30, 1948; *New York Times*, June 4, 1948.

permanent. The following year he appointed a commission on civil rights to investigate and report on rights denied minority Americans; in February 1948 he endorsed all of the committee's recommendations in a special message to the Congress. While congressional opposition, provided by a southern-led filibuster, doomed the FEPC, the president resorted to executive orders to desegregate the armed forces in July 1948 and, at the same time, ban discrimination based on race, creed, color, and religion in federal employment.[37]

The expanded coverage of the president and the Washington news scene by the black press reflected both its keen interest in the role of the federal government in advancing minority rights and opportunities and its ability to bear the expenses involved. During the war the circulation of black newspapers grew tremendously, thanks to the improved economic status of blacks in the civilian workforce and in the military that allowed them to subscribe and purchase newspapers and magazines. The number of subscribers to black newspapers in 1945 exceeded half a million while a pass-along readership swelled the number to an estimated two million readers. In 1945 the timing was right, too, for John H. Johnson of Chicago to launch *Ebony* and attain instant success for his publishing venture in black photojournalism.[38]

With the end of World War II, aspiring black journalists had new opportunities to report for one of several large black newspapers— the *New York Amsterdam News, Pittsburgh Courier, Chicago Defender, Norfolk* [Va.] *Pilot and Guide, Atlanta World, Baltimore Afro-American*—and other smaller black newspapers around the nation. The black press enjoyed expanding circulation and sales until the early 1950s, when it slipped back to prewar circulation. A few black reporters, such as Ted Poston of the *New York Post,* gained jobs with white liberal dailies, and when Butler University of Indianapolis conducted a national survey of hiring practices and opportunities for black journalists in 1949, it reported that the demand for trained journalists for employment with white and black newspapers exceeded the supply. The *St. Louis Post-Dispatch* hired

37. McCoy and Ruetten, *Quest and Response,* passim; McCoy, *The Presidency of Harry S. Truman,* 106–9.
38. Roland E. Wolseley, *The Black Press, U.S.A,* 55–57, 63–64; Geoffrey Perrett, *Days of Sadness, Years of Triumph: The American People, 1939–1945,* 149.

its first black reporter that year, signing on John Henry Hicks, a University of Illinois graduate in journalism.[39]

Carl T. Rowan, graduated from Oberlin College in 1947, headed for Minnesota for graduate training in journalism at the state university that ultimately led to his employment with the Cowles newspapers of Minneapolis. During the election year of 1948 he took an assignment with the *Baltimore Afro-American* to conduct surveys of black support for the Democratic and Republican presidential candidates. Although he found strong support for Truman among blacks, the *Afro-American* wrote headlines for his stories that indicated a voter preference for Thomas E. Dewey. The publisher had been bought by the Dewey camp, something that Truman could understand quite readily. Rowan had earlier come to respect Truman for risking election to the presidency in his own right by advocating a comprehensive civil rights program. The award-winning journalist reaffirmed his high opinion of Truman's political courage and leadership in behalf of civil rights when he published his memoirs in 1991.[40]

Black journalists during the Truman years and beyond often confounded whites who had difficulty in understanding that minorities rightfully belonged in business and the professions. John H. Johnson, enjoying his financial success as the publisher of *Ebony*, recalled later the time when he was driving his expensive car in Chicago and a policeman flagged him to a stop for questioning.

"Does your boss know that you are driving his car?" the policeman asked.

"He sure does," Johnson replied.

"Well," advised the policeman, "you had better get it back to him as soon as you can."

"Sure will!" said Johnson.[41]

Rowan told a story about himself in the 1960s to illustrate the same point. According to his apocryphal tale, while mowing the lawn of his home in suburban Washington during his tenure as Deputy Assistant Secretary of State, a blond white woman in a

39. *Editor and Publisher* (July 2, 1949): 35; Wolseley, *Black Press, U.S.A.,* 56. For a sketch of Poston's work in journalism, see *Editor and Publisher* (September 24, 1949): 28. *Editor and Publisher* (July 2, 1949): 35; (July 18, 1949): 10.
40. Rowan, *Breaking Barriers,* 75–83, 78–79, 159–65.
41. Wolseley, *Black Press, U.S.A.,* 86.

chauffeur-driven limousine pulled to the curb. The woman, assuming that Rowan was a yardman whom she might employ, called to him.

"Boy!"

"Tell me," she asked, "how much do you get for mowing lawns?"

"Well," he replied, "the lady of *this* house lets me sleep with her."[42]

Rowan's ability to look with humor upon the many humiliating and dangerous experiences that he and his fellow black Americans endured offered one measure of the distance that he and the country had traveled from the Truman years to the 1960s.

It was more important, however, in the postwar years for white Americans in a position of leadership and power to feel the pain and the anger and injustice of racial discrimination in order to work toward a more just society. Truman sensed that pain. Acts of violence against black citizens in the postwar period shocked and angered the president and contributed to his decision to establish a commission on civil rights in 1946. Two years later Truman made the commission's recommendations the basis for his civil rights program.[43]

In March 1948 the Negro Newspaper Publisher's Association assessed both the white press and President Truman in its observance of national newspaper week. "If the white press fearlessly and relentlessly crusaded against all injustices and inequalities," said NNPA president Thomas W. Young, one of the fundamental reasons for a black press would be removed. "It is a painful irony," Young asserted, "that the Negro newspapers of today could not exist in the kind of democracy for which they strive." On this occasion, marked by a banquet in Washington, the president had not come to give awards but to receive one himself: the John R. Russwurm Citation, given by the NNPA in honor of the nation's first black newspaper publisher. Truman merited the award for his "uncompromising fight for civil rights," and he accepted the citation in the spirit of Russwurm's earlier fight for the liberation of enslaved blacks.[44]

There were no comparable awards for Truman from women's rights organizations, although he got high marks from social feminists for his support and advocacy of protectionist legislation for

42. Rowan, *Breaking Barriers*, 179–80.
43. McCoy and Ruetten, *Quest and Response*, 44–49.
44. *Editor and Publisher* (March 12, 1948): 52.

women and children. He also appointed a few women to second- and third-echelon positions during his presidency and, to the delight of young women attending a Girls Nation conference in 1949, he predicted that a woman would someday be elected president of the United States.[45]

But he also joked publicly about his chauvinistic views, as he did in a news conference exchange on April 5, 1951, with May Craig. Craig did not want to leave unnoted a statement in a recent article that appeared in *Collier's* to the effect that if congressmen did not think they knew better than the president how to run the country, their wives did. Was it laudable, Craig asked, "for wives to think their husbands know best?" "Of course it is," the president replied, evoking much laughter from the predominant contingent of newsmen.[46]

Female reporters such as Craig, unwilling to accept the patriarchal beliefs that dominated journalism and American society at midcentury, could be expected to carry their struggle for equality of opportunity to the White House itself. The newswomen, determined to change the working relationship between the president and the press still conducted largely as the affairs of gentlemen, would make the most of their opportunities during the Truman years.

45. Franklin D. Mitchell, "Harry S. Truman and the Politics of the Equal Rights Amendment, 1944–1953," unpublished paper read at the 1984 annual meeting of the American Historical Association. In the possession of the author.
46. *Public Papers*, 1951, 216.

6

First Ladies of Journalism

WOMEN BATTLED RESOURCEFULLY for equality of opportunity in the news profession during the Truman presidency. Veteran reporters May Craig and Doris Fleeson led the way in coverage on the president while the youthful correspondent Marguerite Higgins advanced the cause of female journalists on the distant battlefields of Korea. African American reporter Alice Dunnigan opened doors for her gender and race in coverage of official Washington, but she and other women were barred from the private newsgathering preserves of men in the nation's capital. Consequently, female journalists had a dual mission during the Truman administration: to cover the president with opportunity equal to that afforded to men, and to end women's second-class citizenship in the fourth estate.

Female reporters first gained access to presidential news conferences during the Franklin D. Roosevelt administration, but for many years May Craig, representing a chain of newspapers in Maine, and Esther Van Wagoner Tufty, correspondent for a string of newspapers in Michigan, were the only women in regular attendance at Roosevelt's news conferences. Only women attended the news conferences of Eleanor Roosevelt after she extended White House press coverage to her activities and interests in early 1933. Mrs. Roosevelt's decision to meet with female reporters stemmed in large part from her desire to give women, underrepresented among correspondents assigned to cover the president, opportunity to cover the White House.[1]

Manpower shortages during World War II contributed to a proliferation of female journalists both in Washington and throughout the nation. Women who found it difficult or impossible to break into journalism prior to the war readily found entry-level positions in the newspaper business ranging from copy writers to cub reporters as male journalists were drawn into the military services or given overseas assignment. Some women trained for executive positions as managing editors and bureau managers. A few highly accomplished and resourceful women such as Craig, Fleeson, and Higgins won overseas assignments during the war.[2]

The wartime performance of female journalists in the nation's capital itself became a news story. Virginia Irwin, Washington correspondent for the *St. Louis Post-Dispatch,* reported in 1943 that "Washington newspaperwomen have completely exploded the myth that the female of the species in the newspaper business is good only for 'feature' assignments with a woman's angle. They have proved that they can take the pressure of straight political reporting and that they can absorb the intricacies of politics right along with any man reporter."[3]

Irwin could not resist adding an anecdote to illustrate that the ability to attract and hold a male companion also sparked rivalry among some female reporters:

> One day a Washington newspaperwoman, newly divorced, was discussing the clothes question with one of her less attractive colleagues.

1. Virginia Irwin, "Low Down on Top Newspaper Women," *St. Louis Post-Dispatch,* May 2, 1943, Scrapbook 8, Container 1, Craig Papers, Library of Congress; Maurine H. Beasley, *Eleanor Roosevelt and the Media: A Public Quest for Self-Fulfillment,* 38–41.

2. Marion Marzolf, *Up from the Footnote: A History of Women Journalists,* 37; *Editor and Publisher* (September 27, 1947): 36. Craig was an accredited war correspondent from 1944–1945; Fleeson became a war correspondent for *Woman's Home Companion* in May 1943. See their biographical sketches in *Current Biography* for 1949 and 1959 respectively. Marguerite Higgins, two years out of Columbia University School of Journalism in 1944, became a correspondent in the European theater of war that year for the *New York Herald Tribune* after a direct appeal to the publisher, Helen Rogers Reid. Marion Marzolf, "Marguerite Higgins," 340–41. An estimated five hundred to six hundred men were assigned to the war fronts in contrast to approximately two dozen women war correspondents. *Editor and Publisher* (February 17, 1945): 8.

3. Irwin, "Low Down on Top Newspaper Women."

"You really ought to fix yourself up a bit," the divorcee advised patronizingly.

"I'll admit I don't know much about clothes," was her drab sister's reply, "But I am clever at holding my husband."[4]

After the war, societal pressure mounted for male journalists to reenter the news profession at the expense of women in the field. Two aspiring female journalists, Helen Thomas and Sarah McClendon, survived postwar discrimination and ultimately climbed to the top of their profession. Thomas began her journalistic career in 1942 as a seventeen-dollar-per-week copy girl at the now defunct *Washington Daily News;* later she became a cub reporter for United Press. When UPI (United Press merged with International News Service) assigned Thomas to the White House in 1961, she began her rise as eventual "dean" of the White House correspondents with a tenure of more than thirty years' duration.[5]

McClendon had gone to Washington as a member of the Women's Army Auxiliary Corps—the WACS—in 1942. Her training in journalism at the University of Missouri and a decade of experience working for newspapers in her native Texas landed her an assignment as a publicist for the army. After her wartime marriage failed, McClendon, pregnant with her first child, continued to work in her WAC uniform until the eighth month of her pregnancy. She became the first army officer to give birth to a child at Walter Reed Hospital, and when she was discharged from the hospital in June 1944, she was discharged from the WACS, too. Nine days later she found employment as a Washington correspondent for a chain of Texas newspapers. Although she lost her job to a man at the end of the war, she benefited from the advice of her former benefactor who told her, "You should be like May Craig, you should have your own news bureau." McClendon took the advice and succeeded immensely in a career extending over five decades and eleven presidential administrations.[6]

The determination of competent women such as McClendon and Thomas to continue in a profession they loved, as well as the practice of many publishers to employ women at a salary lower than

4. Ibid.

5. Helen Thomas, *Dateline: White House* (New York: Macmillan, 1975), xii–xviii, 6–8.

6. Sarah McClendon, *My Eight Presidents,* 10–23; Dawn Klingensmith, "Rancorous Rose," *Mizzou* 86 (fall 1986): 20–21.

that paid to men, helped to stem the immediate postwar exodus of female journalists; by 1946, the number of women employed by newspapers increased steadily.[7]

The relationship of female journalists to President Truman was conditioned initially by the decision of Mrs. Truman to discontinue the occasional meetings with female reporters begun by Eleanor Roosevelt. While Bess Truman's secretaries, Edith Helm and Reathel Odum, provided weekly information about activities scheduled on the first lady's social calendar, Mrs. Truman maintained a low profile in deference to her own desires and because of her belief that a president's wife should not play a public role in the policies of her husband's administration.[8]

Harry Truman's views on the proper role of wives of public officials happily coincided with the role Bess preferred to play as first lady. While he permitted advocates of the Equal Rights Amendment to publicize his prepresidential statement of 1944 endorsing an equal rights amendment, he privately dismissed the idea of equal rights for women as "a lot of hooey." More important to Truman was the predominant sentiment in the Democratic party and among women themselves for maintaining and extending protectionist legislation for females in lieu of an equal rights amendment. These views of the president, tempered by his official policy to extend political and economic equality of opportunity to all Americans, go far to explain his relationship with female White House correspondents.[9]

Two women, Craig and Fleeson, brought a wealth of journalistic skills and a deep commitment to equality of opportunity for female journalists to their coverage of the Truman presidency. Both had begun their careers in journalism in the 1920s as writing partners with their newspapermen husbands. Craig teamed with her husband, Donald, the Washington bureau chief of the *New York Herald,* and combined rearing two children with the writing of a column for the *Portland Press-Herald* starting in 1923. The following year the column appeared under her byline, and when her husband died in

7. For an authoritative analysis of this trend, see the results of a survey published in *Editor and Publisher* (February 11, 1950): 9, 72–73.

8. Maurine Beasley, "Bess Truman and the Press: A Case Study of a First Lady as Political Communicator," 208–11.

9. Franklin D. Mitchell, "Harry S. Truman and the Politics of the Equal Rights Amendment, 1944–1953."

1936, she was a well-established journalist writing columns exclusively for the Maine newspapers of Guy P. Gannett.[10]

Fleeson's career in journalism began in 1923 in her native Kansas following her graduation from the state university in Lawrence. By 1927, and soon after she landed a job with the *New York Daily News,* Fleeson graduated from local news assignments to reporting on New York politics. Three years later she married John O'Donnell, her colleague in political reporting for the *Daily News.* Their daughter was born two years later, and in 1933, when the *Daily News* opened a Washington bureau to cover the Roosevelt administration, Fleeson and O'Donnell took assignment there. Fleeson, as liberal as her husband was conservative, also embraced an internationalist course as Europe moved toward war. Increasingly her views on domestic and foreign affairs placed her at odds with the editorial position of the *Daily News.* Marital problems arose with her husband, and in 1942 the couple divorced. In 1943 Fleeson left the *Daily News* for a two-year tour as a war correspondent for *Woman's Home Companion.* At the end of the war she began to write a political affairs column for the *Washington Evening Star* and the *Boston Globe.*[11]

Craig had had extensive experience in the ways of Washington and the presidential news conference when the Truman administration began. Her family had left her birth state of South Carolina to make their new home in Washington when she was twelve. She never lost her southern accent, but many of her readers, who associated her with the Maine newspapers for whom she wrote, thought of her as a peppery New Englander with "a mind as sharp as cider vinegar, as retentive as a lobster trap." When she began to write a column with her husband in the early 1920s, Craig covered the entire federal government, but her primary beat was Congress until she began to divide her time between the White House and Capitol Hill during the Roosevelt administration.[12]

10. "Elizabeth May Craig," in Anna Rothe, ed., *Current Biography,* 1949, 127–28. Craig dropped the use of her first name in the early 1940s. Jennifer L. Tebbe, "Elizabeth May Adams Craig," in *Notable American Women: The Modern Period, A Biographical Dictionary,* edited by Barbara Sicherman and Carol Hurd Green, with Ilene Kantrov and Harriette Walker, 171–73. Cambridge: Belknap Press of Harvard University Press, 1980.

11. "Doris Fleeson," in Rothe, ed., *Current Biography,* 1959, 122–23; Mary McGrory, "Doris Fleeson," in *Notable American Women,* edited by Sicherman et al., 239–42.

12. *New York Times,* July 16, 1975; Draft, biography of Elizabeth May Craig, "Correspondents' Kindergarten," 9, Chapter Four folder, Container 2, Craig Papers, Library of Congress.

The twice-weekly Roosevelt news conferences gave Craig many opportunities for verbal jousts with the president. On one occasion the president gave the reporters a tongue-lashing for allegedly failing to report the facts regarding wartime enforcement of price controls that led to the arrest of Avery Sewall, president of the Montgomery Ward merchandising chain. Craig challenged Roosevelt by stating that both the press and radio had reported the facts of the case. When Roosevelt reasserted his view, Craig responded in kind.[13]

On another occasion, Craig endeared herself to fellow reporters who had left unchallenged the president's assertion that columnists were "unnecessary excrescences on civilization." Craig, whose column "Inside In Washington" appeared seven days a week, shot back: "But Mr. President, you've got one in the family!" much to the delight of the reporters. Roosevelt quickly alibied that his wife's syndicated column, "My Day," was a diary rather than a column. Clearly Craig came off better in the exchange. To her friends, she quipped that she didn't mind being called an excrescent—"that's just a wart"—but she didn't want her editor to get the idea that her work was unnecessary.[14]

Craig's complete ease in asking questions of the president made her the subject of both envy and contempt. Some of Craig's fellow reporters believed that she carefully planned her questions in advance of the news conference in order to attract attention to herself. During the Roosevelt administration, FDR, peeved by one of Craig's prickly questions, echoed this belief by remarking that she "must have stayed awake all night thinking that up."

"I did," Craig replied, evoking peals of laughter from both Roosevelt and the correspondents.[15]

Craig came into conflict with Truman over the treatment of women in the Washington press corps early in his administration. In the spring of 1945 the White House Correspondents Association, an exclusive organization for the male journalists accredited to the White House, made plans for its annual dinner, with the president, as usual, the guest of honor. Craig, in behalf of the excluded female journalists, asked President Truman to extend an invitation to them. But Truman spurned the suggestion on the ground that it would

13. Ruth Montgomery, untitled story on Craig, c. January 9, 1945, Scrapbook 1945, Container 10, Craig Papers, Library of Congress.

14. Ibid.

15. Eleanor Harris, "May Craig: TV's Most Unusual Star," 109.

be presumptuous for him, as a guest, to insist on extending an invitation to the women.[16]

Similarly, women were denied membership in other professional and social clubs for men, such as the National Press Club, the Gridiron—an organization of newsmen who subjected the president to good-natured grilling each year—and the exclusive Metropolitan Club and Cosmos Club. Male reporters argued that women such as Craig and Fleeson would "take over" the National Press Club if they were admitted to membership. Despite the annual rebuffs, female reporters continued their efforts to break down the doors to the Washington male preserves during the Truman years. By 1949 the National Press Club had made a concession to white female journalists by providing for them, in the rapidly fading spirit of "separate but equal," a separate cocktail lounge and dining room.[17]

The second-class citizenship accorded to female journalists itself made news when the navy denied Craig permission to travel with the presidential party on the USS *Missouri* for the return trip from Truman's state visit to Brazil in September 1947. The principle of traveling with the president was not the central issue: Craig had journeyed to Mexico earlier in the year to cover President Truman's state visit there. She had flown to Rio de Janeiro to report on the president's activities in the Brazilian capital. The rub came when Craig sought to join the men reporters permitted to travel on the battleship for coverage of the presidential party en route home. Permission denied.[18]

Immediately Craig and other women in the press corps swung into action. In Washington, Fleeson telephoned Press Secretary Ross, who had not accompanied Truman to Brazil, to learn who had denied Craig the opportunity to report on the president whenever that opportunity was afforded male reporters. Ross conceded that the decision had been made in the White House, but shifted the blame to the captain of the *Missouri*, Robert L. Dennison, who,

16. Ferrell, ed., *Truman in the White House*, 76.
17. See preceding chapter on the exclusion of women from professional and social clubs in Washington; Draft, biography, Chapter One folder, Container 2, Craig Papers, Library of Congress; Frederick C. Othman, "Every Day is Election Day," in Phillips et al., eds., *Dateline: Washington*, 254–56. Women were not added to the roster until 1970. *New York Times*, October 28, 1970; S. McBee, "Open Sesame!" *McCall's* 98 (July 1971): 45. The black journalist Louis Lautier broke the color barrier at the National Press Club by gaining membership in 1955. *New York Times*, February 5, 8, 1955.
18. "Elizabeth May Craig," *Current Biography*, 1949, 127–28.

Ross explained, followed the naval tradition of not allowing women aboard a combat vessel. Dennison, in turn, stated that the vessel lacked bathroom facilities for women other than the private accommodations in the president's quarters.[19]

Fleeson blew the battleship "tradition" explanation out of the water in her syndicated column. She pointed out that Mrs. Truman and Margaret were accompanying the president home on the *Missouri*, thus scotching the notion that naval tradition of men only aboard ships at sea was being upheld. Moreover, President Herbert Hoover had traveled with Mrs. Hoover on a battleship during his administration. In addition, she reported that the vessel had a powder room for "senoras" who attended the shipboard state reception hosted by President and Mrs. Truman during the battleship's anchorage in Rio de Janeiro harbor. (She wrote unaware, as Captain Dennison later reported, that the powder room lacked a tub and shower.) The tradition that the military clung to, Fleeson charged, was sob-story journalism—the genre of an earlier era when women wrote heart-rendering accounts as mothers and daughters. In the current era, Fleeson wrote, the military wanted stories to boost the morale of women who must give their sons and sweethearts to the army and navy. The idea that female reporters could not go where their male counterparts ventured, she declared, was a carryover from World War II, when the brass cited the lack of facilities as the reason for the exclusion of women. "The war is over," Fleeson noted, "but somewhere the frame of mind lingers."[20]

Fleeson and Craig quickly gained support from organizations and individuals. The Women's National Press Club sent formal protests to President Truman and to the navy, stating that what had happened to Craig shouldn't happen to any female reporter and must not happen again. The publisher of Craig's columns made the same point and later elicited from her the observation that discrimination against women was discrimination against their publishers to hire.[21]

19. Draft, biography, General Miscellany, Biographical folder, Container 2, Craig Papers, Library of Congress.

20. Doris Fleeson, "They Shy At Women," August 28, 1947, Scrapbook, Box 1, Doris Fleeson Papers, University of Kansas, Lawrence, Kansas; Fleeson's former husband, John O'Donnell, writing about the incident in his syndicated column, called it "The Battle of the Powder Room" (Scrapbook 19, Craig Papers, Library of Congress).

21. John O'Donnell, "Capitol Stuff," c. September 1947, Scrapbook, 1947, Container 17, Craig Papers, Library of Congress; Guy P. Gannett to Truman, quoted in *Editor and Publisher* (September 6, 1947): 8.

One woman, who had administered contracts for the navy's ship-building program during the war, wrote to Craig to suggest that the incident be used to unite women in behalf of equality:

> There must be thousands of women, throughout the country, who did material work on these ships, in factories and in offices. The post-war decline in our precious sense of national unity, so helpful in winning the war, is pushing women back (ala Wylie, Farnham, et al.) psychologically and materially, so your campaign to go forward in a very limited way would well do with reinforcement on this broader front. You want to cover public affairs on an equal footing with men; this is only part of the whole problem—say so, and waken other women to this urgent task.[22]

The latter point provided a key insight into the feminist views of veteran reporters such as Craig and Fleeson. Both wanted equality of opportunity in journalism, but neither had the time nor the inclination to take up the cause of feminism. Years earlier, when Craig had marched with suffragettes and developed a friendship with Alice Paul of the National Woman's Party and its single-cause objective of securing an equal rights amendment, she decided that she could not espouse feminism and carry on her work as an objective reporter. So while she battled discrimination based on sex—she even tried to get male reporters admitted to Eleanor Roosevelt's press conferences without success—she did not take up the cause of feminism per se. Fleeson believed that a competent woman could open any door through individual effort and thus spurned a united approach to overcoming gender discrimination.[23]

22. Eleanor Manning to Craig, undated, General Scrapbook 1947, Container 17, Craig Papers, Library of Congress. The references are to Philip Wylie, who popularized the concept of "Momism" in his 1942 book, *Generation of Vipers,* and Marynia Farnham, coauthor of the 1947 antifeminist study, *Modern Woman: The Lost Sex.*

23. Draft, biography, untitled chapter, 9–10, 14–15. The Press Galleries of the Congress and the White House Correspondents folder, Container 2, Craig Papers, Library of Congress. According to one account, Craig cajoled Congressman Howard Smith (D-Va.) into adding the word "sex" to the landmark Civil Rights Bill of 1964. Smith added the gender category, but not to provide equality of treatment for women; he hoped that adding a gender classification to the categories of nondiscrimination would attract additional negative votes for the defeat of the bill. Bruce J. Dierenfield, *Keeper of the Rules: Congressman Howard W. Smith of Virginia* (Charlottesville: University Press of Virginia, 1987), 19, 194–96. Fleeson's major cause was the profession of journalism and she combatted discrimination based on race and gender vigorously within the

Craig, not unexpectedly, carried her protest directly to Truman when the opportunity arose before the start of the president's news conference on September 25, 1947, following his return from Brazil. While male reporters engaged the president in casual conversation as other correspondents filed into the Oval Office, they swapped stories about the time-honored custom of initiating the passengers abroad the USS *Missouri* crossing the equator for the first time into the court of King Neptune. Craig seized the opening provided unwittingly by the president himself:

"Too bad," Truman joked, "we didn't have May to put through that initiation."

"Why didn't you, Mr. President?" Craig quickly shot back.

"That's a question I can't answer," Truman responded evasively.

"I've never had an answer," Craig replied, keeping the president on the hook.

"Hard to get," Truman admitted, coming off the worst in the exchange and by now probably glad to start the news conference.[24]

Meanwhile, female and male African American journalists intensified their efforts during the early postwar years to gain admission to the congressional press galleries and full access to the news conferences and travels of the president. An earlier chapter in this struggle had been written in Truman's home state by Lucile Bluford, a black newspaperwoman. In 1938 Bluford had sought admission to the graduate program of the prestigious School of Journalism of the University of Missouri. Despite her credentials as a graduate of the undergraduate journalism program of the University of Kansas and managing editor of the *Kansas City Call*, a well-regarded black newspaper, she was denied admission on account of her race. Bluford's successful suit in a federal court required the state in 1942 to establish a school of journalism for blacks at the all-black Lincoln University in Jefferson City. In 1949 *Editor and Publisher* boasted that Lincoln University had the distinction of being the only black school of journalism in the United States, but the boast did more to call attention to limited educational opportunities for aspiring black journalists in the South and Missouri than it did to equal professional training in journalism.

---

profession. She, like May Craig, left to others the broad efforts to extend and expand women's rights.

24. Transcript of the President's News Conference for Press and Radio, September 25, 1947, Box 62, PSF, Truman Papers, Truman Library.

The University of Missouri did not admit its first black student until 1950.[25]

The pianist Hazel Scott was the catalyst for change in racially segregated news centers of official and social Washington in the fall of 1945. Scott, the wife of Congressman Adam Clayton Powell, Jr. (D-N.Y.), challenged both the Daughters of the American Revolution and the National Press Club when the former barred her recital in its Constitution Hall and the latter practiced racial and gender discrimination in limiting its membership to white males working for daily newspapers. Ironically, the press club had opened its auditorium to Scott, and she at first accepted its offer to perform. Later, however, she declined the invitation, citing the membership practices of the organization, which she linked as well to the exclusion of black journalists from the press galleries of the House and Senate. The publicity generated by the incident contributed to the effort of a few black journalists and their white friends in the news profession and Congress to break down the doors of discrimination in the congressional press galleries.[26]

The governing body of white male journalists who set the policy for the Senate Rules Committee and the Speaker of the House on admittance to the congressional press galleries had denied black journalists access on technical grounds. Because the rules limited access to the press galleries of the Senate and House to accredited reporters of daily newspapers—the same policy as at the National Press Club—reporters who wrote for weeklies or weekly periodicals could not qualify. Louis L. Lautier, reporter for the weekly *Atlanta World*, appealed to the Senate Rules Committee for a change in policy in 1947. Craig, who had led the successful campaign for admission of female reporters to the congressional press galleries two decades earlier, endorsed Lautier's application, and Doris Fleeson publicized his bid for representation in her column for March 8, 1947. Within days the Senate Rules Committee ordered a change in policy to permit Lautier and other black reporters access to the Senate press galleries. Independently, and a few days earlier, white male periodical correspondents had voted to admit Percival Prattis, managing editor of the *Pittsburgh Courier* and contributor to *Negro*

25. Lucile Bluford, "Missouri 'Shows' The Supreme Court," 230–32, 242; *Editor and Publisher* (May 21, 1949): 50. The article pointed out that more than a score of black colleges had limited courses in journalism and two schools, Xavier at New Orleans and Texas Tech in Houston, had well-developed departments of journalism. *New York Times*, July 8, 1950.

26. *Editor and Publisher* (March 22, 1947): 13.

Digest; thus the distinction of being the first African American journalist to gain admission to the Senate press gallery belonged to Prattis, followed in a few days by Lautier. They were joined by Alice Dunnigan, a fledgling reporter for the Associated Negro Press, in August 1947.[27] Dunnigan first began to write part-time for black newspapers in her native Kentucky in the late 1930s. During the war she left her primary profession of teaching to work as a typist in a government office in Washington. Eager to become a full-time reporter after the war, Dunnigan sought to become the Washington correspondent of the Chicago-based Associated Negro Press Association (ANP) of Claude Barnett. Barnett, however, kept Dunnigan in the wings until he had first tried to hire an experienced black male reporter at a salary of two hundred dollars per month. When these efforts failed, he agreed in December 1946 to give Dunnigan the job with the title "Washington Bureau Chief," with compensation set on a piece-rate basis.[28]

Dunnigan jumped at the chance to represent the ANP, but when few of her articles were accepted, or were picked up from other sources without any compensation to her, she soon exhausted her government severance pay. She successfully negotiated a weekly salary with the ANP—she settled for twenty-five dollars a week—but that pay, too, forced her to accept greatly reduced living standards. She established living quarters in the basement of a well-located white residence in Washington where she tended the furnace and hauled the ashes as a work contribution to her monthly rent. Food costs taxed her ingenuity, too. In explaining her need for a more substantial weekly wage, she informed her employer that Sunday dinner consisted of pig ears and turnip greens.[29]

Dunnigan's problems compounded when her small weekly check did not arrive every Friday as scheduled, leaving her without food

27. *Editor and Publisher* (January 12, 1946): 42; (March 16, 1946): 79; (March 22, 1947): 13; Lautier to Fleeson, March 25, 1947, Folder L, Box 9, Fleeson Papers, University of Kansas; Dunnigan, *A Black Woman's Experience*, 3–6; Dunnigan to Claude A. Barnett, August 26, 1947, Reel 5, Part II, Claude A. Barnett Papers, Library of Congress.

28. Dunnigan, *A Black Woman's Experience*, 204–5 and passim; Dunnigan to Barnett, November 21, 1946; Barnett to James L. Hicks, November 26, 1946; Dunnigan to Barnett, June 21, 1948; Dunnigan to Barnett, January 1, 1949, Reel 5, Part II, Claude A. Barnett Papers, Library of Congress.

29. Dunnigan, *A Black Woman's Experience*, 205, 298; Dunnigan to Barnett, c. September 1947, Reel 5, Part II, Barnett Papers, Library of Congress.

money for the weekend. Often she had to pawn a few prized possessions Friday night and redeem them, at a hefty rate of interest, when her paycheck arrived on Monday. Her meager salary also permitted the purchase of few new clothes. As fashions changed and the abbreviated hemline of the war years came down after the war, she received criticism from women who considered her short dresses inappropriate for a working reporter.[30]

Still Dunnigan persevered. As a newcomer to Washington journalism, she, unlike established black newsmen, had no network of influential friends and associates who could supply news stories of interest to black Americans. Consequently, Dunnigan had to go to the agencies and departments to develop news leads. She relied on the trolley cars of the segregated Washington transit system for transportation, for cost of a taxi or a personal automobile was prohibitive. Once while en route to Capitol Hill, she discovered that her transit pass had expired; lacking the fare, she walked the long distance to the Capitol. (By contrast, Joseph Alsop, who never learned to drive, relied exclusively upon taxis to get about Washington.)[31]

Dunnigan began her campaign to win accreditation at the White House shortly after she began to cover the capital for the ANP. Louis Lautier had earlier gained his credentials as the successor to black reporter Harry McAlpin, the first of his race to be accredited by the White House in 1944 during the Roosevelt administration. As Dunnigan recalled later, Lautier gave her no assistance in her efforts to win accreditation; in fact, she believed that he was part of the male opposition to female journalists that had to be overcome along with race and class discrimination. In August 1947 the White House Press Office gave Dunnigan accreditation for attendance at the president's news conferences.[32]

Dunnigan earnestly believed that she was making history as well

30. Dunnigan to Barnett, undated, Reel 5, Part II, Barnett Papers, Library of Congress; Dunnigan, *A Black Woman's Experience*, 220–21, 297.

31. Percival Prattis of the *Pittsburgh Courier* and other black reporters had to develop an information network among black employees throughout the federal government in Washington because white information officials refused to serve them. Prattis also socialized and planned assaults on racial barriers with Thurgood Marshall, Robert Weaver, William Hastie, and other influential blacks in official Washington. Robert C. Weaver, Testimonial Address, October 20, 1961, Organizations and Organizational Affiliations folder, Box 144, Percival L. Prattis Papers, Howard University. Dunnigan, *A Black Woman's Experience*, 212–13, 220. Alsop, with Platt, *I've Seen the Best of It*, 480.

32. Dunnigan, *A Black Woman's Experience*, 209, 210–11; Winfield, *FDR and the News Media*, 71–72, note 10.

as reporting the historic events of her time. For this reason she attached great significance to joining the news media representatives on President Truman's western train tour of June 1948. The ANP candidly rejected her request for financial assistance on the ground that the cost, approximately one thousand dollars, was not worth it to the newsgathering organization; it could get the information free from the accounts filed in daily newspapers.[33] Dunnigan managed to secure a loan for the trip and became the first black newspaperwoman to travel with a presidential party.

Unfortunately, Dunnigan became the subject of one of her own news stories based on discrimination against her in Cheyenne. The incident occurred as reporters walked the brief distance on a roped-off section of the street from the train depot to the Wyoming capitol building where Truman was scheduled to make an address. A white military policeman, apparently thinking that Dunnigan did not belong in the president's press entourage, spoke to her rudely and shoved her to the sidelines. A white male reporter, Lacey Reynolds of the *Nashville Tennessean,* quickly interceded in her behalf.

"Watch out there!" Reynolds admonished the officer. "You're messing with the party of the president of the United States. You know Mrs. Dunnigan is with us. She has her badge and she has it on." The MP relented and Dunnigan proceeded with her colleagues.[34]

Later, when Truman heard about the incident, he lauded Reynolds for his action, and personally spoke to Dunnigan when the train had stopped for the night in Tacoma. Dunnigan, sitting barefoot in her compartment and typing out the news story for the day, heard a faint knock on the door. The greatly surprised reporter could only manage to say "Oh, Mr. President, Mr. President" as he entered the room. In response to his question of whether she were being treated all right on the trip, she diplomatically assured him that she was. "That's good," he said. "But if you have any further trouble let me know."[35]

Dunnigan filed her account of the incident and the president's concern about her mistreatment with the Associated Negro Press, but metropolitan newspapers and national newsmagazines took no note of the story.[36]

33. Barnett to Dunnigan, June 3, 1948, Reel 5, Part II, Barnett Papers, Library of Congress; Dunnigan, *A Black Woman's Experience,* 228–33.

34. Dunnigan, *A Black Woman's Experience,* 240–41.

35. Ibid., 242–43.

36. Weekly News Release, Associated Negro Press, June 9, 1948, 12, Reel 8, Part II, Barnett Papers.

If Dunnigan had needed a role model in dealing with discrimination based on gender, she could have found one in the youthful and talented Marguerite Higgins. Barely out of her twenties and already an experienced war correspondent from her European assignment during the final months of World War II, Higgins wrote dispatches from the battlefields of Korea in 1950 and 1951 that had symbolic and real significance for all female reporters at home.

Assigned by the *New York Herald Tribune* in May 1950 to cover Far Eastern affairs from Tokyo, Higgins flew to Seoul on June 27, 1950, two days after the armed forces of North Korea invaded its southern neighbor, to report on the evacuation of American citizens. On the first flight the plane turned back because of reports that Seoul's Kimpo airfield was under strafing attacks from North Korean planes. After arrangements were made for another flight, Frank Gibney of *Time*, one of three male reporters making the trip with Higgins, tried to persuade her from going, arguing that Korea was "no place for a woman."[37]

Higgins refused to stay behind, and subsequently wrote that Korea was more than just a story.

> It was a personal crusade. I felt that my position as a correspondent was at stake. Here I represented one of the world's most noted newspapers as its correspondent in that area. I could not let the fact that I was a woman jeopardize my newspaper's coverage of the war. Failure to reach the front would undermine all my arguments that I was entitled to the same assignment breaks as any man. It would prove that a woman as a correspondent was a handicap to the *New York Herald Tribune*.[38]

The courageous Higgins covered the fall of Seoul and the unsuccessful efforts of the American and South Korean forces to halt the invading North Korean army at considerable risk to her own safety. Despite her good reportage, her own *Herald Tribune* colleague, Homer Bigart, placed her on the defensive when he arrived in Korea from the United States in early July. Bigart, winner of a Pulitzer Prize for his reporting on the fall of Japan in World War II, ordered Higgins back to Japan and warned her that she would be fired if she stayed in Korea to cover the war. Male correspondents representing other newspapers refused to be drawn into the personal

---

37. Marzolf, "Marguerite Higgins," 340–41; Marguerite Higgins, *War in Korea: The Report of a Woman Combat Correspondent*, 17–18.
38. Higgins, *War in Korea*.

controversy, and Higgins cabled her newspaper that the war was big enough for two reporters to share. By the end of the summer Bigart had dropped his opposition to Higgins but never abandoned his cutting remarks about his colleague. Years later, when informed that Higgins and her husband were expecting their first child, he chauvinistically wisecracked, "Who's the mother?"[39]

If the contretemps with Bigart and the dangers of the battlefield were not enough, Higgins also had to overcome the obstacles placed in her way by the American Embassy and army and naval commanders. Ambassador John J. Muccio assembled Higgins and her male colleagues early in the war to tell them they were a nuisance and should leave.[40] Later, when Higgins flew into Suwon, an army colonel informed her, "You'll have to go back, young lady. You can't stay here. There may be trouble."

This reception left Higgins discouraged. As she wrote later, "I had hoped that my performance under fire in the exit from Seoul would have ended further arguments that 'the front is no place for a woman.' But it was to be many weeks before I was accepted on an equal basis with the men." Another officer who had earlier seen Higgins at the front came to her rescue, and she continued to cover the war.[41]

During the battle of Taegu in mid-July, Higgins was stunned to receive an order from Lt. General Walton H. Walker to leave the Korean theater of war at once. She suspected that some of her early stories, written without military guidelines, had offended army censors. In addition, her stories of the frustration and despair of American troops unable to stop the advancing enemy forces may have been regarded as injurious to morale. To her surprise, however, Higgins learned that General Walker had ordered her out because there were no facilities for women at the front.

Higgins had not asked for special consideration because of her gender and later noted that there was "no shortage of bushes in Korea." For a while she stalled until an appeal could be made directly to General MacArthur, but when no word arrived from headquarters, junior officers of Walker's staff placed Higgins on a plane for a flight to Tokyo.[42]

39. Ibid., 25–28, 55–58; Betsy Wade, comp. and ed., *Forward Positions: The War Correspondence of Homer Bigart*, 224.

40. Higgins, *War in Korea*, 30.

41. Ibid., 39, 41.

42. Ibid., 95–107.

Unknown to Higgins and the officers who had placed her on the plane for Japan, MacArthur had rescinded Walker's ban on female reporters in Korea. Interceding for Higgins was another woman, Helen Rogers Reid, president of the *Herald Tribune*. A cable from Reid to MacArthur produced both a reversal of General Walker's ban and praise from MacArthur for Higgins, who, he acknowledged, "was held in highest professional esteem by everyone."[43]

In fact, though, Higgins became the butt of many jokes and vicious tales that implied that she used her sex to curry favor with men to get a story. A comely woman with a winsome smile, Higgins's physical attractiveness and personality were indeed assets; she was vulnerable mainly, her male friends noted, in her lack of self-esteem. Barry Bingham, Sr., publisher of the *Louisville Courier-Journal*, removed some of the sting of these stories with an editorial of praise for Higgins in his newspaper: "Miss Higgins shows no desire to win a name as a woman who dares to write at the spot where men are fighting. Her ambition is to be recognized as a good reporter, sex undesignated."[44]

Later in the war and back in Korea, Higgins experienced trouble with naval authorities who, like their army counterparts, argued that the lack of facilities for females precluded her passage on a troop transport assembled as a part of the armada for the invasion of Inchon on September 15, 1950. Her persistence paid off; the navy relented, and Higgins landed in the fifth wave of the assault. Yet despite her bravery on the beach at Inchon, Admiral James H. Doyle thereafter permitted Higgins aboard naval vessels only if accompanied by a female nurse.[45]

Higgins's courageous reporting did not go unrewarded, nor was her work as a war correspondent over. In 1951, she received a Pulitzer Prize for her coverage of the Korean War, marking the first time a woman had won the award for reportage as a combat correspondent. Fifteen years later, with America engaged in war in Vietnam, Higgins went there for her third war assignment. Tragically, her string of good fortune and achievement ended when she contracted a tropical infection and died at the young age of 45.[46]

---

43. Ibid., 102, 107.
44. Ibid., 108, 109; see Julia Edwards, "The Outrageous Marguerite Higgins," in *Women of the World: The Great Foreign Correspondents*, 188–201.
45. Higgins, *War in Korea*, 140–50.
46. Edwards, "The Outrageous Marguerite Higgins," 199. Technically, Higgins's prize was for her writing as a foreign correspondent. Marzolf, "Marguerite Higgins," 340–41.

May Craig, in Washington, continued her battle with the navy to win access to its ships for coverage of the war in Korea. Earlier, Secretary of the Navy John L. Sullivan gave Craig permission to sail on the aircraft carrier USS *Midway* when several members of Congress joined the crew in the ship's maiden cruise in 1949. During the Korean War, she became the first female correspondent to stay aboard a battleship—the USS *New Jersey*—during its bombardment of the east coast of Korea. These feats earned her the title "admiral" in navy circles and the begrudging admiration of the military. Truman, although sometimes exasperated by Craig, wrote a nice note to her during her coverage of the Korean War expressing his concern for her safety.[47]

Doris Fleeson had an entirely different experience with the president. She earned Truman's wrath by looking quizzically at him during a press conference in mid-December 1951 when reports of corruption in the federal government were rampant. Truman broke off from his explanation of what he had done and would continue to do to clean house to ask Fleeson: "Why are you looking at me like that for? Do you want to write a sob sister piece about it? I don't need any sob sister pieces!"[48]

The column Fleeson wrote for publication the following day fairly burned the president to a crisp. Until scandals in the Internal Revenue Service had broken out recently, she wrote, Truman probably felt he had assured his place in history and that "in Valhalla he would not need to bow to his brilliant predecessor," Franklin D. Roosevelt. Now Truman was in the position to appreciate the philosopher Hobbes's description of Hell as "the truth seen too late." In an interview with other reporters, who led off their coverage of the press conference with an account of Truman's waspish remarks to Fleeson, she stated that she was unaware of looking at the president in any special way. In sorting out what he had said about corruption in government, it struck her, she said, as being contradictory, "as it did to other reporters." And in her own distinctive way of turning attention to her advantage, she added impertinently: "But as for how I was looking—I thought I looked pretty good. I had a new Sally Victor hat on."[49]

47. "Elizabeth May Craig," 1127; Draft, biography, General Miscellany, Biographical, p. 3, Container 2, Craig Papers, Library of Congress; Truman to Craig, June 29, 1952, PPF 5772, Truman Library.

48. *Public Papers*, 1951, 641.

49. *St. Louis Post-Dispatch*, December 14, 1951.

Publishers around the country who carried Fleeson's column, and who shared her private views that Truman had been lax in dealing with corruption in the federal government, quickly sprang to her defense. An editorial in the [Portland] *Oregonian* affirmed that "One thing she is not is a 'sob sister'—as a girl reporter who goes all out on emotional stories is known in the trade. No wonder our Doris blinked and was speechless. It was a nasty swipe at her reputation as a serious and very good reporter." The editorial concluded that while it regretted the president's "petulant attacks" on reporters, "Miss Fleeson will be comforted in the knowledge that she is in distinguished company in the 'Denounced by Truman Club.'"[50]

To his great credit, and probably with the urging of Mrs. Truman, who enjoyed a warm personal relationship with Fleeson, Truman got along well with the reporter for the rest of his presidency, even including her among a few journalists granted individual interviews in the closing days of his presidency.[51]

It was important to Fleeson and Craig that they not incur the president's enmity for both professional and personal reasons. Their sharp exchanges with Truman offered opportunities for his and their detractors such as Walter Trohan of the *Chicago Tribune* and Fleeson's former husband, John O'Donnell, to impair the newswomen's working relations with the president. Consequently both reporters did not allow minor skirmishes with Truman to escalate. Both wanted to enjoy the president's goodwill and friendship, and each demonstrated that they wanted to be counted among the president's friends. Craig requested that Truman be photographed with her, and he readily consented, inscribing the photo to "A Great Reporter." In her column of April 21, 1952, Craig wrote an admiring sketch of the president and explained away their skirmishes at press conferences as merely a professional relationship. "I am sure he likes me," she wrote. "There is a look in his eye and a note in his voice, even when he is angry because I ask an embarrassing question, that shows he likes me."[52]

50. Editorial, [Portland] *Oregonian,* December 15, 1951, Scrapbook, Box 1, Fleeson Papers, University of Kansas.
51. Fleeson also attended the news briefings of the first lady's social activities. Harry and Bess exchanged friendly letters with Fleeson after they returned to private life in Independence. See Truman correspondence folder, Box 9, Fleeson Papers, University of Kansas.
52. See, for example, O'Donnell's column for January 4, 1951, that took note of Truman's angry exchanges with women reporters. Scrapbook 1950–51, Craig Papers, Library of Congress. Trohan, no fan of Craig's, speculated

Fleeson paid a tearful farewell to the Trumans when they boarded the train that would carry the now former president and first lady back to Independence on January 20, 1953. She even warmly embraced another well-wisher, General Vaughan, one of her targets in articles on corruption in the Truman administration, lamenting to Vaughan that Washington would never be the same without the Trumans.

"Well," Mrs. Vaughan exclaimed, as much surprised as her husband by Fleeson's action, "that's a *switch!*" ("At least that is the word I think she said," Vaughan wrote Truman.)[53]

Fleeson, as Craig had done earlier, wrote a moving tribute to the now former president in her syndicated column.[54] Presidential approbation thus ranked alongside of journalistic awards received by women during the Truman presidency.

The formal and informal honors accorded female journalists during the Truman years were impressive even when the list is limited to Craig, Fleeson, and Dunnigan. Craig, praised by an admirer as the "First Lady of Journalism" when she retired in 1965, had won that accolade in recognition of her years as a syndicated columnist and long-standing role as a regular panelist on "Meet the Press," a popular Sunday news interview destined to become one of the institutions of the Washington news scene after its inauguration on radio in 1946 and on television starting in 1949. Her ability to ask pointed questions of significant news makers, a skill honed to perfection at presidential news conferences, won for her immense respect and great popularity. The pert and fearless reporter with her trademark bonnet adorned with pink flowers had become a celebrity in her own right.[55]

Fleeson attained prominence and distinction as a writer of lead articles on important news-breaking stories. In 1951 *Time* hailed Fleeson as the leading newswoman in Washington for her exclusive stories and skillful political reporting. A few years later she

that her voice, which he described as "like the scraping of a faulty grain of chalk on a slate blackboard," irritated Truman more than her pointed questions (*Political Animals*, 261). "Inside in Washington," April 21, 1952, Scrapbook 1952, Container 1, Craig Papers, Library of Congress.

53. Vaughan to Truman, January 29, 1953, Harry Vaughan folder, PPNF, Truman Library.

54. *Washington Star*, January 21, 1953.

55. "Elizabeth May Craig," *Current Biography*, 1949, 127–28; Harris, "May Craig," 109–10, 112, 118. A reference to Craig as "the first lady of journalism" is in the letter of John B. Conway to Craig, February 25, 1964, "Decline and Fall of the American Republic" folder, Container 1, Craig Papers, Library of Congress.

won the prestigious Raymond L. Clapper award for distinguished journalism. Her political commentary column had an enormous readership through its national distribution to newspapers by the Bell Syndicate.[56]

Both Craig and Fleeson admired the pluck and energy of Alice Dunnigan as the fledgling reporter faced daily hardships and discrimination during the Truman years. The social and economic status of the two women alone put great distance between themselves and Dunnigan. Craig entertained news makers such as Clare Boothe Luce and Senator Richard B. Russell, Jr. (D-Ga.) in her Capitol Hill townhouse and occasionally vacationed with Eleanor Roosevelt at Hyde Park or at the Roosevelt summer home in Maine. Fleeson, owner of a comfortable old house in Georgetown, moved in high Washington social circles, too, and married former Navy Secretary Dan Kimball in 1958.[57]

Neither Craig nor Fleeson, who probably drew more salary in a month than Dunnigan earned in a year, could have imagined the basement room that served as Dunnigan's living quarters and the space she called an office, equipped with a typewriter but no telephone. Her circumstances made day-to-day living so difficult that on occasion she lacked the fifteen-cent postage needed for special delivery of copy to the Associated Negro Press in Chicago.[58]

In 1947 both women tested the waters for Dunnigan's membership in the lily-white National Women's Press Club. While this proposal got sidetracked for several years, Craig and Fleeson insisted that Dunnigan be included in a dinner in 1950 hosted by Fleeson's future husband, Dan Kimball, as a spoof of the exclusive dinners for male reporters of the White House Correspondents Association. The dinner, booked at a Washington hotel that still practiced segregation, was itself billed as an attempt to get a fair deal for female reporters at the White House. To avoid insult to Dunnigan and embarrassment to her friends, private arrangements were made with the hotel

56. *Time* 58 (September 11, 1951): 55; "Doris Fleeson," *Current Biography,* 1959, 123.

57. See correspondence file with named individuals, Container 1, and scrapbooks for 1946 and 1952, Craig Papers, Library of Congress. "Doris Fleeson," *Current Biography,* 1959, 123.

58. No specific salary figures are available for Craig and Fleeson, but at twelve thousand dollars per year, their annual income would have been ten times more than Dunnigan's income for 1948. Dunnigan to Barnett, January 10, 1949, Reel 5, Part II, Barnett Papers, Library of Congress. A. J. Liebling estimated that White House correspondents earned between $150 and $200 per week in 1950. See "The Press," *Holiday* 7 (February 1950): 124.

to admit the black reporter. However, Fleeson and Craig took no chance that an incident might occur. When Dunnigan entered the hotel lobby, they swarmed to her side and swiftly escorted her to the banquet hall.[59] The trio thus transcended, for the evening at least, the barriers of race, class, and gender that governed social Washington.

Dunnigan in time became an accomplished reporter and winner of numerous awards from her peers, but the distinction of being the first black newswoman accredited to the White House gave her greatest pleasure. She prized, too, being the first black female reporter to travel in the president's party when Truman made his cross-country tour in June 1948. She ardently believed that these activities did more than advance the cause of black women in journalism. Her presence, she later wrote, served as a visible reminder to all Americans of the president's commitment to political and economic equality for all citizens, and demonstrated, by her inclusion in the presidential travel party, a degree of social opportunity as well.[60]

When the Truman administration ended, women were still denied membership in the National Press Club and barred from Washington's exclusive social clubs. They were excluded from the Gridiron Club—where the "women are always present" rule governed the conduct of the men in telling stories but not the organization's membership policy.[61] Women remained unrepresented among the White House wire service reporters, and none served as White House correspondents for the major newspapers and radio networks that maintained weekday coverage of the president.

These policies and practices of exclusion assured female journalists of future battles to be fought in their efforts to overcome barriers to opportunity and equality in their profession. Still, the task would be made easier by the impressive accomplishments of the newswomen of the Truman years.

59. Dunnigan, *A Black Woman's Experience*, 257–58, 460–62.
60. Ibid., 5, 469–76.
61. Harold Brayman, *The President Speaks Off-The-Record: Historic Evenings with America's Leaders, the Press, and Other Men of Power, At Washington's Exclusive Gridiron Club*, xii.

7

Still Photography and Newsreels

HARRY TRUMAN DELIGHTED in the American pastime of taking candid photographs with a simple, inexpensive camera and in posing for the camera himself. His appreciation of visual imagery, evidenced in his youth by his fondness for picture postcards and photographs, increased when he entered politics; his customary modesty in most things yielded readily to a willingness, even an eagerness, to be photographed for publication in newspapers. As president, he maximized opportunities for still and motion picture photographers to document the events of his life and his administration, contributing in a small but significant way to both acceptance and respectability for photojournalists and to prolonging the newsreel era.

Truman's openness and receptivity to still photographers contrasted significantly with the guarded relationship developed between Franklin D. Roosevelt and the cameramen. Press Secretary Steve Early summoned the photographers assigned to the White House to his office at the beginning of the Roosevelt administration and spoke candidly: "President Roosevelt is crippled; there's nothing secret about that. And he has a favor to ask of his friends in the media . . . and that is not to photograph him when he's being carried, or when he is in some of the more compromising positions." In return, Roosevelt pledged to make himself more readily available to the photographers than his immediate predecessor, Herbert Hoover.

The photographers agreed and, with few exceptions, honored the request, but Roosevelt did not keep his end of the bargain.[1]

Truman personally ordered photographers admitted to the White House press room, to permit greater coverage of his daily activities. Years before, photographers sent to the White House had to stand on the street outside the Executive Mansion; during FDR's presidency the lensmen were housed in "the dog house," a small room of a grounds building near the West Wing entrance. When Truman learned, soon after he became president, of the exclusion of photographers from the White House press room, he ordered their admission to both the White House and his news conferences and thereby earned their warm gratitude.[2]

In the absence of an official White House photographer—a position created during the Gerald R. Ford administration—still camera coverage of the president came largely from the lensmen assigned by major news organizations and photographic services. Acme Newspictures, Associated Press, Harris and Ewing, International News Photos, and the *New York Times* provided daily coverage of the Truman White House. On press conference days and special occasions the number of still photographers representing local and out-of-town newspapers increased considerably; more than two hundred civilian photographers and a few army and navy cameramen were accredited to the White House in 1949. The civilian photographers were members of the White House Photographers Association, formed in 1921 during the presidency of Warren G. Harding.[3]

Unlike the men of the Washington press corps, male photographers admitted women to their ranks without discrimination. Women belonged to the White House Photographers Association, attended its annual dinners, and competed successfully with the men. Marion A. Carpenter, photographer for International News Photos, won first prize in the annual photo competition of the University of Missouri School of Journalism in 1946 for her "Spring

1. Tames oral history, 5–6; Winfield, *FDR and the News Media*, 16, 85–86, 111–17.

2. Tames oral history, 8–9.

3. *Editor and Publisher* (December 25, 1948): 36. In 1950, the photographers for the aforementioned studios and the *New York Times* were Milton Frier (successor to Frank Cancellare), Byron Rollins, Walter N. Jacobus, Al Muto, and George Tames. "Famed Byline," undated clipping, folder 1, Box 10, Ayers Papers, Truman Library; *Editor and Publisher* (November 23, 1946): 48. The figures for the White House photojournalism corps were supplied to the author by Pauline Testerman, audio/visual archivist, Truman Library. Winfield, *FDR and the News Media*, 16.

Comes to the White House" photo of a smiling president admiring a camellia blossom. The same year Charlie Ross basked in the glow of an alumni award given by his alma mater's journalism school to *Life* photographer Marie Hansen. He boasted in remarks prepared for the occasion that women were "members on an equal footing with men in the White House News Photographer's Association and take part in all annual events."[4]

Hansen recalled, however, that in 1939 her employer, the *Louis-ville Courier Journal*, had serious reservations about permitting a woman to develop pictures in the darkroom with male photographers. She used the occasion of the alumni award to invite other women to photojournalism as a field of equal opportunity. Nevertheless, of the photographers accredited to the Truman White House, the men outnumbered the women by almost one hundred to one.[5]

The president's excellent rapport with the photographers resulted in a friendly association with them throughout his administration. In mock recognition of their frequent requests for "one more" photo, he organized for them the "One More Club."[6] George Tames, a photographer, explained how the term itself originated:

> This was in the days when you used a 4 x 5 Speed Graphic and [flash] bulbs. The fastest photographer took six seconds from the time he fired the shot until he was ready to fire the next one. And while you were reversing your holder and putting in your bulb and cocking your shutter and getting ready, things were happening that you would see with your eye and you were missing. So, you'd always shout, "one more."[7]

In 1946 the photographers held a birthday party in the president's honor, and Truman, posing with the cake, blew out the candles and served his hosts. The appreciative photographers presented him with a movie camera and a Speed Graphic still camera for his personal use.[8]

---

4. *Editor and Publisher* (May 18, 1946): 35; Remarks of Charles G. Ross, undated, Marie Hansen folder, Box 3, Charles G. Ross Papers, Truman Library.
5. Marie Hansen, remarks, Marie Hansen folder, Box 3, Charles G. Ross Papers, Truman Library. The preponderance of male photographers accredited to the White House is evident from a photograph taken of the group on the occasion of Truman's birthday in 1947 and reprinted in this book.
6. "Truman and the 'One More Club'," *Whistle Stop* 20, no. 2 (1992): 3. See also Jack Price, "Truman is Photogs 'Best Friend,'" *Editor and Publisher* (October 20, 1945): 68.
7. Tames oral history, 34–35.
8. *Editor and Publisher* (December 25, 1948): 36.

Occasionally Truman would take the camera and photograph White House visitors. He expertly maneuvered his subjects to the proper stance for a good picture and gave instructions to members of a large group on how to identify themselves by location in the picture. He joked that while he was president and commander in chief of the armed forces, he took orders from no one except the photographers.[9]

The close bond between the photographers and the president extended to holding in confidence the casual and private conversations of Truman and his guests during a photo session. Tames recalled that "we heard many, many secrets; many, many good stories, and we never repeated them when we came out because there was an unwritten rule that anything said in there was privileged, so we never said anything."[10] Operating without the later intrusion of sound cameras that recorded conversations as well as visual images, the still photographers let their photographs tell a story.

The regularly assigned White House photographers committed one breach of trust, however, on one particular Wednesday afternoon routinely used for what the photographers called "dog and cat" sessions. Congressmen and their constituents who wanted to pose with the president and business and trade association representatives seeking publicity for their product were typical Wednesday afternoon callers. At the end of the session a few of Truman's World War I buddies came in for a photo only to have the photographers go through the motions without film in their cameras. When the president later asked for the photo, the lensmen had to confess what they had done. Truman called the photographers into his office, allowed them to stand for several seconds like errant schoolboys, then dismissed them with a single admonition: "Don't ever do that again."[11]

Truman's willingness to pose with out-of-town visitors brought embarrassment to him on one occasion after wide news coverage of a photo showing the presentation of a desk set from the Lions Club of Kansas City by a club member. The Associated Press photograph, taken early in 1946, was featured in newspapers around the nation and also appeared in *Life*. *Time* published the photograph too, and in a story entitled "The Man Who Knew Harry" revealed that the

9. *Editor and Publisher* (March 15, 1952): 52; "Truman and the 'One More Club,'" 1; Tames oral history, 35–36.

10. Tames oral history, 70–71.

11. Ibid., 59–61.

Kansas Citian had left town the day his wife had filed for divorce, leaving behind not only his spouse but also his accounting firm with an indebtedness of eighteen thousand dollars and creditors holding worthless checks. His arrest in Salt Lake City for passing a bad check to a fellow Lion brought these details to light for *Time.* The magazine left no question about the unsavory character of Truman's visitor in its closing line: "[He] was what the cops call a two-time loser. He had served prison terms for forgery in Michigan and California." He had taken the president for a photograph as well, and gave *Time* an opportunity to present Truman in a bad light.[12]

Truman understood and expected that the photos taken of himself and others were subject to the whim of editors and publishers. He expressed his displeasure with the *Washington Times-Herald* and its owner, Eleanor Patterson, when the newspaper failed to join other metropolitan newspapers in a front-page display of his conferring of the Medal of Honor to General Jonathan Wainwright in September 1945. The *Times-Herald,* a staunch supporter of General Douglas MacArthur, apparently did not want to detract from MacArthur's stature by publicizing Wainwright's reward for his heroic defense of the Philippines in 1942 before becoming imprisoned by the Japanese for the duration of the war. When Truman called the omission to the attention of his aides, he castigated the conservative Republican newspaper as the "sabotage press," a term he used frequently during his presidency to characterize archconservative, isolationist newspapers.[13]

Truman correctly believed that Henry Luce's publications, particularly *Life,* sought to sabotage his election bid in 1948 through selective photojournalistic coverage of his preconvention western trip. The magazine had published a motley assortment of photos of the president's appearances in Omaha and Sun Valley to document its claim that the president's western trip was a fiasco. It continued to promote this view by providing no coverage of the huge crowds that turned out to see and hear the president in his Pacific Coast appearances.

During his extensive campaign trip that fall, Truman lost no opportunity to correct any lingering impression of public apathy to his campaign. When a large crowd of ten to twelve thousand people turned out to see him after 11 P.M. in Ogden, Utah, on September 21, 1948, he asked a photographer to capture the scene. "I never

12. *Time* 47 (March 25, 1946): 7.
13. Ferrell, ed., *Truman in the White House,* 76.

expected to see a crowd like this at this time of night," he said. "Somebody I hope will take a picture of it and send it to all the eastern newspapers." He repeated this theme in a near midnight appearance in Toledo, Ohio, recalling for the audience the *Life* photo of "a soldier facing a vacant lot and [saying] that was the kind of reception I got." During his retirement he recalled how the Luce publications had used photographs "trying to disprove there weren't any crowds turning out for my speeches, which was a damn lie, of course. . . . Pictures can lie just as much as words if that's what the big editors and publishers set out to do."[14]

Still, even antiadministration newspapers and magazines could not easily ignore the large crowds that turned out to see the president during his famed "whistlestop" campaign. And Truman was a willing subject. Even after he had retired for the evening he pleased a hopeful crowd in Barstow, California, by pulling a robe over his pajamas and greeting the well-wishers and curious assembled at the nonscheduled speaking stop. On other occasions he posed with a baby, an Indian chief, and a little girl clutching an ear of corn.[15] Photographer Tames, responsible for staging the latter picture, recalled the conversation that ensued.

"Well," the president said to the child, "I understand you have a gift for me, this ear of corn." "No, sir," the small girl replied. "I happened to be walking past the pigpen and picked it up." Tames photographed Truman in uproarious laughter over the child's honest disclosure and the newspapers got a good picture of an unpretentious and affable president.[16]

Probably no photograph gave Truman greater satisfaction than the one showing him holding aloft a copy of the *Chicago Tribune* and its mistaken banner headline "Dewey Defeats Truman." The photograph, taken after his victorious election while en route by train to Washington, served as a fitting climax to Truman's triumph over the biases and misinterpretations that marked much of the journalistic coverage of his 1948 campaign. Years later the publisher of the *Tribune*, in a spirit of nonpartisanship and generosity unlike the days when Colonel McCormick published the newspaper, presented

14. *Public Papers*, 1948, 473, 529. Martin, *Henry and Clare*, 280.
15. For an assortment of Truman campaign poses, see *Time* 52 (November 1, 1948): 23; Tames oral history, 49, 50–51.
16. Tames, *Eye on Washington*, 36.

the Truman Library with a bronze engraving of its famous front page for permanent display.[17]

The attempt on the life of President Truman by Puerto Rican nationalists in the early afternoon of November 1, 1950, gave the White House photographers action shots aplenty. The lensmen had already loaded their equipment into a car parked outside the White House for a trip to Arlington National Cemetery, where Truman was scheduled to dedicate a memorial to British Field Marshal Sir John Dill. As the cameramen chatted among themselves, awaiting the departure of the president from his temporary living quarters in the nearby Blair House, a pistol shot rang out. The photographers dismissed the first shot as a leftover firecracker from the previous night's Halloween, but as more shots were fired and sirens began to wail, they jumped from their cars, eyewitnesses to the shootout between the president's guards and the three assailants. Before taking cover in the shrubbery, Charles Corte of Acme Newspictures braved one quick picture of a guard on one knee shooting at the attackers. Bruce Hoertel of the *New York Times* photographed the corpse of an assailant felled by a guard's bullet. Within minutes graphic pictures of the assassination attempt moved on wire circuits, in time for newspapers to publish afternoon extras detailing the most dangerous episode in journalistic coverage of the Truman presidency.[18]

As the Truman presidency ended in January 1953, the golden era of photojournalism neared its zenith before its swift decline. Relatively few years had elapsed since Henry Luce achieved instant success in photojournalism with the launching of *Life* in 1936, followed a year later by Gardner Cowles's highly successful *Look*. The public's appetite for photos that told the developments and events of World War II, coupled with wartime prosperity, boosted circulation of *Life* and *Look* to more than five million and three million respectively, and millions more read current and back issues of the magazines available in waiting rooms and libraries.[19]

Television's growing popularity, however, began to be felt by the weekly photojournals during the last years of the Truman presidency. *Life* formed an alliance with the new visual medium in

17. There are several good versions of the "Dewey Defeats Truman" photo, including Milton Frier's photo for Acme published in *Time* and *Newsweek*. Wendt, *Chicago Tribune,* 654, 682–84.

18. *Editor and Publisher* (November 4, 1950): 10–11.

19. Baughman, *Henry R. Luce,* 89–96, 133–34. Association of National Advertisers, Inc., *Magazine Circulation and Rate Trends, 1937–1952.* Supplement (n.p., 1953): 12.

its coverage of the 1948 Democratic and Republican presidential nominating conventions, boasting that "the word-and-picture journalism that has won for *Life* the continuing interest of the world's largest weekly magazine audience will be applied to television." Its photographers and reporters joined forces with the National Broadcasting Company. *Life's* postwar circulation remained high, actually increasing into the early 1950s. Eventually, though, television's popularity spelled the decline of both readership and advertising dollars for magazines, ending the classic period of photojournalism by the early 1970s.[20]

The still photographer's access to the White House and the president also underwent change with the introduction of video cameras that recorded sound as well as visual images. Conversations of substance between a president and his guest were replaced with amiable chit-chat after the intrusion of sound equipment, and reporters, finding their access to presidents limited by few and irregular press conferences during the late 1960s, pressed for admission to the photo sessions of the president and the White House photographers. During the Nixon and Reagan administrations, when the president's meetings with the press became rare, reporters attempted to turn the "photo opportunity" into a news conference by shouting out questions to the president. (One of the frequent questions during the Reagan administration was "Mr. President, when are you going to have a news conference?") The staffing of the White House Office of Communications with official photographers during the Ford administration placed further distance between the president and the small but representative group of photographers who had covered the daily activities of the president during the Truman years.[21]

Motion picture journalism, known popularly as newsreels to millions of Americans, began earlier than the golden era of magazine photojournalism, but the two media went into decline at about the same time, after the advent of television. In 1911, the French-owned

20. *Life* 24 (May 7, 1948), unnumbered double page advertisement. *Life's* decline began in the 1960s. *Look* ceased publication in 1971, followed by *Life* a year later. Baughman, *Henry R. Luce,* 169, 195.

21. Tames oral history, 70–72. President Nixon held forty-three meetings with the news media during his sixty-eight-month presidency; President Reagan met with the news media thirty-nine times during his two terms. Helen Thomas, among others, frequently asked Reagan during his coming and going at the White House when he would hold a news conference. Telecast, "Sixty Minutes," CBS, June 26, 1988. John Herbers, *No Thank You, Mr. President* (New York: Norton, 1976), 167.

Pathé's Weekly, the first newsreel produced, assembled, and released in the United States, boasted that "the moving picture theaters of this country will go into active and . . . successful competition with the illustrated periodicals and magazines, for they will be able to show the important news of the world not in cold type or in still picture but in actual moving reproduction." Newsreels exaggerated their claim of authenticity, however; well into the Truman years, the motion picture firms still faked scenes and fabricated news stories from old footage.[22]

Still the uncritical public welcomed the "press of the screen," and within days after Pathé's Weekly began to exhibit in August 1911, the Vitagraph Company began producing its monthly newsreel. Over the next decade and a half several individuals and firms attempted to produce or exhibit newsreels, but only five famous newsreel companies emerged: Pathé, Universal, Fox, Metro-Goldwyn-Mayer (produced by Hearst), and Paramount. *The March of Time*, an offspring of Henry Luce's *Time, Life,* and *Fortune,* joined the ranks later, in 1935, and ceased production earlier, in 1951. In 1942 *All-American News,* the newsreel firm of independent producer E. M. Glucksman, began coverage of black America for the nation's racially segregated theaters and remained in business until the mid-1950s. Among the last firms to organize was Telenews. Begun in 1939 as an exhibition house, it later turned to production for its developing chain of newsreel theaters. According to newsreel historian Raymond Fielding, by the early 1950s, Telenews was supplying more than 90 percent of television's news film across the nation. Its demise came quickly as newsgathering and broadcast technology made it possible for stations to film or broadcast live their own coverage of local stories while national and international events were televised either by direct feed or film. By 1967, all the newsreel firms had ceased production, a victim of the American people's preference to watch the day's news on home television sets.[23]

Long before Truman's presidency, motion picture cameras had begun to record presidential inaugurations and parades, starting with

22. Raymond Fielding, *The American Newsreel, 1911–1967,* 72–73, 37.

23. Ibid., 80–81, 187–88, 296, 307–9. According to Fielding, "The March of Time" was not a newsreel; rather it was "a kind of documentary film whose structure represented a compromise between the traditional newsreel and the socially consciously discursive forms of the British and American documentary traditions" (231). See also Fielding's *The March of Time, 1935–1951.*

William McKinley in 1897. Newsreel coverage of the presidents became standard fare during the presidency of Woodrow Wilson. Franklin D. Roosevelt, however, was the first president to make calculated and skillful use of the newsreel medium, which, with the advent of sound, had only gained its voice in 1927. Roosevelt permitted newsreel cameras into the White House in light of his special needs for easy access to the popular news medium. The large and cumbersome motion picture cameras were housed in a little-used basement room in the East Wing of the White House until the medium's demise in the mid-1960s.[24]

The Roosevelt administration's carefully controlled newsreel coverage of the president maximized FDR's policies and personality. The newsreels, providing visual as well as sound coverage of Roosevelt, contributed powerfully to the image of a robust, mobile president unafflicted by the polio that had left him crippled for life after he contracted the disease in 1921. The motion picture cameramen operated under the same rules as the still photographers—they were forbidden to take any shots of the president that would reveal his disability. Instead, the coverage of FDR at the wheel of his touring car, erect at a ship's rail with the wind blowing back his hair and his cape, or standing erect with leg braces locked into position at the rear of his moving railroad car, contributed to the public's perception of a fully mobile president.[25]

The newsreel coverage of FDR's addresses and fireside chats conveyed to the president's viewers a feeling of intimacy, as though he were in their presence. Peter Arno's cartoon for the *New Yorker* caught this spirit in a negative light by depicting two obviously wealthy couples attired in formal evening dress (all of Arno's cartoon characters were dressed in formal attire) calling from the sidewalk to another couple standing in the window of their mansion. "Come along," the caption read. "We're going to the Trans-Lux and hiss Roosevelt." FDR's supporters were as mesmerized by his performance before the newsreel cameras as they were captivated by his voice on radio.[26]

24. Fielding, *The American Newsreel*, 25, 91, 184, 201; Winfield, *FDR and the News Media*, 116–18; Eben A. Ayers diary, September 1, 1945, October 30, 1945, Diary 1945 folder, Box 16, Ayers Papers, Truman Library.

25. Tames oral history, 5–7; Winfield, *FDR and the News Media*, 116.

26. Arno's cartoon is reproduced in Doris Kearns Goodwin, "The Home Front," *New Yorker* 70 (August 15, 1994): 55; Winfield, *FDR and the News Media*, 111–18; Fielding, *The American Newsreel*, 184, 201.

By contrast, Truman's use of the newsreels seemed bland and ordinary, due, in part, because his freedom of movement permitted coverage of ordinary activities. Universal's first newsreel of the new chief executive released in April 1945 emphasized Truman's daily routine. The opening scene showed a smiling president walking briskly in the company of Secret Service agents from the family's temporary living quarters in the Blair House to his office in the White House. Interior scenes showed the president at his desk, signing papers and meeting with his new aides. The newsreel's focus on Truman's everyday activities conveyed to viewers a sense of the down-to-earth, undramatic new chief executive as well as seemingly unrestricted access to the White House and the president.[27]

The uncoordinated appearances of Truman in the newsreels owed much to Press Secretary Ross. He displayed little interest in securing effective portrayal of the president in newsreels. During the railroad strike of 1946, when officials of newsreel companies found reason to complain of the administration's regulations governing the news media, they bypassed Ross. George Dorsey of Pathé wrote directly to the director of the motion picture office in Washington to express his puzzlement over the failure of government regulators to include the "press of the screen" in its policies for press and radio. Newsreel firms, Dorsey explained, were unable to ship newsreels by plane during the railroad strike despite the fact that they contained a message from the president to the public asking cooperation in the emergency. Only after unnecessary delays and discussions, Dorsey concluded, were orders issued allowing the shipment of the newsreels.[28]

The unsystematic portrayal of Truman in the newsreels prompted advice from many quarters to limit the president's appearances. Hollywood producer Darryl F. Zanuck, production chief of Twentieth Century Fox, the distributor of "Movietone News," conveyed that advice to Edwin Pauley, secretary-treasurer of the California Democratic Committee, in a letter of January 11, 1946. Truman's appearances in the newsreels, Zanuck wrote, "should be saved until crucial issues are at stake."[29]

27. This analysis is based on the author's viewing of the Universal newsreel housed at the Truman Library.

28. Dorsey to Arch C. Mercey, August 9, 1946, Newsreels folder, Box 4, Dallas C. Halverstadt Files, Truman Papers, Truman Library.

29. Zanuck to Pauley, January 11, 1946, Edwin W. Pauley folder, PSF 320, Truman Papers, Truman Library.

Similar advice that "the president was being used too much in the reels" and "imposed upon by too many interested groups in and out of the Government" came forward in the spring of 1946 from other representatives of newsreel companies. The complaints partly reflected the movie industry's feeling that the federal government no longer needed its help in making and disseminating propaganda. The industry had cooperated magnificently with the government during the war, but in the postwar period the film studios saw no need for mobilizing public opinion behind the government's objectives. The newsreels also wanted to "avoid the sameness which prevailed during the war."[30]

Creative reconstruction of one White House news story brought a quick rebuke from Ross. When the press secretary denied newsreel companies permission to film an announcement by Truman on September 23, 1949, that an atomic explosion had occurred in the Soviet Union, Metro-Goldwyn-Mayer's "News of the Day" decided to recreate the momentous news by drawing upon stock footage of Truman presiding at a cabinet meeting with commentary supplied by an off-camera narrator. Outraged, Ross wrote a stern letter to MGM to complain that "this picture makes it appear that the Cabinet laughed and joked in the face of the tremendous news given them by the President." Ross characterized the newsreel as "irresponsible . . . pictorial journalism." His complaint drew an apology from an official of MGM with a weak explanation that the levity of the cabinet officers, not so apparent in the negative, was offset by the stern countenance of the president. "News of the Day" had been on friendly terms with the White House for a long time, the letter writer continued, and hoped that "this cooperative relationship will not be disturbed by one unfortunate incident."[31]

Ross was on the receiving end of a complaint earlier that year when Pathé Newsreel almost missed the White House retirement ceremony for Admiral William D. Leahy. Pathé's Dorsey pointed out to Ross that because newsreel companies did not keep cameramen there at all times, they needed advance notice of important White House announcements and ceremonies. "I assure that it is our desire to portray the President in the best possible light at all times,"

30. Arch C. Mercey to Anthony Hyde, memorandum, May 1, 1946, and Notes of White House Conference with Francis Harmon of the Motion Picture Association, May 7, 1946, Notebook folder, Box 7, Halverstadt Files, Truman Papers, Truman Library.

31. Ross to M. J. Clofine, October 11, 1949, and M. D. Clofine to Charles G. Ross, October 13, 1949, OF 73, Box 334, Truman Papers, Truman Library.

Dorsey wrote, "and an arrangement of this kind would help us to do this."[32]

The initiative for improving Truman's appearances in the newsreels depended less upon his press secretaries than the technical assistance provided by newsreel and television companies and broadcast journalists. Radio adviser J. Leonard Reinsch devised a system of typing Truman's speeches so that the natural rhythm was indicated by limiting the phrasing on a line. To assist Truman in following his script, his secretary used a large-type speech typewriter for the president's reading copy. White House aide George Elsey improved upon this technique by asking the Signal Corps to prepare large cue cards of significant passages so Truman could look up from his script and appear to be looking straight into the camera without aid of a text. The application of a coating to the lenses of the president's glasses corrected the problem of light reflection. These techniques improved Truman's appearances before the motion picture cameras, but they were slow in coming. Truman believed that the use of the teleprompter, new in 1952, would make him appear to be faking his sincerity of communication.[33]

Meanwhile, the rapid development of video technology and the slow but measured growth of television stations ensured the demise of newsreels. By 1949, television "newsreels" produced with a relatively small camera and an on-site narrator could be broadcast within minutes. The film produced by the television newsreel team required no development because, through the process of electronic reversal of polarity, the negative appeared as positive film on a home television set. By contrast, newsreel negatives required preparation of several duplicate negatives for printing hundreds of positive films. This time-consuming task, in addition to distribution of the newsreels to movie theaters, lent itself only to twice-a-week releases. Moviegoers, except in a few metropolitan areas where the film

32. Dorsey to Ross, March 25, 1949, OF 73, Box 334, Truman Papers, Truman Library.

33. Reinsch, *Getting Elected*, 13; Hechler, *Working With Truman*, 224–25, 215; Charles G. Ross to Charles de N. Barnes, June 1949–July 1950 folder, OF 73, Box 335, Truman Papers, Truman Library. Ross reported that the cards prepared by the army for use in making newsreels "are of real assistance." The suggestions for improving Truman's appearance on camera ranged from the helpful to the zany. See OF 136-b, Truman Papers, Truman Library. White House photographers gave Truman a pair of glasses without lenses to eliminate reflection caused by flashbulbs; Truman, however, considered their use artificial and would not use them. Tames, *Eye on Washington*, 38–39.

processing and distribution could be accomplished in a day, saw news two or more days old.[34]

Television "newsreels" also enjoyed an advantage in covering stories overseas. By August 1950, Charles de Soria of KTTV, the *Los Angeles Times* CBS-affiliated station in Los Angeles, sent television newsreels of the war in Korea to Los Angeles for broadcast there and in a score of other communities.[35]

Eventually, television's live coverage of events, including Truman's address on his efforts to combat inflation, transmitted directly to an audience in the Keith Theater in the nation's capital on June 14, 1951, spelled the end of the newsreels. By midcentury, competition from television forced most newsreel theaters to close. Among these once-popular exhibition houses was New York City's Embassy Newsreel Theater, which closed out two decades of operation with an estimated overall viewing audience exceeding eleven million. The last of the newsreel companies quietly went out of business in 1967.[36]

Truman, in sharp contrast to his pronounced views on newspapers and radio, did not become personally embroiled with newsreel firms during his presidency. He relied upon the White House Press Office to make the decisions on what portions of his addresses and press conferences, if any, would be repeated before the motion picture cameras. This arrangement gave the White House a large degree of control over the subject matter and content of newsreel coverage of the president. Moreover, the twice-weekly release schedules of the major newsreels and the inclusion of international as well as national news, entertainment, and sports events made the president merely one contributor, albeit an important one, to the newsreels. The exclusive single-theme format of "The March of Time" mixed heavy coverage of the nation's Cold War enemies with postwar social and cultural topics as diverse as "Problem Drinkers," "Marriage and Divorce," and "Schools March On." This emphasis and monthly production and distribution of "The March of Time" made the president and the presidency an infrequent topic of coverage for Henry Luce's film documentary.[37]

---

34. Fielding, *The American Newsreel*, 306–7.

35. *Editor and Publisher* (August 12, 1950): 40.

36. Hechler, *Working With Truman*, 213–14; Fielding, *The American Newsreel*, 307–9.

37. Press Assistant Eben A. Ayers has described this process in his diary. See Ferrell, ed., *Truman in the White House*, 206. Fielding, *The March of Time*, 335–42.

Truman enjoyed looking at the newsreels throughout his presidency; when time permitted he and members of his personal and official family viewed newsreels each Thursday after lunch in the basement projection room of the White House.[38]

The White House Press Office, by refusing to grant access to television for live telecasting of the presidential news conferences throughout Truman's administration and by its continued reliance upon newsreels made for movie theater and television viewing, contributed in a small measure to prolonging the life of the once-popular news medium. The relentless advance of television technology and the declining number of moviegoers dependent upon the newsreels for an audiovisual treatment of the news, however, were forces too powerful even for the traditionalists.

Time had indeed marched on.

38. *New York Times*, February 6, 1947.

8

Radio and Television

DURING TRUMAN'S PRESIDENCY radio peaked as the preferred evening entertainment medium of the American people, while television rose in popularity and eventually surpassed radio as the supreme broadcast medium. Both radio and television enjoyed continued growth as a news source at the expense of newspapers.

The rivalry, even hostility, between newspaper reporters and radio newscasters revealed itself at the outset of the Truman administration. In the first instance, Press Secretary Steve Early forbade live radio coverage of the swearing-in of the new president in the White House Cabinet Room on the apparent ground of impropriety. Only with considerable difficulty did radio gain permission to broadcast the East Room funeral ceremonies for Franklin Roosevelt. Secondly, the successful opposition of newspaper journalists to the appointment of a radio man to handle press and radio affairs, recounted in an earlier chapter, demonstrated the determination of the print journalists to maintain their dominance over broadcast journalists in news coverage of the president.[1]

Truman's extensive use of radio first began with his nomination as vice president on the Democratic ticket in 1944. Because World War II demanded the attention and energy of President Roosevelt,

1. Charter Heslep, diary, April 12, 1945, Box 2, Charter Heslep Papers, Truman Library. Heslep was the Mutual Broadcasting System newscaster sent to the White House to cover the swearing-in ceremony.

the active campaigning in the presidential election fell to the Missouri senator. The campaign train carried Truman into several sections of the country, but the message of his personal appearances reached voters everywhere via radio.

Regrettably, Truman possessed neither an attractive voice nor a polished speaking style. Recognizing these weaknesses, the Democratic National Committee hired J. Leonard Reinsch to coach the candidate. With additional support from Tom Evans, Truman's Kansas City friend and owner of radio station KCMO, Truman practiced delivering speeches on a wire recorder.[2]

Reinsch had a formidable assignment. Truman tended to rush through a manuscript, placing false emphasis on the beginning of sentences while slurring the syllables in some words. He pronounced individual "indivual," production "perduction," and running "runnen." Reinsch instructed his willing pupil to enunciate every syllable, thus slowing the pace of his delivery while increasing the listener's comprehension. Coaching Truman for a radio address thus differed greatly from the preparations made for Franklin Roosevelt's broadcasts; radio technicians only had to check the microphone placement for FDR.[3]

Reinsch remained on call for several months to assist Truman with many radio speeches. He kept especially busy during the first weeks as Truman delivered major addresses to a joint session of the Congress, the United Nations Conference, and separate broadcasts to the armed forces and the American people announcing the surrender of Germany. By 1947 Reinsch's coaching had produced a noticeable improvement in the president's radio delivery and, in the process, lowered Truman's voice one-half octave for a pleasing tone.[4]

Reinsch's association with Truman declined sharply in the summer of 1947 after rumors circulated that he would be appointed to a vacancy on the Federal Communications Commission. *Broadcasting,* a radio trade journal, carried a favorable story touting Reinsch as an example of the practical broadcasters needed for the FCC, namely persons "who have met a payroll and who know the practicalities of

2. J. Leonard Reinsch oral history, by J. R. Fuchs, March 13, 1967, 2–3, 7–11. Truman Library.

3. Ibid., 23, 143; Robert Underhill, *The Truman Persuasions,* 335–36; Winfield, *FDR and the News Media,* 17–18, 106–9.

4. See *Public Papers,* 1945 for the radio addresses of the first month of Truman's presidency; *Time* (June 23, 1947): 62.

business operations." If Reinsch received appointment to the FCC, the journal noted, he would be required to withdraw an application then pending before the agency for a license to operate a new radio station in Cincinnati. The liberal New York newspaper *PM*, however, published a story insinuating that CBS president Frank Stanton had given Reinsch a car, with the hope that Reinsch, as an FCC member, would repay Stanton with favors. In fact, Reinsch had purchased Stanton's car after CBS signed a large contract with Ford that required the CBS executive to drive a Lincoln automobile. Nevertheless, Charles Ross and other White House aides, unhappy about Reinsch's influence with the president and convinced that he was angling for appointment to the FCC, effectively curtailed his role as "radio adviser" to the president.[5]

Truman maintained a relationship with the FCC remarkably free of controversy and involvement given his strong views on the communications media. Indeed, in 1940, while in the Senate, Truman had expressed his opinion that radio and television would in time undercut the power of the newspapers to the benefit of the people. He readily accepted the independent character of the FCC and the unwritten rule established shortly after the regulatory agency was created in 1934 that it would be a nonpartisan body. In practice this meant that, under a Democratic administration, Republicans were entitled to three of the seven seats on the commission. In this manner Truman made his first appointment to the FCC in June 1945 by selecting former Republican governor William H. Wills of Vermont to succeed Republican Norman S. Case. "It's a case of one Republican taking the place of another. Vermont is surely a Republican State, so they couldn't accuse me of playing politics up there," he stated at a news conference. Wayne Coy, appointed commissioner in 1947, had come from the Bureau of the Budget and more recently from WINX-TV, the capital television station of the *Washington Post*. Frieda Hennock, one of the conspicuous examples of the Truman administration's few appointments of women to high-level positions, became a champion of allocating a large number of channels to public television stations during her tenure as an FCC commissioner, and Truman endorsed this priority. He turned to FCC

5. *Broadcasting* (August 11, 1947): 86 in J. Leonard Reinsch folder, Box 321, PSF, Truman Library; Reinsch to Truman, August 28, 1947, Reinsch folder; Ferrell, ed., *Truman in the White House*, 10–12, 34, 144, 150, 174–75, 190.

Counsel Rosel Hyde when another Republican vacancy occurred on the commission.[6]

The closest Truman came to a pure political appointment to the FCC was his selection of Robert T. Bartley of Texas. A reporter who apparently knew the answer to his question before he asked wanted to know Bartley's home state.

"Texas, I guess. Yes, he comes from Bonham, Texas," the president replied.

The most famous citizen of Bonham, Democratic House Speaker Sam Rayburn, was also the best-known bachelor in Washington. The reporter pressed on: "Bonham?"

"Yes," Truman replied.

"A son-in-law of the Speaker, is he, sir?" another reporter volunteered.

"That's right," Truman agreed.

"Nephew, isn't it?" someone corrected. Reporters were laughing now as Truman agreed, tentatively:

"He's a nephew—I guess."

Now more laughter and more clarification.

"All right," Truman conceded, "he's a nephew. A son of the Speaker's sister."[7]

Truman cited his final appointment, Eugene H. Merrill, trustee of Brigham Young University and member of a prominent Mormon family in Utah, as evidence that he had sought the "right man" to fill a position on the FCC.[8] On balance, these appointments attest to Truman's strong belief that the FCC should function in the interest of the public on a nonpartisan basis.

This belief, however, did not prevent a few members of Truman's inner circle from making inquiries and representations to the FCC in behalf of political friends in the early years of the administration. Appointment Secretary Matthew Connelly obligingly wrote to FCC Commissioner Charles R. Denny in November 1946 conveying House Majority Leader John McCormack's pitch in behalf of a Brockton, Massachusetts, firm's application. Truman's military

6. Truman to H. W. Lanigan, August 23, 1940, quoted in *Editor and Publisher* (September 24, 1949): 34; *Public Papers*, 1945, 119; Obituary, Wayne Coy, *New York Times*, September 25, 1957; Maryann Yodelin Smith, "Frieda Barkin Hennock," in *Notable American Women*, edited by Sicherman et al., 332–33; Truman to Paul C. Walker, June 26, 1952, OF 136-B, Truman Papers, Truman Library; *Public Papers*, 1946, 163.

7. *Public Papers*, 1952–1953, 171.

8. Ibid., 720.

aide, General Harry H. Vaughan, also directed inquiries and requests to the commission for parties seeking favorable action on pending licenses; however, in a frank letter to a St. Louis friend in May 1947, Vaughan conceded that "my record to date with the FCC is practically zero. I will not go into what I think of the Federal Communications Commission at the moment," he added, "as there are definite rules in the Post Office Department as just what kind of material can go through the mail." Connelly veered from an advocacy role, informing a friend in 1947 who had asked for assistance on a matter with the commission that "in all questions affecting the Federal Communications Commission we are extremely careful not to make any recommendations whatsoever. About all I am free to do," he explained, "is to refer papers to that organization purely on their merits."[9]

Truman made his own representation to the FCC when he learned late in his full term that Kansas City, Missouri, had been denied a second television channel. In his letter to Chairman Wayne Coy, Truman stated that it appeared to him "there is rank discrimination there—probably brought about by my good friends at the *Kansas City Star* who are now in complete control of nearly every means of distribution of information." Why, Truman wondered, was the metropolitan area of Kansas City treated differently from the Dallas–Fort Worth and Minneapolis–St. Paul areas? As though he needed to be more explicit, Truman added, "I don't like this arrangement one little bit."[10]

Truman's letter may have been prompted by his belief, now borne out in practice, that newspapers had undercut competition from radio and television by entering the field of broadcast journalism. "I had thought that pictures [television] and the radio would cure the news liars," he wrote to his sister in 1948, "but they—the liars—have taken over both." In fact, newspapers, including the *Kansas City Star*, had entered the field of radio and television broadcasting from the inception of both media; in 1948 one-third of the nation's radio stations had press affiliation.[11]

9. Connelly to Denny, November 25, 1946, OF 136, Box 571, Truman Papers, Truman Library; Vaughan to Oscar A. Zahner, May 15, 1947, OF 136, Box 571, Truman Papers, Truman Library; Connelly to C. Edward Rowe, February 17, 1947, OF 136, Box 571, Truman Papers, Truman Library.

10. Truman to Coy, April 24, 1951, Lou Holland folder, Box 313, PSF, Truman Library.

11. Truman to Mary Jane Truman, May 12, 1948, quoted in Robert Donovan interview, Thompson, ed., *Ten Presidents and the Press*, 31. The *Kansas City*

Still, Truman agreed with the Democratic National Committee (DNC) that Republican control of the press in many parts of the country made use of the radio imperative. According to Sam O'Neal, director of publicity for the DNC, some of these newspapers wanted the Democrats to purchase ads to refute Republican claims printed by them free of charge as news. Radio thus helped to mitigate the power of the Republican-biased press.[12]

But the investment in radio time did not produce the desired results in the 1946 congressional election. Moreover, Truman played only a marginal role in the campaign. As the president's popularity nosed downward in the face of labor-management strife and mounting inflation that year, DNC Chairman Robert E. Hannegan worried about how to keep disaffected Democrats from staying away from the polls or from voting for Republican candidates. He hit upon the idea of featuring a recording of the late President Roosevelt in purchased air time. Truman's voice was used in the radio programming, too, but Roosevelt's voice and message was emphasized. GOP National Chairman Carroll Reece, who had hoped to capitalize on Truman's unpopularity in the off-year election, denounced the use of FDR's voice as "one of the cheapest and most grisly stratagems in the history of American politics."[13] GOP fears of the DNC's radio strategy were exaggerated, for the Republicans regained, for the first time since 1930, majority control of Congress.

In the fall of 1947 the DNC began experimenting with radio rallies to generate enthusiasm for the party. In September the committee received free air time from the American Broadcasting Company for a half-hour program. Billed as the first national radio rally of any political party, the program featured Democrats who stressed the party's liberal heritage. Truman's absence from the program underscored the fact that the DNC, as in 1946, had taken the lead from the White House in the use of radio to advance liberal Democratic interests. The success of the program prompted party officials to schedule another broadcast in December, this time courtesy of the Mutual

---

Star began operation of WDAF radio in 1922 and WDAF-TV in October 1949. William James Ryan, "Which Came First?—65 Years of Broadcasting in Kansas City," *Missouri Historical Review* 82 (July 1988): 414–17: *Editor and Publisher* (September 17, 1949): 44 and (March 20, 1948): 40.

12. *New York Times*, October 29, 1946, as consulted in folder "Use of FDR's Voice in Radio, 1946," Box 196, Democratic National Committee Clipping File, Truman Library; *Public Papers*, 1948, 854, 61–62.

13. *Washington Post*, October 27, 1948, in "Use of FDR's Voice in Radio, 1946."

Broadcasting System. Both ABC and Mutual expected Democrats and Republicans to purchase air time in the 1948 campaign.[14]

Meanwhile, President Truman conducted a media experiment of his own. On October 5, 1947, television cameras were invited for the first time inside the White House to broadcast the president's appeal for food conservation to assist famine-stricken western Europe. Despite the direction of Charles Luckman, chairman of the Food Conservation Commission and an experienced television hand, the telecast was poorly staged. Truman rarely looked up from his script and distracted the viewers by visible turning of pages. Awkward camera angles brought only the lower quarter of a portrait that hung in the background into view.[15]

Thereafter the president's television performances gradually improved. His aides ordered huge cue cards printed with inch-high lettering. This technique, first used with the motion picture camera, was a case of an obsolete media assisting its visual successor. Also, Truman's delivery of written speeches benefited from the use of a script that fitted sentences on the page so that his penchant for false emphasis and rushing forward could be better controlled. Improved delivery resulted, too, when Truman spoke extemporaneously on radio and television with an outline script as back-up. The networks themselves contributed with improved lighting, camera placement, multiple camera use, close-up and distant shots, microphone design and placement, visual props and appropriate background, and in 1952, the teleprompter. None of this technology transformed Truman into a gifted performer, but the improved results pleased viewers and gratified the president.[16]

An estimated four hundred thousand homes and offices, including the White House, had television sets in the summer of 1948, and the television industry projected that the public's interest in the

14. Publicity release, August 22, 1947, and December 18, 1947, Radio Rally folder, Box 190, Democratic National Committee Files, Truman Library.

15. See videotape of the president's address, Truman Library. The text of the message is published in *Public Papers*, 1947, 456–58.

16. The first experiment with cue cards, in 1947, failed. However, by 1950, the use of larger print and larger cards proved useful. Clifford, with Holbrooke, *Counsel to the President: A Memoir*, 74–75, 199. See previous chapter on use of cue cards for Truman's newsreel appearances. Edward Lockett to Don Birmingham, April 19, 1945, News stories filed *Time* folder, Box 1, Lockett Papers, Truman Library. For correspondence on these matters, see OF 136b, Truman Papers, Truman Library; Reinsch, *Getting Elected*, 72. Reinsch to Truman, April 30, 1947, J. Leonard Reinsch folder, Box 321, PSF, Truman Papers, Truman Library.

political conventions and the fall campaign would stimulate sales of one million new sets by Christmas. The same generous television industry figures calculated that more than ten million viewers would watch the national political conventions.[17]

Both the Democrats and Republicans had selected Philadelphia for their conventions because of the city's location within the large television region served by coaxial cable, microwave, and radio relay. Linkage of these transmission systems for the first time in the summer of 1948 provided direct convention coverage to viewers of eighteen eastern and upper southern stations. In addition, television broadcasters filmed the proceedings for daily air shipment to points west.[18]

But radio was still king. In 1948, 94.4 percent of American families owned one or more radios, while the number of television sets in homes and bars reached an audience estimated at only 10 percent of the potential viewers. While television executives and producers were excited about the challenge of televising the conventions, their budgets and allocation of news personnel demonstrated that the 1948 convention coverage was a dress rehearsal for the political conventions of 1952, when millions of new viewers would make television the preferred news media of the American public. According to ABC's vice president for engineering, the significance of television's coverage of the 1948 conventions lay in its technical achievements, accomplishing for television "what the last war did for radio electronically."[19]

17. Edward Bliss, Jr., *Now the News: The Story of Broadcast Journalism,* 209, 211; Jack Gould, television writer for the *New York Times,* calculated the number of television sets in use in the summer of 1948 at 375,000 with 50,000 sets added each month; he estimated the number of viewers at 1,750,000, or about 20 percent of the figure cited by an industry source. "Television Builds for a Future of Boundless Promise," *New York Times,* June 13, 1948, TV Clippings folder, Box 15, Democratic National Committee Files, Truman Library.

18. The Progressive Party of America, formed to advance the presidential ambitions of Henry A. Wallace, also convened in Philadelphia to take advantage of the television industry's staging of the political conventions of 1948 (Bliss, *Now the News,* 208–13). Gould, "Television Builds for a Future of Boundless Promise."

19. *Editor and Publisher* (June 26, 1948): 55; Bliss, *Now the News,* 212. In 1948 the Democratic National Committee, for example, allocated about 10 percent of its broadcast budget of nearly one million dollars to television. Ken Fry to Jack Redding, July 23, 1948, Current Budget, 1948 Campaign folder, Box 11, Publicity Division Files, Records of the Democratic National Committee, Truman Library. News Release, "ABC's Radio and Television Facilities Held Ready for Democratic Convention," June 25, 1948, 4, Radio Coverage 1948

Radio thus far outpaced the television media in its coverage of the president's electioneering of 1948. Local and network radio strategically provided coverage of the Truman "whistlestop" campaign through direct broadcasts and taped recordings for delayed broadcasts. Radio correspondents recorded material when local broadcast facilities were nonexistent and broadcast live when area stations could feed the correspondents' reports and the president's remarks into a regional or national hookup. On one occasion the campaign train's late arrival in Oklahoma City gave Truman only ten seconds of margin when he arrived at the state fairgrounds for a national address on radio. He had no trouble getting off the air: when he failed to finish within the paid amount of air time, the networks unceremoniously broke away on the second. Television reporting on the campaign tour reflected the new medium's limited development and capabilities. When the president visited cities served by television, local stations fed their brief reports as an unpaid news story directly to the station via mobile transmission trucks. The newly opened television station at Fort Worth, authorized by the FCC to broadcast a few days earlier than originally planned to permit coverage of the president's visit there in mid-September, used this mode of transmission. The president, and a future president—senatorial candidate Lyndon B. Johnson—apparently already ahead of their rivals among Texas voters, swept to victory there with the limited assistance of television. Only a few of the president's major addresses, such as his appearance in Chicago on October 28, were televised. That speech, carried over a recently linked network of stations extending westward to St. Louis and east to Buffalo, New York, gave the president access to the television viewing audience in the important electoral states of Missouri, Illinois, Wisconsin, Michigan, Ohio, and New York.[20]

Democratic Convention folder, Box 10, Democratic National Committee Files, Truman Library.

20. "ABC's Radio and Television Facilities"; Charter Heslep to Sol Taishof, c. September 23, 1948, Campaign Broadcast folder, Box 2, Heslep Papers, Truman Library. The networks demonstrated their nonpartisanship by supplying their own announcer, who informed the audience at the beginning and end that the president's talk had been paid for as a campaign address by the Democratic National Committee. Helen Sioussat to Joe Bernard, September 28, 1948, Truman at Oklahoma City September 28 folder, Box 13, Publicity Division File, Democratic National Committee Records, Truman Library. The television crew of newly opened WBAP-TV, Fort Worth, Texas, provided live coverage of Truman's remarks at the railroad station when he arrived there September 27, 1948. Heslep to Tasshof, c. September 28, 1948, ibid; *Public Papers*, 1948,

Elsewhere, in the thirty-three states still unserved by television, voters unable to see the president in person and wanting to see Truman "give 'em hell" viewed newsreels shown in a local movie theater. In all, an estimated thirty million American weekly movie-goers watched Truman, Dewey, and the other presidential candidates in newsreels.[21]

The president's upset victory in 1948 thus represented an effective combining of old and new ways of reaching the American people. Truman's triumph sustained his belief that personal appearances and his use of the broadcast media helped him to overcome the power of newspapers and radio commentators opposed to his administration. He openly criticized the news media late in the campaign, claiming that 90 percent of the newspapers and radio commentators were opposed to his candidacy. Biased reporting, misleading headlines, and slanted editorials, he believed, had been overcome with a direct appeal to the people through personal appearances that also became the occasion for addressing a much larger audience via radio and television.[22]

During Truman's full term from 1949 to 1953, television technology increased significantly but slowly. CBS and RCA, each offering different technology for color television, lobbied with the Federal Communications Commission to make its mode the industry's standard. The FCC also wrestled with the issue of determining how many channels to allocate for educational broadcasting. Consequently, the commission imposed a freeze on allotment of new channels from late 1948 through July 1952 until these issues could be resolved.[23]

587–88, 848–53; *Editor and Publisher* (October 9, 1948): 28. *New York Times*, November 4, 1948. Publicity Release, October 22, 1948, Truman at Chicago, October 25 folder, Publicity Division Files, Box 13, Records of the Democratic National Committee, Truman Library.

21. This estimate is calculated from the viewing audience for *The March of Time. Time* 52 (April 19, 1948): 17.

22. See chapter 2 for Truman's charges that most of the press and radio commentators were opposed to his candidacy. On the one notable occasion when a small audience turned out for an address—the president's June 1948 talk in Omaha—Truman pointed out that the chief audience was midwestern farmers who tuned in to hear him on radio. Edward D. McKim oral history, by J. R. Fuchs, 82, Truman Library.

23. Erik Barnouw, *Tube of Plenty: The Evolution of American Television*, 112–14; Emery and Emery, *The Press and America*, 367.

Meanwhile, existing stations and networks developed local broadcasting facilities and network linkage. The television system serving the eastern seaboard was extended to the Midwest and the lower South for live broadcasts, while Los Angeles and a few cities in between were linked to Miami. Finally, on September 4, 1951, American Telephone and Telegraph completed the coaxial and microwave relays necessary for coast-to-coast television from Washington and New York to West Coast cities. This first live and direct transmission featured President Truman speaking from San Francisco, where he presided over ceremonies for the signing of the Japanese Peace Treaty.[24] By 1952 the country was well on its way to having national television.

Television's expansion in the early 1950s also resulted from the greatly improved programming that attracted millions of new viewers and allowed the new medium early in the new decade to surpass radio as the preferred source of news and entertainment. Television viewers who had formerly got into listening range of the radio to hear the evening news broadcast by Elmer Davis on ABC; Lowell Thomas, Edward R. Murrow, and Charles Collingwood on the CBS network; H. V. Kaltenborn and Morgan Beatty on NBC; and Gabriel Heatter and Fulton Lewis, Jr. on Mutual switched on their television sets to see and hear the news of the day. CBS television began its news telecast, "Douglas Edwards with the News," in August 1948, starting Edwards on his fifteen-minute, five-nights-a-week schedule for the next fourteen years. NBC Television inaugurated its fifteen-minute "Camel Caravan" evening newscast with John Cameron Swayze on February 16, 1949, originating in New York City with pickups from Washington, D.C., and other stations of the network.[25]

The outbreak of war in Korea in June 1950 and the nation's involvement there brought television cameras into the White House with increased frequency. Truman's initial address in late July on the conduct of the war, carried on all major networks of television and radio, attracted the biggest audience in history for any single personage. *Television Daily*, observing that the telecast marked the

24. Barnouw, *Tube of Plenty*, 112–13; *Time* 52 (May 24, 1948): 72–77; Emery and Emery, *The Press and America*, 367.

25. Barnouw, *Tube of Plenty*, 155, passim; Bliss, *Now the News*, 185, 188–89; "Television," *The Daily Breeze/Outlook/News Pilot* [Santa Monica, Calif.], August 7–13, 1990, 9; *Editor and Publisher* (March 12, 1949): 50 and (February 5, 1949): 44. See also Bliss, *Now the News*, 218–29.

first use of the medium by the president for addressing a matter of great national importance, reached an audience upwards to 30 million people.[26]

Television returned to the White House on December 15 for a further report on the precarious nature of the war following the intervention of Chinese Communist forces. Ben Gross, television critic for the *New York Daily News,* commenting on the still novel media presentation that gave TV superiority over radio and newspapers, noted in his column, "The grim look, the steely glance, and the play of expression on the President's face conveyed far more than his words." The male patrons of a Chicago bar who viewed the president's televised speech, properly impressed by the solemnity as well as the novelty of the occasion, removed their hats and stood at attention as the National Anthem concluded the telecast.[27]

The White House relied heavily upon radio to explain the president's decision to fire Douglas MacArthur. Addressing the nation on April 11, 1951, Truman reviewed the differences between himself and MacArthur. Speaking in his now familiar cadence and with the tone of authority, the president explained that the general did not agree with his policy to limit the war in Korea. It was essential, Truman said, to relieve General MacArthur "to end confusion as to the real purpose and aim of our policy"—to prevent a third world war.[28]

However deliberate and painstaking the process of the presidential decision to fire MacArthur, the announcement itself was rushed by a report that the *Chicago Tribune,* informed by a news leak, would publish the story before the general could be informed personally. In order to prevent the president's nemesis from scoring a journalistic scoop, the White House called in reporters at 1 A.M. for the news. Hurried preparations for the president's radio address that evening precluded the additional planning and arrangements for live television. Filmed excerpts for television and movie theaters were released the following day.[29]

26. *Television Daily,* July 20, 1950, in OF 136-b, Box 575, Truman Papers, Truman Library.

27. Ben Gross, "Televiewing," *New York Daily News,* December 18, 1950, in OF 136-b, Truman Papers, Truman Library; Albert Gore, Jr., "The Impact of Television on the Conduct of the Presidency," master's thesis, Harvard College, 1969, 3.

28. *Public Papers,* 1951, 223, 226.

29. Ibid., 223–27. Presidential aide George Elsey believed that Press Secretary Joseph Short's handling of the matter, including the preparation of documents

A storm of criticism over the relief of General MacArthur swept the nation as a majority of Americans denounced the president's action in letters, telegrams, and paid advertisements. Ministers condemned the president's decision from the pulpit, and civic and veterans groups passed censuring resolutions. Protesters assembled in town squares and on college campuses. House Minority Leader Joseph Martin telephoned MacArthur's Tokyo headquarters to invite him to address a joint session of Congress. Senator William Jenner (R-Ind.) expressed the view of the anticommunist right: "I charge that this country is in the hands of a secret inner coterie which is directed by agents of the Soviet Union. Our only choice is to impeach President Truman."[30]

For the next several days the president's political enemies and detractors dominated the news media. Television and radio carried MacArthur's emotional farewell speech to millions. Congressman Martin, asked by reporters to comment on the general's address in the chambers of the House of Representatives, commented wittily, "Well boys, all I can say is that there wasn't a dry eye on the Democratic side and there wasn't a dry seat on the Republican." "It was," reporter Cabell Phillips later wrote, "Douglas MacArthur's finest hour, the zenith of his career as a master of dramaturgy, as a national hero, and as a symbol of a nation's wrath. Thereafter, everything was anticlimax."[31]

The administration, thrown off stride by the powerful initial support for MacArthur and condemnation of Truman, eventually regained its footing as its side of the dispute between the president and the general became better known through the news media. Ultimately, Truman counted on the ability of the American people to see the correctness of his military and foreign policies and in his assertion of civilian supremacy over the military. Public opinion slowly swung back toward Truman's side on the dismissal of MacArthur, but public dissatisfaction over the administration's limited war objective in Korea continued to get a powerful hearing in the antiadministration press until the presidential election of

---

to buttress the president's case, had unnecessarily slowed the initial announcement of MacArthur's dismissal. Elsey oral history, by Hess, 59. Warner-Pathé's newsreel release on the president's address and public reaction to MacArthur's relief is housed in the audiovisual collection of the Truman Library.

30. This account is derived from Phillips, *The Truman Presidency*, 344–45.

31. Ibid., 347, 348. Martin is quoted in Tames, *Eye on Washington*, 40.

1952 finally ended twenty years of Democratic control of the White House.[32]

Despite President Truman's growing ease with the use of the electronic media, his weekly press and radio conferences during the last years of his administration remained securely in the domain of the print journalists, thanks to the vigilance of his press secretaries. Ross, who had his hands full with guarding Truman from unwise "shoot from the hip" comments, feared verbatim quotation of the president by radio and television would compound his problem. His reputation as an overly cautious custodian of White House news led Doris Fleeson to quip that Ross never permitted a syllable of news to pass his lips until it had first been published in the *World Almanac*. When a newsman asked Ross early in 1950 if television would be admitted to the press conferences with the move from the Oval Office to more spacious quarters in the old State Department building, Ross dismissed the question with an emphatic "No!"[33]

Ross's successors also followed a protective policy for guarding the president's comments in conferences with the press and radio. When Telenews, supplier of 90 percent of the nation's television stations with newsreels, asked for permission in the spring of 1951 for weekly access to the president, Press Secretary Joseph Short, Jr., declined on the ground that the president lacked the time for the newsreels. Short broke new ground, however, in permitting the release of a transcript prepared from the news conference stenographic sound recording. His office also arranged for the Signal Corps to make a high-quality magnetic tape of both news conferences and the president's informal White House talks for occasional radio "outtakes" and for the historical record.[34]

These policies continued through the end of the Truman administration. Television taping of presidential news conferences for later editing and release began in 1955 during the Eisenhower presidency,

32. Phillips, *The Truman Presidency*, 349–50. The decline of public support for MacArthur is discussed in Hechler, *Working with Truman*, 182–84.

33. Doris Fleeson column, *Boston Globe*, February 18, 1950, Scrapbook 1, Fleeson Papers, University of Kansas. Ross is quoted in Herbert Lee Williams, "Truman and the Press" (Ph.D. diss., University of Missouri, 1954), 198.

34. Irving Perlmeter to Short, May 18, 1951, and Short's unsigned and undated attached note, August 1950–May 1951 folder, OF 73, Truman Papers, Truman Library; Short to Louis Seligson, June 16, 1951, January–September 1951 folder, OF 36, Box 195, Truman Papers, Truman Library; W. H. Lawrence, "Taping the Talk," *New York Times Magazine*, October 14, 1951; Hechler, *Working with Truman*, 209, 218–19; *Washington News*, June 8, 1951.

and in 1961 John F. Kennedy inaugurated regular live telecasts of his meetings with the news media.[35]

At his next-to-last news conference Truman announced that his farewell address to the nation would be broadcast "on the radio." Would his talk be on TV, too, a reporter inquired? Truman replied that he did not know, but Press Secretary Roger Tubby quickly volunteered that the address would indeed be telecast. The president's lack of interest in whether he would be seen as well as heard by the American people hardly foreshadowed the "television president" and "video politics" that have come to characterize American politics since Truman left office.[36]

The president and the first lady, except for their enjoyment of newsreels and feature movies, preferred the printed page. They did not share the public's enthusiasm for television despite the medium's continually expanding news, entertainment, and sports programming. Sometime before June 1947 a small screen set had become part of the White House furnishings; that month the general manager of WTTG-TV in Washington offered to replace the set with a large screen receiver housed in a handsome cabinet available in "waxed knotty pine, golden honey selected maple, and natural brown mahogany." The station would also send men to the White House to install the set and its antennae. President Truman personally declined the offer, and he followed the same course in 1948 when an executive of Philco wanted to elicit a statement from the White House to the effect that "the President thinks well enough of television to use it as a means of keeping abreast of current events." The answer telephoned back by a White House aide was a polite "No." Earlier, in October 1947, an RCA television set was acquired for the White House living quarters; later CBS supplied a color television set to the Blair House when the Trumans lived there during the reconstruction of the White House.[37]

35. For operation of the press secretariat by Tubby see his oral history interview by Jerry N. Hess and the oral history of Tubby's assistant, Irving Perlmeter, by Charles T. Morrissey, Truman Library. Gore, "The Impact of Television," 8–9, 37. President Eisenhower conducted the first live news conference on radio and television on August 22, 1956. Reinsch, *Getting Elected*, 104–5.

36. *Public Papers*, 1952–1953, 1105. For the terms and concepts of the "television presidency" and "video politics," see Thomas E. Cronin, *The State of the Presidency*, 2d ed. (Boston: Little, Brown, 1979), 100. See also the theme issue on "The Media and the Presidency" of *Presidential Studies Quarterly* 16 (winter 1986).

37. Leslie G. Arries to Matthew Connelly, June 26, 1947, OF 136b, Box 575, Truman Papers, Truman Library. Reinsch has written that Truman watched

While the Trumans devoted little time to television viewing even after they left the White House, they could definitely be counted on to watch television when their daughter, busy with her singing career and guest appearances on popular entertainment programs, appeared on the medium. Truman made that admission when asked about his viewing habits in 1951.[38] Later, in March 1952, a reporter who wanted to know if the president was going to watch a program featuring the homecoming of General Dwight D. Eisenhower engaged Truman in this exchange:

> Reporter: Mr. President, do you intend to be near a television set Wednesday at seven?
> The President: Wednesday at seven?
> Reporter: That is when Ike has his homecoming at Abilene.
> The President: I didn't know it. I hadn't heard about it. I usually watch the television show, particularly watch it when Margaret is on.
> Reporter: I didn't know . . . she'll be on then.
> The President: She is going to be on Thursday (laughter).[39]

The Truman house in Independence did not have a television set during his presidency despite programming begun in the fall of 1949 by WDAF-TV in Kansas City. When the first lady was in Independence and wanted to see the president and her daughter on television, she walked down the street to watch on the set of her neighbor, Henry Bundschu. The Trumans did not acquire a "television machine"—Harry's term—for their home until Margaret purchased a set for her parents in the mid-1950s.[40]

---

the opening of the Eightieth Congress in January 1947 on a ten-inch RCA set in the Oval Office (*Getting Elected*, 46). Penciled on the letter offering the television set to the president was the notation "This Television set finally refused by the Pres. July 16, [1947]." R. B. George to Charles Ross, August 9, 1948, Connelly to Earl H. Gammons, February 3, 1950, and William M. Rigdon to E. F. McDonald, Jr., January 28, 1949, TV 1945–49 folder, OF 136b, Box 575, Truman Papers, Truman Library. Zenith Radio also supplied a television set to the White House that ended up in the president's private railroad car.

38. *Public Papers*, 1951, 203.
39. *Public Papers*, 1952–1953, 391.
40. WDAF-TV inaugurated the first programming for Kansas City in October 1949 and within months was linked to a national network. *Editor and Publisher* (September 17, 1949): 44; Truman's reference to watching programming on the "television machine" is in his letter to Mary Jane Truman, March 30, 1948, quoted in Ferrell, ed., *Off the Record*, 128; Bess Truman's viewing of television at the Bundschu home is recounted in Helen Worden Erskine, "The Riddle of Mrs. Truman," 61; Margaret's gift of a black-and-white television

Although the president had come to reject his view of 1940 that radio and television, once perfected, would leave newspapers "without a leg to stand on," he never abandoned his belief that a president could, through personal appearances, get his message across by going directly to the people. In this spirit Truman responded to a reporter who asked at a news conference if he would go on television in the 1952 presidential campaign. "I put on a pretty good show myself," he replied, "with or without television."[41]

As a half-joking, half-serious assessment of his own role during the revolutionary changes brought by radio and television to the American news scene at midcentury, Truman's comment is close to the mark. It captures the strong personal force and vitality the great democrat brought to American life in personal appearances via railroads—the greatest transportation invention of the nineteenth century—that carried him to the whistlestops and the still-bustling union stations of the nation's cities. And it makes room, too, for radio and television, the twentieth century's two greatest inventions of news communication, as media that allowed him to go directly to the people and thus bypass the antiadministration newspapers that opposed his foreign policies and domestic programs—the same press that had called for his defeat in 1948 and, failing that, for his impeachment. Truman's good fortune, and America's too, was to stand, for the last time, at a juncture in history when railroad transportation and electronic media could be effectively linked as major vehicles for presidential communication with the American people.

---

set to her parents in 1955 (the date was calculated by a photo of the Truman home showing an antenna approximately a year before Margaret's marriage) is recounted in her interview by Ron Cockrell, 45, Truman Library.

41. Truman's views about the power of radio to leave newspapers "without a leg to stand on," cited earlier in this chapter, comes from a letter he wrote in 1940 that was published in *Editor and Publisher* (September 24, 1949): 34; *Public Papers, 1952–1953*, 417.

9

First Family and Kin

HARRY, BESS, AND MARGARET TRUMAN received a foretaste of the attention they would receive from the press and the public as the presidential first family soon after Truman's nomination as the Democratic vice-presidential candidate in July 1944. After delivering his brief acceptance speech in the Chicago Convention Hall, Truman needed a cordon of police to return to the box where his wife and daughter were engulfed by well-wishers and a phalanx of photographers. As a police escort ushered them to the safety of a waiting limousine, Bess, in a pique of anger, asked Harry, "Are we going to have to go through this for the rest of our lives?"[1]

The reporters' quest for personal information on Truman, keen during the presidential campaign, increased after the brief inaugural ceremonies for Roosevelt's fourth term clearly revealed the deteriorating health of the president. Walter Trohan, chief of the Washington Bureau of the *Chicago Tribune*, in an irreverent voice loud enough to turn his fellow reporters away in revulsion, said "Till death do us part" as Roosevelt affirmed the oath of office. George Rothwell Brown, veteran Hearst correspondent, noting the gaunt neck of the president, added his own malediction: "He's a gone goose." A few weeks later Trohan and John O'Donnell of the *New York Daily News* sneaked a physician into the White House

1. Margaret Truman, *Bess W. Truman*, 231.

184

Correspondents Annual Dinner to get an expert's evaluation of FDR's rapid decline.[2] The journalistic deathwatch was on.

In the process, reporters unfamiliar with the vice president sought information about him and his family. A correspondent for the *Boston Globe* traveled to Independence after the inauguration to gather background information on the Trumans. In Washington Helen Essary interviewed the vice president so she could share her impression with the readers of her *Washington Times-Herald* column. She had expected to find the Missourian a sour, dour man; instead, she reported he had a vigorous, lively personality.[3]

With Roosevelt's death and Truman's assumption of the presidency eighty-two days into FDR's fourth term, the preoccupation of the press with the Trumans became constant and unrelenting. The president, of course, received primary attention from the news media. During the next seven-plus years, journalists, motivated by noble as well as malicious interests, dug into all aspects of his past and present personal life. The search involved matters as diverse as his ancestry, education, reading interests, finances, tastes in music and art, religious practices, and marital fidelity.[4]

Trohan sought information for the antiadministration *Chicago Tribune* that might reveal any private vices of the new chief executive. "When Truman became President," he wrote in his memoirs, "it became important to me to know about his sex life . . . for future guidance." The *Tribune* reporter gathered both incriminating stories and revealing photographs of national politicians for political purposes, and he apparently hoped to accumulate private derogatory information on Truman for use at a critical time. He had heard rumors of sexual high jinks that occurred on the junket to Central America and Mexico in 1939 when Truman and other senators and congressmen visited the region to assess hemispheric defenses. In an account obtained from Republican Congressman Paul Shafer of Michigan, a member of the junket, Trohan learned that ladies of the evening had entertained the American visitors in Costa Rica and Mexico City. Truman had discreetly absented himself from the group in these activities, retiring to his hotel room to write Bess

2. Trohan, *Political Animals*, 1, 201.

3. Margaret Truman, *Bess W. Truman*, 245; Helen Essary, "Dear Washington," *Washington Times-Herald*, December 4, 1944, in Craig Scrapbook, General Clippings, 1942–1945, Craig Papers, Library of Congress.

4. A listing of the entries under the president's name in the *New York Times Index* reveals the large variety of personal data published in the *Times* during the Truman presidency.

about the cavorting by some members of his party and of his own fidelity to her. Although Trohan provided the readers of his memoirs with a graphic account of the frolics that had taken place on the 1939 trip, he expressed pleasure in learning from the errant congressman "that Truman had never thought of cheating on his wife."[5] The fidelity and love of Harry and Bess was the real news story, but Trohan could not use it for partisan advantage.

Truman's enjoyment in playing poker and moderate drinking of bourbon and scotch required that he exercise vigilance to avoid offending Americans whose religious scruples forbade playing cards and drinking alcohol. Both private pleasures made him the subject of controversy among members of the Texas Baptist Convention at its annual conclave in November 1945 in connection with the plans of Baylor University, a Southern Baptist school, to confer an honorary degree upon the president. A majority of the delegates to the convention gave a negative answer to the question in the resolution that asked, "Shall a school that calls itself a Christian school confer honorary degrees upon men whose names are in the public's eye as poker players and drinkers of bourbon whisky?" The *Houston Post*'s extensive coverage of the story drew letters from its readers that both denounced and supported the action of the Texas Baptist Convention.[6]

Baylor eventually got its way and conferred an honorary doctorate of law upon the president in March 1947. A White House aide who was a member of the presidential party housed in the home of Baylor University's president, apparently unaware of the earlier quarrel among Baptists on this matter, left a bottle of bourbon under the pillow of the bed in the guest room as a present for their host. When Truman learned about the gift, he ordered its immediate retrieval for fear that news of the ill-considered gesture would get the university president fired.[7]

Truman let his own guard down in 1948 when a photographer for *Life* aboard the campaign train attempted to associate the president

5. Trohan, *Political Animals*, 216–17, 208–9. Trohan provided a photograph of liberal Senator Claude Pepper (D-Fla.) embracing Paul Robeson and Eleanor Roosevelt at a New York political rally to Pepper's opponent, George Smathers, in the racist-charged Democratic 1950 senatorial primary in Florida. See also the chapter of his memoirs titled "Sex Spices Capital Life and Policy," 132–56.

6. P. C. Williams to the *Houston Post*, December 3, 1945, 1945–46 folder, Box 31, PPF, Truman Papers, Truman Library.

7. *Public Papers*, 1947, 167–72; Stanley Woodward statement, February 8, 1955, 4, "Memoirs" File, Box 2, PPF, Truman Library.

with both alcohol and poker in an unauthorized photograph. Merriman Smith, who did not write about the incident until the last year of the Truman presidency, disclosed that Truman had walked into the club car where the newsmen were playing poker. As the president approached the card players, a friendly reporter offered him a glass of bourbon and water. Truman laughed and took the drink, only to be surprised by the click of a camera's shutter. Turning, he saw a Secret Service agent remonstrating with the photographer. The president set his drink on a table, bid the reporters a polite "goodnight," and left the club car. He did not return there for the rest of the campaign. *Life* failed to get its incriminating photograph and its sister publication, *Time,* had to settle for an oblique reference to the president's visit to the club car.[8]

Truman was not hypocritical on his moderate daily use of alcohol. He did not hide the fact that he drank a cocktail for social relaxation, and, in retirement, disclosed that he consumed, on the average, two ounces of bourbon a day as medicine to improve circulation caused by chronic low blood pressure. He bolted down a shot glass of whiskey in the morning; in the evening Bess joined him in a cocktail of bourbon and water. As in most of his personal habits, the president exercised moderation in drinking alcohol, but on occasion and under stress, he took an extra drink. The columnists Joseph and Stewart Alsop observed but did not report that Truman, while waiting backstage to make his acceptance speech at the 1948 Democratic National Convention, "at long intervals . . . took a pull on a half bottle of liquid that was in his pocket." Joseph Alsop accepted the explanation that the president had a nervous stomach that night and speculated that "in all likelihood, [the liquid] was some form of medicine." In a widely reported statement Senator Joseph R. McCarthy insinuated that the president was intoxicated when he fired General MacArthur, resulting, the senator said, in "a Communist victory won with the aid of bourbon and Benedictine."

8. Merriman Smith, "Watch Your Step, Mr. President," *This Week* (November 2, 1952): 24, "Memoirs" File, Box 2, PPF, Truman Library. Smith's account of this incident does not shed any light on what happened to the film that apparently recorded the scene, but the use of a candid camera for an unauthorized snapshot violated the working rules of both the White House Press Office and the ethics of White House photographers. Press Secretary Short on another occasion registered a complaint involving *Life* photographer George Skadding and Bob Phillips of *Time* for an undisclosed breach in coverage of the president. Jim Truitt to Joe Short, September 12, 1951, OF 271, Truman Papers, Truman Library.

In his own profane way, McCarthy added: "The son of a bitch should be impeached."[9]

Truman's liberal use of "hell" and "damn" and its reportage in the press gained for him a reputation as a profane man. A reporter who traveled with him during the 1944 campaign noted that the vice-presidential candidate was "a little more profane than the average man"; and in the 1960 presidential campaign, candidate Richard Nixon, still years away from uttering expletives in the White House, admonished Truman for language unbecoming to a former president. Truman, always scrupulous in his speech when women were present, occasionally sprinkled his conversation with scatological phrases and military barracks talk in the company of men.[10]

As a God-fearing Baptist, Truman cherished religious beliefs that transcended the fundamentalist prohibition on swearing and the use of alcohol. He firmly believed that God had destined the United States to lead the world toward peace. He regularly read the Bible and drew upon the moral code of the Ten Commandments and the Christian ethics of the New Testament in his own life. He attended Sunday religious services fairly regularly and, preferring to worship without public notice, informed reporters and photographers that he did not want them to accompany him when he went to church. The press representatives did not fully comply, however, remaining a discreet distance in the background. Ministers found it difficult, too, to resist the publicity attendant to having the president at a

9. Shortly after Truman became president he provided answers to an extensive set of personal questions submitted to him by NBC radio newscaster Morgan Beatty. He acknowledged that he drank bourbon and ginger ale and, on occasion, scotch and plain water. HST Personal Data, Morgan Beatty's Questions c. November 9, 1945, 7, Confidential File, Truman Papers, Truman Library. See also McClendon, *My Eight Presidents*, 30–31. Harry S. Truman, *Mr. Citizen*, 67; his drinking of a shot glass of whiskey before breakfast is implied in W. E. Worthing to Truman, July 16, 1947, "W" folder, Box 327, PSF, Truman Papers, Truman Library. See also Williams, *The Newspaperman's President*, xi; McCullough, *Truman*, 468. Clifford, with Holbrooke, *Counsel to the President*, 71, 220. Alsop, with Platt, *I've Seen The Best Of It*, 296. Clark Clifford described Truman's ailment as gastrointestinal upset. *Time* 57 (April 23, 1951): 26.

10. Edward B. Lockett, undated report, news stories filed in *Time* folder, Box 1, Lockett Papers, Truman Library; televised debate with John F. Kennedy, October 13, 1960, quoted in *Time* 103 (May 20, 1974): 71; Margaret Truman, ed., *Letters from Father*, 137. Beth Short, correspondence secretary in 1952, has related how Truman had used the word "damn" while entering an elevator at the White House. When he saw her, he apologized immediately. Underhill, *The Truman Persuasions*, 331. Ferrell, ed., *Truman in the White House*, 17, 83, 266, 315.

worship service. In time, Truman worshiped where he could not be followed by the press and the public, finding privacy in the chapels of the Bethesda Naval Hospital and Walter Reed Army Hospital.[11]

While Truman tolerated reasonably well the seemingly inexhaustible interest of journalists and the public in all facets of his life,[12] he strongly disliked publicity of his family calculated to reflect criticism upon them and the presidency. To an extraordinary degree, with only minor exceptions, all the Trumans and members of his wife's family, the Wallaces, conducted themselves with propriety. In a few well-publicized situations, Truman himself had to learn how to govern his conduct to meet the expectations of the public and the press.

The president's aged mother, Martha Ellen Truman, gave entirely proper remarks to reporters upon receiving the news that Franklin Roosevelt had died and that her son was now president. "I can't really be glad he is president," she told inquiring reporters, "because I'm sorry that President Roosevelt is dead. If he had been voted in, I'd be out waving a flag, but it doesn't seem right to be very happy or wave a flag now." A press agent, Truman later noted, could not have written a more appropriate response.[13]

The public's interest in the president's mother required security measures by the Secret Service to assure her personal safety and to protect her from well-meaning sightseers. When an agent informed Mrs. Truman that a Secret Service detail must now guard her house, she said that it would be all right, but to remember what the song said. The agent, puzzled by this remark, asked for an explanation. "Don't Fence Me In," she chuckled, with reference to the popular song of 1945. Truman wrote to his mother and sister a few weeks after he had become president to commiserate with them over the public attention that now came their way. "It is a . . . terrible nuisance to be kin to the president of the United States. Reporters have been haunting every relative and purported relative I ever heard

---

11. Truman expressed this view often during his presidency. See, for example, his remarks at the presentation of the Medal of Honor, March 27, 1946, *Public Papers*, 1946, 170–71. Hillman, *Mr. President*, frontispiece photograph, 104–6, and 134. Smith, *Thank You, Mr. President*, 86. Truman to D. E. Kucharsky, April 28, 1961, Letters to Hold folder, Box 305, PPF, Truman Papers, Truman Library.

12. When reporters and photographers for the *Kansas City Star* spied on Truman with binoculars during one of his visits to Independence, the exasperated president gave one of the newsmen a detailed and graphic account of his morning visit to the bathroom and demanded that the surveillance be stopped. Ferrell, ed., *Truman in the White House*, 155–56.

13. Hillman, *Mr. President*, 114.

of and they've probably made life miserable for [you and] mother. I am sorry for it, but it can't be helped." He added, "Don't let the pests get you down."[14]

Mrs. Truman's only visit to her son at the White House in May 1945 received extensive press coverage. When the old woman deplaned in Washington and saw the crowd of reporters and photographers present, she protested good-naturedly, "Oh fiddlesticks! Why didn't you tell me there was going to be all this fuss. If I had known, I wouldn't have come."[15]

Although the president's sister, Mary Jane Truman, had accompanied her mother to Washington, the journalists and photographers focused their stories and pictures on Harry and his mother. Years later it still rankled her that photographers had framed some of their shots to exclude her from the photographs that appeared in many newspapers. The press, she complained, must have thought that she was the maid.[16]

The press embroidered the story that the president's mother, as a southerner and Confederate sympathizer, had refused to sleep in the bed of Abraham Lincoln. In fact, she and her daughter occupied the beds in the rooms used by Queen Wilhelmina of the Netherlands during her visit to the White House years before. The Queen's bed, like the bed of Lincoln, was too high for Truman's mother, so she selected a smaller one in an adjoining room.[17]

Truman's attempts to keep his relationship with his mother private and low-keyed drove home to him just how much of a nuisance the press could be. As Mrs. Truman's ninety-second birthday approached, Press Secretary Ross, in response to a reporter's question asking if the president would fly to see her, stated that Truman had no such plans. Then on Sunday, November 25, 1945, the day of her birthday, Truman, without public notification, flew to her home in Grandview, Missouri. Apparently regretting that he had given the slip to White House reporters, the president telephoned

14. Richard Eaton and LaValle Hart, *Meet Harry S. Truman* (Washington, D.C.: Dumbarton House, 1945), 91; Truman to Ethel Noland, August 13, 1949, printed in Ferrell, ed., *Off the Record*, 161.

15. Truman, *Harry S. Truman*, 244.

16. Mary Jane Truman oral history, by Stephen and Cathy Doyal and Fred and Audrey Truman, 53.

17. Ibid., 58–59; Press Secretary Ross held up the ceremonies at Baylor University for awarding an honorary doctorate to the president until the reference to Truman's mother and the "Lincoln bed" could be removed from the university president's citation. Ferrell, ed., *Truman in the White House*, 171–72.

the publisher of the *Kansas City Star* from his mother's house to announce his presence. Word quickly spread to Washington radio and newspaper reporters, and they were waiting for the president when he returned to the capital that evening. An exchange between Merriman Smith and the president made it clear that the reporters were miffed at him, and he, in turn, was miffed at them for their insistence on being notified of his travel plans. Newspaper editorials on the subject sided with Truman's right to visit his mother whenever he so desired, and Smith privately apologized for his line of questioning at the airport, stressing that he "was not trying to pry into Truman's relations with his mother, but only posing the question of whether he should make secret plane trips." Truman dismissed the matter, insisting that he was not angry and realized that the reporters were just doing their job.[18]

The following month Truman's flight to join his mother and family for Christmas in Missouri produced yet another round of controversy based on the belief that the president had unnecessarily endangered his life and the life of the reporters assigned to cover his trip by flying in bad weather. May Craig, writing in her daily column of January 6, 1946, bluntly asserted that "the president has to learn how to be President, and one of the lessons is that he cannot do just as he likes, personally." Craig elaborated her criticism to include a gratuitous swipe at the president's mother: "He wanted to be with his mother on Christmas day, and she apparently does not want to come and spend the Winter in the White House. She may have to bend the stiff neck he inherited, if she expects to see much of him. His strength and his life belongs to the Nation for the next three years." Craig concluded with more advice: "A president has to learn to sacrifice his own preferences to the necessities of his office, and flying in bad weather is one thing Mr. Truman will have to stop." Similar criticisms arose in the press when Truman made yet another plane trip home for Christmas in 1946 in stormy weather.[19]

Truman's trips to Grandview became more frequent in the spring and summer of 1947 as his mother, bedridden with a broken hip and weak from two heart attacks, entered her final illness. The press reported sympathetically on the president's sad journeys to his mother's bedside and her imminent death. But on July 26, 1947,

18. Smith, *Thank You, Mr. President*, 231–33.
19. Craig, "Inside in Washington," January 6, 1946, Scrapbook 1946, Container 13, Craig Papers, Library of Congress; *New York Times*, December 26, 27, 1946.

the day his sister summoned the president home after he signed into law the National Defense Establishment Act, the *Chicago Tribune's* front-page cartoon for the day, standard fare of the highly editorialized newspaper, depicted Truman as an errant schoolboy about to set off a firecracker as part of a crisis to produce World War III to help his election bid in 1948. Truman permitted the ill-timed editorializing of the *Tribune* to go unrebuked; but years later in a draft and unpublished portion of his memoirs, he remembered, apparently mistakenly, that the newspaper had criticized him for taking a needless vacation at the taxpayers' expense. After his mother's death, Truman called in the White House reporters and photographers to thank them personally for respecting his privacy and the privacy of his family in press coverage of Mrs. Truman's final illness and funeral.[20]

Truman's protectiveness of Bess Truman earned for two of her critics—Clare Boothe Luce and Adam Clayton Powell, Jr.—a permanent ban from the White House during his administration. Luce first incurred Truman's wrath in 1944 by noting in a column that Washingtonians had nicknamed Mrs. Truman "Overtime Bess," a reference to her well-compensated service on the senator's office staff. When the press reported correctly that Luce was persona non grata at the White House, the congresswoman appealed to House minority leader Joseph W. Martin (R-Mass.) to intercede in her behalf. His appeal, as well as her own, were of no avail, and with the Trumans seemingly on their way out of the White House after the next election, Luce ridiculed the president and Mrs. Truman in her address at the 1948 Republican National Convention. She called the president "a gone goose"—the same term a Hearst reporter had used to describe Roosevelt in his final months of life—and Bess "an ersatz First Lady."[21] With these cutting remarks Luce

20. A search of the *Chicago Tribune* for an editorial criticizing Truman for taking a needless vacation during the illness of his mother turned up nothing; Truman may have seen an edition of the *Tribune* not available in my research. The unpublished account of the offending editorial as remembered by Truman, characterized by him as the "sewer point" of American journalism, is entitled "The Press," 3, Box 647, PPF, Truman Papers, Truman Library. *Public Papers, 1947*, 365.

21. Norma Lee Browning, "Why Clare Boothe Luce Went Home," *Chicago Sunday Tribune*, January 5, 1947, 1947–July 1949 folder, Box 31, PPF, Truman Papers, Truman Library. Truman explained and defended his wife's working arrangement in an interview published in the *St. Louis Globe-Democrat*, undated, c. August 1944, Clippings Concerning Mrs. HST folder, Box 1, Mary Paxton Keeley Papers, Truman Library. Congresswoman Luce sought to see Truman

completely wrote herself off the White House invitation list for the next four years.

The president's White House ban on Congressman Adam Clayton Powell, Jr., resulted from the adverse publicity that came to Mrs. Truman in mid-October 1945 for her acceptance of an invitation to a tea hosted by the Daughters of the American Revolution. Powell's wife, the pianist Hazel Scott, had been denied permission to play in the DAR's Constitution Hall—reminiscent of the ban in 1939 for another black artist, singer Marian Anderson. Unlike Scott, whose protest to others was recounted earlier, Powell wired a protest to the president, and when the press reported that Mrs. Truman would attend the DAR social event, he wired the president again urging the first lady to decline the invitation. Mrs. Truman, through her social secretary, released her reply to Powell that she would honor a commitment she had made to attend the tea before the DAR's ban on the use of its hall for Scott's recital. The president's special counsel sent a diplomatic letter to Powell that affirmed Truman's belief that talent knew no racial boundaries but left unchallenged the racial exclusion policies of the DAR. Powell, displeased with these responses, blasted the first lady as the "last lady."[22]

The president, with more ground to cover in the development of an understanding view of social discrimination against blacks, referred to Powell in a letter to his mother and sister as a "high brow preacher" from New York. In the company of his inner circle, he joked that he wanted George Allen—a native of Mississippi and a White House insider without portfolio—to look up that "damn n------ preacher" who had said things about "the Madam" and kick him around.[23]

Although black newspaper publishers had little affection for Powell, who had joined their ranks as cofounder and editor-in-chief of a bombastic Harlem weekly, the *People's Voice,* they supported his call for a rebuke of the DAR's discriminatory practices. The black

---

on several pretexts, including the presentation of a delegation of Scottish Rite Masons. The White House response was always that time did not permit the appointment requested by Luce. See Harry S. Truman folder, Box 519, Clare Booth Luce Papers, Library of Congress; Luce to Matthew J. Connelly, March 13, 1946, and Connelly to Luce, March 22, 1946, "P" January–June 1946 folder, Box 75, PPF; undated memorandum, Luce folder, Box 1480, General File, Truman Papers, Truman Library. Margaret Truman, *Bess W. Truman*, 321.

22. Margaret Truman, *Bess W. Truman*, 278–79; *Public Papers*, 1945, 396.

23. Truman to Martha Ellen and Mary Jane Truman, October 13, 1945, quoted in Ferrell, ed., *Off the Record*, 69–70; Ferrell, ed., *Truman in the White House*, 88–89.

press also protested Truman's ban on Powell at the White House as an unfair closure of personal communication between an elected representative of the people and the president. To reinforce the point, black newspapers pointed out that the Harlem congressman provided de facto representation in Congress for people of his race denied the right to vote in southern states. Nevertheless, Truman maintained his ban of Powell throughout his presidency.[24]

Drew Pearson, who had access to the president as a newsman accredited by the White House, also incurred the president's wrath for his unfavorable reports on Mrs. Truman. Pearson had written that Mrs. Truman had lacked the stamina of Eleanor Roosevelt as the two women received guests at the White House on inauguration day in 1945. There was truth in this comment as Bess never mastered the deep-grip handshake to prevent guests from squeezing her hand. This criticism did not draw a personal rebuke from her husband, but Pearson's false report that the first lady and Margaret had traveled in a private railroad car at a time when returning servicemen were unable to get transportation home for Christmas in 1945 drew his fire. Pearson received a dressing-down at the conclusion of the president's news conference on January 9, 1946, as other reporters filed out of the Oval Office. Adding to the president's ire was his belief that Pearson had irresponsibly lent his broadcasts to the complaints of discontented servicemen who had demonstrated in the Philippines over the slow return of the troops to the United States.[25]

Over time, Truman's rebuke of Pearson took on an added dimension with the inclusion of a threat from the president to shoot the columnist. Reporter Charles J. Greene of the *New York Daily News*, who said he heard an account of the incident from the president while aboard the *Williamsburg*, related the story in its classic form in his oral history interview for the Truman Library. According to Greene, Truman told Pearson: "You've been writing some nasty things about my family. I want you to know that down in Missouri we put our women on a pedestal, and *my* women are on a pedestal, and I'm going to keep them there." The president continued: "Over in that desk I've got a gold-plated automatic pistol that was given to

24. Charles V. Hamilton, *Adam Clayton Powell, Jr.: The Political Biography of an American Dilemma*, 119–20, 154–56, 163–66, 179–85; Wil Haygood, *King of the Cats: The Life and Times of Adam Clayton Powell, Jr.*, 128–32, 135.

25. Margaret Truman, *Bess W. Truman*, 233, 282, 295; Drew Pearson, "Confessions of 'an SOB,' " 38; Ferrell, ed., *Truman in the White House*, 113–14.

me as a present, and you son-of-a-bitch, if you write one more line derogatory about *my* women, I'm going to take that pistol and use it on you."[26]

Years later, Pearson denied that the president had ever threatened to shoot him. In any event, the stern rebuke served its purpose. At the time, Pearson apologized in his column for having his facts wrong on the travel arrangements for Bess and Margaret and, for the remainder of Truman presidency, kept the president's wife and daughter out of his columns.[27]

Bess effectively distanced herself from an inquiring press by delegating her social secretary, Edith Helm, and her personal secretary, Reathel Odum, for weekly meetings with female reporters accredited to the White House. When she met with the press at the beginning of the Truman administration to explain that she would not personally hold news conferences, a reporter remonstrated, "But Mrs. Truman, how are we ever going to get to know you?" Bess replied, "You don't need to know me. I'm only the president's wife and the mother of his daughter."[28]

Editors and reporters persisted, however, in seeking information about Bess for what it would reveal about her and, in turn, the president and other members of the family. Odum developed a good sense of what information to give out or to keep under wraps. "Keep on smiling and tell 'them' nothing," Bess instructed Odum. When Washington society reporter Betty Beale insisted that Odum telephone Mrs. Truman in Independence to learn what activity kept Margaret in Missouri and away from the instructional classes of the Junior League of Washington, Bess instructed Odum to explain that Margaret was finishing a course in voice lessons. She added, "I'd prefer telling her it's *none of their d-business.*"[29]

The managing editor of the *New York Times Magazine*, apparently unwilling to accept the difficulty of extracting information from Mrs. Truman, and unpleased with the lack of specifics in an article on a typical day in the Truman White House submitted by White House correspondent Bess Furman, telegraphed several

26. Charles J. Greene oral history, by Jerry N. Hess, 31–33.

27. Pearson, "Confessions of 'an S.O.B.,'" 74. The following chapter covers the gossip and rumor columnist's attacks on several members of the president's official family.

28. Jhan Robbins, *Bess and Harry: An American Love Story*, 82.

29. Truman to Odum, c. July 1945, President Truman, newspaper clippings folder, Box 5, Reathel Odum Papers, Truman Library. The italics are Mrs. Truman's; Odum to Truman, October 11, 1946, ibid.

questions for a rewrite: "What's the routine? Does Mrs. Truman ring for coffee at 6:30 in the morning? Is it carried up on a tray? Does someone have the job of arranging flowers at the breakfast table . . . ? Who consults on planning the day's menu? While this is going on is someone washing the windows? Later is the floor waxed for a dance that night? We want all this sort of detail. . . . Is this clear?" Most of the answers were not forthcoming, and when Furman's article was published, it appeared under the title "The Independent Lady from Independence."[30]

In the summer of 1947 Bess responded to a questionnaire submitted by several female journalists to elicit her views on the presidency. "Would she like to be the president?" the reporters asked. She gave a resounding "No" to the question, nor did she want her daughter—or a son if she had had one—to ever become president. Her responses may have reflected her desire for privacy as much as a reluctant willingness to be helpful to the reporters. When her responses made the front page of many newspapers, it prompted Harry to write his daughter: "It looks as if [Bess] has gone 'Potomac' as all people do who stay in the White House long enough." "When you write to her," Truman suggested, "you might ask her what caused this outburst."[31]

Truman had little to worry about Bess "going Potomac"—his term for egotistical Washingtonians—and he asserted his belief that he should be the head of his household in a letter to his wife in March 1947. He also vented his irritation over a lengthy letter Eleanor Roosevelt had written to him with advice on who should be appointed Democratic party chairman and treasurer. "Thank heaven," he wrote, "there are no pants wearing women in my family." And while he introduced Bess to audiences who turned out to see the first family during the 1948 campaign as "My boss," her visible presence personified a loyal wife standing by her husband.[32]

30. [Lewis] Bergman to [Cabell] Phillips, March 25 [no year], folder 1, Container 59, Bess Furman Papers, Library of Congress; Bess Furman, "The Independent Lady from Independence," 20, 47.

31. The questions for Bess Truman were drawn by three reporters for the wire services. The brief story appeared on the front page of the *New York Times*, October 15, 1947. Truman to Margaret Truman, October 30, 1947, Margaret Truman folder, Box 325, PSF, Truman Papers, Truman Library.

32. Truman to Bess Truman, September 22, 1947, September 1947 folder, Box 9, Family, Business, and Personal Affairs, Truman Papers, Truman Library. See Truman's folksy introductions of his family in the "whistlestop" speeches of his 1948 campaign in *Public Papers*, 1948, passim.

Further efforts by reporters to draw out Bess as first lady during Truman's full term were largely unsuccessful. Furman continued to submit pieces on both Bess and Margaret to her editors at the *New York Times*, but she chafed under the revision her pieces received from the editors. In 1952 Furman tried to enlist Bess for articles based on the first lady's private papers similar to Harry's sharing of his private papers for William Hillman's book, *Mr. President*. But Bess had no desire to share her papers with anyone, and, lacking the need of her husband to correct and refute his detractors in the news media, politely declined. With the exception of Helen Worden Erskine's speculative and mildly critical piece of February 9, 1952, for *Collier's* on Mrs. Truman's influence on the career and presidency of her husband, Bess had been treated quite well by the press, especially in honoring her desire to remain out of the limelight.[33]

The president's relationship with the press on its coverage of Margaret ran both harmonious and stormy over the course of seven-plus years. When he began his administration, Margaret, then a junior at George Washington University, lived in the White House and the family summer residence in Independence. The inquiries of female reporters who covered the social activities of the White House were routine and predictable: What was her college major? (history); Does she have a dog, and if so, what is the dog's name? (yes, she had a dog, an Irish setter given to her by Democratic National Chairman Robert Hannegan and called "Mikey" by Margaret and "Michael Joseph Casey" by the president); Did she have plans to marry her current boyfriend? (a perennial question and one that Margaret tired of very quickly); Had a New York physician performed surgery on her nose? (no, a false rumor reported by Walter Winchell).[34]

Press coverage became more penetrating and critical when Margaret launched her singing career following graduation from college in 1946. As she stepped onto the stage in 1947, music critics of metropolitan newspapers and political columnists without portfolio

---

33. Furman to Margaret Truman, August 7, 1947, Margaret Truman folder, Box 34, Furman Papers, Library of Congress; Furman to Bess Truman, April 8, 1952, Bess Truman folder, Library of Congress; Erskine, "The Riddle of Mrs. Truman," 11, 61–62 in President Truman, Newspaper Clippings folder, Box 5, Odum Papers, Truman Library.

34. Eaton and Hart, *Meet Harry S. Truman*, 91; Bess Furman to Raethel Odum, July 15, 1946, Mrs. Truman 1946–47 folder, Box 5, Odum Papers, Truman Library; Odum to Margaret Truman, September 19, 1946, Margaret Truman folder, Box 5, Odum Papers, Truman Library.

brought Margaret into their columns. Her debut in Washington, D.C., in December 1947 allowed music critic Paul Hume his first opportunity to write a critique of Miss Truman's singing for the *Washington Post*. He complimented the president's daughter for filling the auditorium—something world-famous artists had failed to do in the season—and for projecting her personality "most appealingly." "But the point of the evening was supposed to be musical," Hume wrote, "and it was in this respect most disappointing. She is intelligent, hard working and admirably ambitious. Her failure to acquire the rudiments of good singing must be laid directly at the feet of her teacher." The president may have found the criticism constructive, as he did a review of his daughter's performance in Pittsburgh that October; over the next three years Margaret changed teachers twice.[35]

The columnist May Craig reviewed Margaret's Washington debut with devastating bluntness, declaring that "there was no depth, no power, no feeling in her singing. No more than the yellow canary singing in your kitchen window." After someone sent the column to the president, Truman spoke to Craig privately at the end of a press conference and gave her, as she remembered it, a "personal, kindly, sad reproach."[36]

Three years later, on December 5, 1950, Hume took a second measure of Margaret's performance at Constitution Hall in Washington. While the president's daughter was "extremely attractive on stage," he wrote in his review, "Miss Truman cannot sing very well. She is flat a good deal of the time—more last night than any time we have heard her in the past years. There are few moments during her recital when one can relax and feel confident that she will make her goal, which is the end of the song." Hume concluded that he either had to report on such "unhappy facts" or omit comment on her programs altogether.[37]

When Truman read the review the following morning, he wrote one of the angriest letters of his presidency. The whole tone of the

35. *Washington Post*, December 22, 1947, Scrapbook, 1947, Container 17, Craig Papers, Library of Congress; Harry S. Truman to Mary Jane Truman, October 21, 1947, as quoted in Ferrell, ed., *Off the Record*, 117–18; *New York Times*, November 28, 1950.
36. Craig, "Inside in Washington," December 28, 1947, Awards folder, Container 3, Craig Papers, Library of Congress; Craig, draft of biography, From the Sidelines folder, Container 2, Craig Papers, Library of Congress.
37. *Washington Post*, December 6, 1950.

letter was abusive, but the most offending portion threatened Hume with a severe beating: "Some day I hope to meet you. When that happens you'll need a new nose, a lot of beefsteak for black eyes, and perhaps a supporter for down below." Ironically, Hume first intended to pocket the letter and keep quiet about it, but when he revealed it to his editor, the *Post* called the White House Press Office to determine its authenticity. After the White House confirmed that the letter was genuine, the newspaper published portions of it in a front-page story. The antiadministration *Washington Daily News* printed the letter in full.[38] Thus the personal became political news for everyone.

The president's detractors immediately cited the letter as further evidence of his inability to uphold the dignity of the presidency. "I ask an apology not to Hume," a woman in Hollywood wired Truman, "but to all Americans whom you again insult by uncouth vulgar unsportsmanlike behavior. You are indeed a small man." Other commentators found other grounds for criticizing Truman and even merit in his stout defense of his daughter. Craig, perhaps in belated defense of her own criticism of Margaret's singing in 1947, took Truman to task for lacking a "proper conception of the freedom of the press which requires a reporter to write what he thinks is fact." But she fended off another presidential reproach with the fair-minded comment that "you can't be too hard on a man who defends his daughter," a position endorsed by others in the press and widely shared by the public.[39]

The president's outburst, however, invited serious analysis. A few columnists began to see a pattern in presidential indiscretions extending back to September, when another Truman letter received extensive newspaper coverage. The objects of Truman's wrath at

38. Truman to Hume, December 6, 1950, reprinted in full in Ferrell, *Harry S. Truman: A Life*, 442, note 34; Eben A. Ayers oral history, by Jerry N. Hess, 181–83, Truman Library; *Washington Daily News*, December 8, 1950, in Margaret Truman–Paul Hume Letter folder, Box 3, PPF, Truman Papers, Truman Library.

39. Mildred G. Heredeen to Truman, telegram, December 10, 1950, Correspondence file, Box 19, Gordon L. McDonough Papers, Regional Cultural History Center, University of Southern California. This was the tenor of several letters to the editor published in newspapers and newsmagazines on the president's letter to Hume. Craig, "Inside in Washington," *Portland* [Maine] *Press-Herald*, c. December 10, 1950, December 1950, Scrapbook, 1950, Craig Papers, Library of Congress; the White House mail ran about 80 percent in favor of Truman's right as a father to defend his daughter. Margaret Truman, *Harry S. Truman*, 503.

that time were the Marine Corps and its zealous advocates who sought a large role for the marines in the postwar defense establishment. When Congressman Gordon McDonough (R-Calif.) wrote to the president to advocate maintaining the strength of the corps, Truman dispatched his undiplomatic reply with its offending charge that "The Marine Corps is the Navy's police force and as long as I am President that is what it will remain. They have a propaganda machine almost the equal of Stalin's." The public outcry over this characterization of the marines by their commander in chief required nothing less than a public apology from Truman, which he offered personally at the annual convention of the Marine Corps Association in early September.[40]

The letters to McDonough and to the music critic, placed in the context of his heated exchanges with White House correspondents over the possible use of atomic weapons in Korea and the president's authority to send troops to Europe, contributed to press speculation that the president was coping poorly with the stress of his office. At the time of the incident with the Marine Corps, columnist Dorothy Thompson had pointedly addressed the question of Truman's lack of self-control. His outburst against the marines and their defenders, Thompson wrote, revealed the president's "deplorable state of mind."[41]

The Hume letter, viewed as more evidence of an ill-tempered president, brought the question of Truman's health into public view. An editorial in the antiadministration *Dallas Times-Herald* in mid-December 1950 frankly asserted that the letter "served the more important purpose of placing the American people on notice that their President's mental competence and emotional stability are in question." Whatever the explanation for the president's condition may be, the editorial declared, "the symptoms are genuinely alarming. . . . President Wilson was not himself in the closing months of his Presidency; Mr. Roosevelt was not himself even before Yalta." "In each case," the editorial concluded, "the President's entourage protected him rather than the country, with results which

---

40. Truman to Gordon L. McDonough, August 29, 1950. McDonough inserted the letter in the *Congressional Record* where it was noted by the press. Franklin D. Mitchell, "An Act of Presidential Indiscretion: Harry S. Truman and the Marine Corps Incident of 1950," 565–75.

41. Dorothy Thompson, "On the Record," *Washington Evening Star*, September 14, 1950, in Truman Marine Corps Letter Story folder, Box 19, McDonough Papers, University of Southern California.

are too well known to require comment. That history must not be repeated."[42]

David Lawrence, a presidential observer since the Wilson administration, offered a sympathetic analysis of the causes of the president's bad temper and a prescription for its relief. The strain of the presidential office, compounded by the November 1950 assassination attempt, the death of Press Secretary Ross the following month, and the casualties among American troops in Korea, he wrote, "cannot be imagined by persons on the outside. It is a time for patience, for forbearance, for tolerant understanding—and indeed for prayer for the man who carries the greatest burden of our time." However, as Bert Andrews, White House correspondent for the *New York Herald-Tribune* noted, reporters wished that the president "would try to get back into the mood he was in when he became President: the mood which made him ask for help from the reporters and which helped him to get that help."[43]

Truman's ability to rebound from these embarrassing episodes, with assistance from his family and aides, helped him to avoid sustained criticism and more pointed inquiries into his mental health. He and Margaret were all smiles when they appeared at the father-daughter banquet hosted by the National Press Club on December 12. Margaret also wisely held a press conference shortly after her father's letter to Hume became public. She met the questions head on; when a reporter asked her if the president's letter to Hume would hurt her career, she replied, "It will help to sell tickets."[44]

One especially irritating question for Margaret from reporters concerned the propriety of the first lady's personal secretary, Reathel Odum, drawing a White House salary while serving as her traveling companion during the concert season. Ruth Montgomery, a syndicated columnist for the Hearst newspapers, kept the story in the news from the time it first broke in 1949 until the end of the Truman administration. According to Montgomery, Margaret's income from singing exceeded the $125,000 annual salary of the

42. Editorial, *Dallas Times-Herald,* December 14, 1950, HST Letter to Music Critic folder, Box 3, Records of the Democratic National Committee, Truman Library.

43. David Lawrence, "Today in Washington," *New York Herald Tribune,* HST Letter to Music Critic folder, Box 3, The Democratic National Committee Records, Truman Library; *New York Herald Tribune,* December 10, 1950, HST Letter to Music Critic folder.

44. *New York Times,* December 12, 1950; Margaret Truman, *Harry S. Truman,* 502–3.

president, yet Odum's salary came not from Miss Truman, but from the "Executive Office of the President" section of the federal budget. As Margaret put it, the disclosure implied that she was chiseling on the taxpayers.[45]

Odum, with considerable justification, defended the unorthodox arrangement. She explained that during her absences from Washington she continued to function as a personal secretary to Mrs. Truman, handling mail pouches of correspondence forwarded to her by the first lady. Her travel and hotel expenses were paid not by the taxpayers, but by Margaret. When Margaret assessed her treatment by the news media in the spring of 1950, she cited the attack from "an anti-Administration newspaper" on her arrangement with Odum, along with criticism of her singing ability made for partisan purposes, as the major exceptions to otherwise "friendly and enjoyable" relations with the press.[46]

Montgomery also published criticism of Truman's spinster sister, Mary Jane. Her ultimate target, of course, was the president, and earned for her his private name of "Miss Cyanide." In her column for May 25, 1952, Montgomery reported that despite the law calling for protection of the immediate family—wife and children—of the nation's chief executive, a detail of the Secret Service provided protection for the president's sister at her Grandview, Missouri, home. In addition, the agents chauffeured Miss Truman in her travels in a government-owned Cadillac limousine. This arrangement, Montgomery wrote, allowed the president to save the expense of buying a car for his sister.[47]

Truman had first assigned a Secret Service detail at the home of his mother and sister in the early days of his presidency to ensure their personal safety. Threats had been telephoned to Mary Jane that the house would be set afire in order to burn the president's mother to death, and similar threats were apparently made on the life of Mary Jane after Mamma Truman had passed away. In the twelve-month period of 1949, for example, the Secret Service investigated 1,925 threats, written and oral, made against the

45. Ruth Montgomery, "Capital Circus," *New York Daily News*, December 2, 1949, Newspaper Clippings folder, Box 4, Odum Papers, Truman Library; *Editor and Publisher* (April 22, 1950): 66.

46. Montgomery, "Capital Circus," *New York Daily News*, December 2, 1949; *Editor and Publisher* (April 22, 1950): 65.

47. Ruth Montgomery, *Hail to the Chiefs: My Life and Times with Six Presidents*, 147; Montgomery, "D.C. Wash," May 25, 1952, Newspaper Clippings folder, Box 4, Odum Papers, Truman Library.

president and members of his family. This point was never made by Montgomery; instead, she stressed how "mighty nice" it was for "Miss Mary Jane" to have a government car chauffeured by Secret Service men "even though it does cost you taxpayers $50,000 or so a year."[48]

Montgomery's column in 1952 had dredged up a news story about Miss Truman and the Secret Service–chauffeured car that first appeared in the *New York Times* immediately after the disclosure of a speeding incident reported by Congressman Kenneth S. Keating (R-N.Y.) on the House floor on May 15, 1951. Keating told his house colleagues that a Secret Service guard driving a government-owned car transporting the president's sister had recently been arrested and fined twenty dollars for speeding through Hopewell, New York. The incident demonstrated, Keating charged, "callous disregard for the legitimate interests of taxpayers and wage earners who must foot the bill for government cars, chauffeur and bodyguards." He reported also that the driver had told the arresting officer that the president would be "distressed if his sister is detained." The Republican congressman condescendingly excused the president's sister of any personal blame, calling Miss Truman "a thoroughly estimable lady of high character who had no reason . . . to question the propriety of a sightseeing trip in a government car with a driver and companion, all compensated out of the pay envelope of American workers." "Indeed," Keating asserted, "there was every reason for her to accept that as the norm of conduct for one with deep roots in the White House. The President has been taking everybody else in the country for a ride for six years. Why not his own sister?"[49]

Although the White House made no public comment on the incident, Truman was outraged that Keating had made his sister the object of a news story that cast aspersions upon her character by insinuating that she was traveling alone in the company of two men. In fact, she had gone east in her capacity as Missouri Grand Matron of the Order of the Eastern Star to attend the organization's national convention in Washington and to participate in lodge ceremonies in Boston. Two friends, past grand matrons of the order, had accompanied her, and the trio were en route home through New York when a policeman ticketed their driver for speeding.

48. Mary Jane Truman oral history, by Jerald L. Hill and William D. Stilley, 20, Truman Library; *Time* (September 23, 1950): 11; Montgomery, "D.C. Wash."
49. *New York Times*, May 16, 1951; *Congressional Record, House,* 82d Cong., 1st Sess., May 15, 1952, vol. 97, pt. four, 82d Cong., 5357.

As Miss Truman recalled the incident years later, "It got into the papers. And Harry really had a fit." Because the news report based on Keating's remarks in Congress failed to mention that Miss Truman was accompanied by two other women, it caused her considerable embarrassment: "I liked to never lived it down. I was Lady Grand Matron . . . of the Eastern Star of Missouri. And there I was . . . joy riding with two secret service men. Two of them mind you . . . from Texas."[50]

The *New York Times* story of the speeding incident reported that the justice of the peace who had fined Miss Truman's driver commented wryly at the close of the proceedings in his court that he would probably now receive a letter from the president.[51]

Indeed, a draft of an unsigned typewritten letter, addressed not to the justice of the peace but to Congressman Keating, may have been dictated by Truman. The letter, less vitriolic than the one dispatched to Hume, nevertheless heaped scalding sarcasm upon Keating for causing pain and embarrassment to Miss Truman. Perhaps a realization that further airing of the matter could open the door to a full investigation of Secret Service protection for Mary Jane kept the letter unsent and the draft consigned to the files of a presidential aide.[52] Truman thus left unanswered, then and later, the charge of unauthorized Secret Service protection for his sister. He probably rationalized that while his economy-minded opponents in Congress were willing to place his sister in jeopardy, he would not, law or no law.

Truman's only brother, Vivian, also came under the watchful eyes of the opposition press despite his low profile as a farmer and administrator in the Kansas City office of the Federal Housing Agency. Although Vivian believed he had received an appointment to the FHA in 1935 without any political "pull," in fact, his brother's secretary had made the necessary arrangements. Vivian turned down an offer to go to the Washington headquarters of the agency after his brother's election in 1948, preferring to remain on the farm where he could combine both farming and his duties with the FHA.[53] When

50. Mary Jane Truman oral history, by Stephen and Cathy Doyle and Fred and Audrey Truman, 60–62.

51. *New York Times*, May 16, 1952.

52. George M. Elsey oral history, by William D. Stilley and Jerald L. Hill, 33–34; Elsey provided a copy of the letter (Draft 5/22/51) to the author without attributing its authorship to Truman. Elsey to author, October 2, 1995.

53. J. Vivian Truman, Obituary, *New York Times*, July 9, 1965; Steinberg, *The Man from Missouri*, 168.

his farming and administrative activities turned up nothing that might be used against the president, a few journalists focused their attention on Vivian for family traits that he shared with his famous brother.

The journalist William Bradford Huie, who visited Jackson County in 1951 to collect information for a virulent anti-Truman article published that April in the Hearst-owned *Cosmopolitan*, described Vivian as an honest man who paid his debts. Harry was the dishonest deadbeat in the family. The two men were alike, according to Huie, in taking after their combative father. Huie quoted anonymous sources who said that Vivian "would just as soon hit you as look at you." In truth, Vivian had been handy with his fists during his youth, and he declared in a letter to his brother that he would trash Westbrook Pegler if he ever met up with him for charging the president with responsibility for the theft of ballots cast in the August 1946 Kansas City primary election. The mature Vivian, however, exhibited shyness and reticence in public speaking. Brother Harry, wrote Huie, was the "cusser" and "hater."[54]

Vivian and Harry were both drawn into the efforts of Bela Kornitzer to write an article about their father, John Truman. The journalist enlisted Truman's endorsement of his research with family members, friends, and acquaintances for an article intended to recognize and honor the contributions of the elder Truman to the qualities of his famous son. The president, sentimental about the task to memorialize his father, a farmer who had died at the age of sixty-three in 1914, gave his blessing to the project.[55]

However, when Kornitzer finished his piece and submitted it to Vivian and the president for review, both reacted sharply to quotes collected from Jackson County residents unfriendly to the Trumans. Some, with considerable truth, remembered John Truman as a sometimes angry, even violent man who had been a failure in his business endeavors. After Vivian detailed the shortcomings of

54. William Bradford Huie, "The Terrible Tempered Mr. Truman," *Cosmopolitan* (April 1951): 32ff; Henry A. Bundschu to Bela Kornitzer, October 22, 1949, PPF 5928, Truman Papers, Truman Library; Vivian Truman to Harry Truman, July 3, 1947, Vivian Truman folder, number 1, Box 332, PSF, Truman Papers, Truman Library. Huie's charges and characterizations were refuted by a longtime acquaintance and friend of both Harry and Vivian Truman, Rufus Burris. Burris to Huie, April 5, 1951, Defense of HST and John Truman folder, Box 306, PSF, Truman Papers, Truman Library.

55. Charles G. Ross to Henry A. Bundschu, July 11, 1949, PPF 5928, Truman Papers, Truman Library.

the article to Harry, the president asked Kornitzer to abandon the project.[56]

But Kornitzer persisted; interviews from Truman family members and their friends helped him to produce a draft that won their approval and that of the president as well.[57] Truman, summarizing his experience with Kornitzer and the press for Vivian, emphasized his belief that "the objective of these Metropolitan Newspapers is to find something detrimental to the President of the United States."

> The man who wrote an article about our father, after he had seen old man Woodson and a lot of other old nuts over in Independence, he was right down their alley and they [*Cosmopolitan*] offered to give him $8,000 for the article. After Charlie Ross and I read it and told him it was not factual and he went back and got the facts they refused to take it because their frank statement was they didn't want anything that was favorable to the President or his family.[58]

Kornitzer eventually placed his article with *Parents Magazine* in March 1951. Unrecorded in the favorable essay was an earlier affirmation of Truman's judgment of his progenitor: "My father was not a failure. . . . He was the father of the President of the United States."[59]

The interest of the press in the president's in-laws, the Wallaces, and especially Bess's mother, Madge Gates Wallace, who shared her home in Independence with the Trumans and lived with them in Washington, never developed much beyond polite inquiries into their plans for the holidays, their health, and other innocuous subjects.

Stories persisted, however, that Truman's mother-in-law held a lifelong belief that Harry Truman was not quite good enough for her

56. The combative personality of John Truman, particularly on election day, and his unwise speculation in wheat futures in 1902 that wiped out most of his considerable property are documented by Harry Truman's biographers, David McCullough and Robert Ferrell. Their balanced portrait of John Truman corrects the one-sided view offered by Huie. See McCullough, *Truman*, 47–48, 66–67 and Ferrell, *Harry S. Truman: A Life*, 5–7, 37. Ross to Kornitzer, December 21, 1949, PPF 5928, Truman Papers, Truman Library.

57. Ross to Kornitzer, February 20, 1950, PPF 5928, Truman Papers, Truman Library; Joseph Short, Jr. to Kornitzer, February 27, 1951, OF 2940, Truman Papers, Truman Library.

58. Truman to Vivian Truman, May 29, 1950, Vivian Truman folder, Box 332 PSF, Truman Papers, Truman Library.

59. Steinberg, *The Man from Missouri*, 15.

daughter. The *Washington Times-Herald* took note of these stories in its account of Mrs. Wallace's life, stating that even after Harry Truman became president his mother-in-law had not completely abandoned her original view that he was unworthy of her daughter's hand. The *Washington Star* more charitably reported, "Since Mr. Truman first succeeded to the presidency, Mrs. Wallace often has laughed at her faint disapproval to the engagement in 1917 of her daughter, fifteen years out of a girls' finishing school, to Harry Truman—whose mother said he could 'plow the straightest furrow in Missouri.' " The writer Merle Miller related in his oral biography of Truman an account of how members of the White House household often heard Madge Wallace remark that other men would have made better presidents than Harry and that Harry should not have fired that nice general, Douglas MacArthur. Truman denied stories that he did not enjoy a good relationship with his mother-in-law, and when she died, he penned a private tribute to a "grand lady."[60]

Interestingly, surely to the great relief of Bess and Harry, the press did not explore the circumstances surrounding the suicide of Bess's father while they were in the White House and during their retirement years. The reporters who covered the first lady may have given her pause, though, in extensive written inquiries submitted through her secretary in August 1947. Near the bottom of a long list compiled by two wire service reporters came the question: "What was her father's business?" The penned response: "Govt. position. K[ansas] C[ity] office of Collector of Customs."[61] Whether by politeness or an assumption similar to Margaret Truman that Bess's father had died a natural death, no additional inquiries were made by the distaff side of the White House press corps into the life and death of David Wallace.

Moveover, when Madge Wallace died in the Truman family quarters of the White House at the age of ninety in December 1952, the extensive news accounts of her life stated without elaboration that her husband had died in 1903. President Truman allowed a few reporters, photographers, and newsreel cameramen to accompany

60. *Washington Times-Herald*, December 6, 1952; *Washington Evening Star*, December 5, 1952, Newspaper Clippings folder, Box 4, Odum Papers, Truman Library. Merle Miller, *Plain Speaking: An Oral Biography of Harry S. Truman*, 17. For a challenge to the authenticity of Miller's oral biography, see Robert H. Ferrell and Francis H. Heller, "Plain Faking?" 14–16. Truman, diary, December 6, 1952, in Ferrell, ed., *Off the Record*, 279.

61. Dorothy Williams to Reathel Odum, August 29, 1947, Mrs. Truman 1946–47 folder, Box 5, Odum Papers, Truman Library.

the family on the train as they returned the body of Mrs. Wallace to Missouri for burial. However, he effectively limited news coverage of the sad homecoming by asking the press party to remain aboard the train when the family departed at Independence and to continue their journey to nearby Kansas City. The occasion revived Truman's perhaps imperfect memories of press criticism of his absence from the capital during his mother's final illness and death, provoking him to record once again his contempt for the "sabotage press" of McCormick and Hearst. "To hell with them," he wrote. "When history is written they will be the sons of bitches—not I."[62]

The news stories and editorials on Mrs. Wallace's passing, funeral, and burial that appeared in the metropolitan press reported with great respect on the personal loss that had come to the nation's first family. The news accounts stated that Madge Gates Wallace was buried in the Gates family lot beside her mother and father, leaving unsaid that the widow of almost half a century was not interred in the Wallace family plot beside her late husband.[63] The family's suppressed "secret" thus remained out of the public realm until 1986 when Margaret Truman revealed its significance in her biography of her late mother.

Fortunately for Truman, the members of his immediate and extended family lived decent, conventional lives. Although he shared Bess's worry that her brother Fred's drinking problems and business dealings might embarrass the first family, he was thankful that his relatives were well-behaved. In a 1949 letter to his cousin Ethel Noland, he also acknowledged the burden imposed by an inquiring public and press upon the lives of his relatives. "It is a terrible handicap these days to be a close relative of the President of the United States," he wrote. "I feel sorry for Margy, Vivian's children, sister Mary and my cousins. People are always watching for something mean to say because they think it will hurt me." "It only hurts," he explained, "because I don't want anyone close to me hurt. Personally," he concluded, overstating the matter, "it runs off me like water off a duck's back."[64]

62. Madge Gates Wallace folder, Vertical File, Truman Library. *New York Times*, December 8, 1952; *Kansas City Times*, December 8, 1952, Wallace folder, Vertical File, Truman Library. Diary, December 6, 1952, Ferrell, ed., *Off the Record*, 79.

63. See press clippings in the Madge Gates Wallace folder, Vertical File, Truman Papers, Truman Library.

64. Fred Wallace's alcoholism and its significance for Bess and Harry is discussed in Margaret Truman, *Bess W. Wallace*, 118, 212, 284–85, 411; when

The president's official family—the members of the cabinet, White House staff, and his inner circle, extending outward to all members of the executive branch of the government and back to the president himself—gave the news media much to write about that ruffled feathers aplenty.

---

a Missouri friend informed Truman that a reporter for the *Chicago Tribune* was probing into Truman's brother-in-law's business dealings in an apparent effort to link him to an alleged Kansas City criminal, Truman replied that if the reporter "comes out with a pack of lies about Mrs. Truman or any of my family his hide won't hold shucks when I get through with him." Joseph J. McGee to Truman, November 17, 1950, "Mc" folder, Box 316, PSF, Truman Papers, Truman Library; Truman to McGee, November 22, 1950, ibid. After he left the White House, Truman wrote that "Not a single member of my family or the family of Mrs. Truman ever embarrassed me in any way as President of the United States. I hope they can say the same about me." Harry S. Truman, *Mr. Citizen*, 149. Truman to Ethel Noland, August 13, 1949, printed in Ferrell, ed., *Off the Record*, 161.

10

The President's Official Family

THE JOURNALISTIC WATCH OF the Truman administration, like the attention news reporters gave to the president and his personal family, became at times intense and unrelenting. Cabinet officers and members of the White House office staff received the greatest coverage because of their importance in formulating and executing presidential policies. Bureau heads and lower-echelon officials, even secretarial personnel and anyone privileged with a pass to the White House, were also potential subjects for close scrutiny of official and personal actions. While each member of the administration was individually responsible for his or her personal reputation, as members of the presidential family their actions contributed to Truman's public standing, measured his ability to judge character and select competent individuals, and tested his personal loyalty to the members of his team. Ultimately, the public performance and private behavior of the official family influenced Truman's ability to govern and reflected upon his own reputation.

Collectively, the negative issues that swirled about some members of the Truman administration involved charges in three broad categories: personal corruption, involving alleged payoffs ranging from thousands of dollars to piddling sums of money and small gifts; psychological or intellectual unfitness for holding a government post; and disloyalty to the nation. The first category of charges led initially to calling Truman's inner circle the "Missouri gang" and culminated in a broader characterization of alleged and real corruption in the administration as the "mess in Washington." The second category of accusations impugned the suitability of the president and his official family to discharge competently their duties and responsibilities. Finally, some members of the administration came under attack for alleged disloyalty to the nation by failing to provide a strong defense establishment and a government free of communist influence. When the administration's foreign policies and defense capabilities fell short of the expectations of its critics, the political opposition and the antiadministration news media branded Truman and several of his secretaries of state and secretaries of defense as "mental misfits" and "traitors" who should be fired or impeached and removed from office.

While Republicans in Congress leveled many of the charges against officials and friends of the Truman administration that found their way into the news media, the press also originated stories that sometimes correctly, sometimes erroneously, implicated members of the administration in wrongdoing. At one extreme, journalists called the public's attention to improprieties that won for them prestigious awards within their profession; at the other, they irresponsibly hurled accusations that reflected dishonorably upon themselves and their craft.

Truman readily involved himself in conferring both praise and blame upon the journalists who reported on his official family. But the operating principle that guided him in dealing with most criticism of his administration rested on a belief that the critics were primarily motivated by a desire to injure his effectiveness as the national leader. Often when administration officials came under attack, he pointed out that he was the real target. His concept of personal loyalty to members of his official family allowed for their indiscretions and laxity that even his friends and associates considered unwise. Within this context Truman battled frequently with his antagonists.[1]

Journalists labeled the president's inner circle of appointed officials and friends the "Missouri gang" within days after Truman took office. Eben A. Ayers, a White House press assistant held over from the Roosevelt administration, took note of the newcomers in his diary entry for April 17: "There seem to be all sorts of strange people

---

1. This point and my account of Truman and his personnel problems in domestic affairs draws heavily upon Andrew J. Dunar, *The Truman Scandals and the Politics of Morality.*

coming and going. Missourians are most in evidence and there is a feeling of an attempt by the 'gang' to move in." Talk was in the air, Ayers observed, of a Democratic "Harding administration."[2]

White House reporters were especially mystified by the apparent lack of duties of two newcomers at the White House, John Maragon of Kansas City and Edward R. McKim of Omaha. Ayers informed the correspondents that Maragon (whom he privately described as a "strange figure . . . of foreign appearance [who] might easily pass for a gangster of the prohibition era"), was "handling transportation" while McKim, for the moment, had no official role but was a friend of the president. Truman soon unwisely and inappropriately designated McKim, his World War I buddy and an honest businessman, "chief administrative assistant." McKim's lack of tact in getting the Trumans settled in the White House required his transfer to another office; he voluntarily returned to private life within weeks. Maragon, a shadowy figure, enterprising businessman, and erstwhile passenger agent for the Baltimore and Ohio Railroad, led a charmed life of White House intrigue until April 1946, when he was finally exiled as an influence peddler.[3]

Although the press exaggerated the importance of Maragon and McKim, its interest in them demonstrated an important principle: those with access to the president and the White House serve as a barometer of the moral climate and competency of the administration. As Truman gathered his staff, drawing heavily upon friends and associates from both his World War I days and Senate years, the seeming preponderance in the new administration of Missourians with no particular talent or ability other than their ties to the president solidified the concept of the "Missouri gang." By extension, even natives of other states serving in the administration were lumped with the Missourians.[4]

If President Warren G. Harding and his cronies came to mind for some watchers of the Truman presidency, the early 1946 Senate

2. Ferrell, ed., *Truman in the White House*, 11–12.

3. Ferrell, ed., *Truman in the White House*, 12, 138; Eben A. Ayers, unpublished diary, April 18 and 19, 1945, Ayers Papers, Truman Library; Eaton and Hart, *Meet Harry S. Truman*, 95; Hamby, *Man of the People*, 302; Dunar, *The Truman Scandals*, 46, 74.

4. Drew Pearson, "The Washington Merry-Go-Round," George E. Allen folder, Box 17, Ayers Papers, Truman Library. Charles G. Ross offered a humorous analysis of the "Missouri gang" by pointing out the numerous non-Missourians on the White House staff and in the president's cabinet in a speech of c. May 1950 to University of Missouri alumni. Quoted in Farrar, *Reluctant Servant*, 212.

confirmation hearings of Edwin W. Pauley as undersecretary of the navy suggested the infamous Teapot Dome scandal of the twenties. Pauley, a wealthy California oilman, had been slated for the undersecretaryship by President Roosevelt in 1944. Following Roosevelt's death, Truman offered his own nomination of the Californian with the view that the successful businessman would ultimately replace Navy Secretary James V. Forrestal. Pauley had raised hundreds of thousands of dollars for the Democratic party. The question of his fitness for the post turned not on his competency, but on the power he would wield on matters pertaining to naval oil reserves and the status of tideland oil deposits. The latter was of keen interest to oil companies, such as Pauley's California firm, located in the coastal and gulf states. These firms wanted offshore oil rights assigned to the states rather than to the federal government.[5]

Although Truman consistently favored the assignment of tideland oil deposits to the federal government, his position was lost from sight during the hearings on Pauley's nomination. Instead, Pauley's past attempts to influence Democratic party politics through campaign donors linked to state control of tidelands oil surfaced. This damaging evidence came from Harold Ickes, secretary of the interior in Roosevelt's cabinet and held over in that position by Truman. Ickes admitted that he did not like Pauley's nomination and wondered aloud what he was doing at the confirmation hearing: "I am a member of the Cabinet. I don't know why, but I am. This nomination was sent here by the man I'm working for, President Truman."[6]

Democratic Senator Tom Stewart of Tennessee wondered instead why Pauley had not withdrawn his nomination and why the Democratic National Chairman had not requested his withdrawal. In a statement released to the press, Stewart candidly assessed the situation: "To continue to embarrass the Democratic party is bad. We have had other Teapot Dome experiences in this country, and I hope we do not have another one. You cannot mix oil, water and politics." Pauley withdrew his name from nomination on March 13, 1946.[7]

The episode had produced another casualty a few days earlier with the announcement from the president that he had accepted the resignation of Secretary Ickes. In a press conference called by Ickes

---

5. Dunar, *The Truman Scandals*, 23, 25–33.
6. Tris Coffin, *Missouri Compromise*, 48–52.
7. Ibid., 53; Dunar, *The Truman Scandals*, 33.

to explain his departure, "Honest Harold," a sobriquet he had gained during the thirties as head of the Public Works Administration, seemed to impugn Truman's integrity. "The President, in principle," Ickes explained, "tried to give an honest administration in the Roosevelt tradition. But he was unfortunate in the choice of certain appointments. There were some very regrettable appointments." A reporter asked: "Do you think Truman was responsible for the selections?" Ickes replied: "As Cal Coolidge used to say, 'He did 'em, didn't he?' "[8]

Ickes's departure, along with the firing of Henry A. Wallace from his position as secretary of commerce in September 1946, removed the last of the holdovers of the Roosevelt cabinet from Truman's administration. The *Chicago Tribune* understandably considered their departure salutary, while heaping abuse upon Truman and his appointees in general. For Truman, it was a no-win situation. In the 1948 presidential election his "Missouri gang" appointments were offered as evidence by Truman detractors that he and his appointees were men of mediocre talents and questionable integrity who should be turned out of office.[9]

Truman's defiant and successful quest for nomination and election in his own right momentarily turned the tables on his critics, but brought no relief to several members of his official family. The central figure in the news media's attacks upon the Truman administration initially and continuously centered on Major General Harry H. Vaughan, whose alleged misuse of his White House connections made him the subject of a congressional investigation in 1949.

Truman and Vaughan first became friends after their meeting as junior national guard officers during World War I. They continued their friendship in the army reserve during the twenties and thirties. In 1940, Vaughan served as treasurer of the Missouri senator's uphill battle for renomination, and after Truman won a second term in the Senate, he followed him to Washington to serve as his executive assistant. During World War II Vaughan served briefly in Australia until he injured his back in a plane crash; upon his return to Washington, he was assigned as army liaison to the Truman committee. When Truman became vice president in 1945, he designated Vaughan as his military aide and retained him in that capacity after assuming the presidency.[10]

8. Coffin, *Missouri Compromise*, 57–59.
9. Dunar, *The Truman Scandals*, 33–34.
10. Ibid., 40–43.

The position of military aide to the president carried little weight or responsibility. Vaughan served as a liaison to the army, accompanied Truman for Memorial Day wreath-laying ceremonies at Arlington National Cemetery, made arrangements for presentations of the Medal of Honor, and traveled with the president at home and abroad. Legend had it that Vaughan, as Truman's close friend with daily access to the president, wielded enormous influence, particularly in military affairs. In fact, Vaughan had very little involvement in decision-making and a large capacity to involve himself in minor affairs that brought embarrassment to himself and to the president.[11]

Reporters quickly discovered that while Vaughan possessed no hard information, he freely offered strong opinions on many persons and subjects. Thus his remarks made him a convenient means of attacking the president. In a postpresidential introduction to Vaughan's never-published memoirs, Truman offered a characteristically biting explanation of malicious press interest in Vaughan and other members of his administration that began early in his administration:

> Such slick purveyors of untruth as *Time, Newsweek,* and the *United States News and World Report,* along with Billy Hearst's sewer press and Bertie McCormick's sabotage sheets . . . began a campaign of misrepresentation and vilification hardly ever equalled in this country's history. *Time* put a special reporter on the job to follow Harry Vaughan with instructions to distort and misquote every action and statement of my military aide. . . . But it is to the everlasting credit of [Secretary of State Dean] Acheson, [Secretary of the Treasury John W.] Snyder, [Secretary of State George C.] Marshall and Harry Vaughan that they faced the lies and misrepresentations with fortitude and did their jobs as duty called for with honor and credit to this great 'free press' Republic of the United States of America.[12]

Truman overstated the charge against distortion and misquotation of Vaughan by the press; at times to quote the general verbatim produced the greatest injury. But there is substance to Truman's charge that the news reporters eavesdropped on Vaughan for the purpose of gathering information on the bumptious military aide to embarrass the president.

11. Ibid., 42–43. For a detractor's view of Vaughan, see Robert Ferrell's edition of Eben A. Ayers diary, *Truman in the White House,* passim.
12. Quoted in Dunar, *The Truman Scandals,* 158.

The first public controversy involving Vaughan came in September 1945 after the disclosure of his remarks to the women's auxiliary of the Presbyterian church he attended in Alexandria, Virginia. Vaughan characterized Protestant chaplains in the armed services as "dull" in contrast with Catholic chaplains, whom he characterized as "regular" fellows. This unfavorable comparison appeared in the *Washington Post* when a member of the church, a reporter for the newspaper, wrote an account of Vaughan's remarks. *Time* gave the story national coverage and touched off an angry outburst from the public and the General Commission on Army and Navy Chaplains, an organization representing Protestant churches. Complaints from the commission to the president led Truman to disassociate himself from the general's remarks.[13]

Vaughan's critics failed to take note that he attended church services regularly, taught a Sunday school class, and shunned both profanity and drinking. Indeed, he conveyed a quite different image to his detractors, who cast the portly and jocular cigar-smoking general as a profane man given to vulgar stories, cheap cigars, and bourbon. This false characterization of Vaughan's personal habits made it easier for Truman to dismiss more serious criticism of his old friend. And because Vaughan was one of the few men with whom he could relax without the stifling formality that governed many of his personal relations, he kept him around for his entire presidency.[14]

Vaughan's greatest indiscretion as the president's companion and military aide involved the assistance he extended to personal friends and other members of the administration. The general's poor judgment in "helping the customers"—a term that Truman often used as a carryover of his haberdashery days and years as a dispenser of political patronage, got him in trouble early and often with the press, especially with Drew Pearson.[15]

Pearson stood at the height of his power in the Truman years, with a widely syndicated newspaper column and a Sunday evening radio commentary broadcast nationally by the American Broadcasting Network. The muckraking journalist, careless with the truth and a purveyor of both information and misinformation, alternately delighted and outraged his listeners with stories of human foibles.

13. Ibid., 43–44.
14. Ibid., 41–43; McCullough, *Truman,* 745–46.
15. Dunar, *The Truman Scandals,* chap. 3.

Truman did not like Pearson's free-swinging journalism and character assassination and did not hesitate to tell him so.[16]

Truman's stout defense of General Vaughan in 1949 occurred
after Pearson broadcast a story that the president's military aide
was scheduled for a decoration from the Argentine government of
dictator Juan Perón. Pearson even staked out the Argentine Embassy
to collect the names of Truman officials who attended the conferring of a medal to Vaughan for revelation on his popular Sunday
broadcast.[17]

While the public and the press took little note of Pearson's she-
nanigans—perhaps because ranking military officers, including
General Omar Bradley, had received similar medals—the episode
prompted Truman to attend an Army Reserve dinner in February
1949 honoring Vaughan as its "Officer of the Year" and level a
blast at Pearson. "Now, I am just as fond and just as loyal to my
military aide as I am to the high brass," Truman declared, "and . . .
any S.O.B. who thinks he can cause any of those people to be
discharged by me, by some smart aleck statement over the air or in
the paper, he has got another think coming." While the president's
stenographer deleted "S.O.B." and inserted the words "anyone" in
the official transcript, editors wrote creative headlines for the news
story written by reporters present at the affair that did little to soften
the president's unfortunate outburst. And, while the president did
not refer to Pearson by name, journalists correctly assumed that he
was Truman's target.

Pearson, for his part, responded graciously, explaining that the
president's reference was to "servant of brotherhood."[18] Years later,
in an article for the *Saturday Evening Post* titled "Confessions of 'an
S.O.B.,'" he revealed that he had privately retaliated at the time by
naming one of the young bulls on his farm "Harry Truman." When
the once-docile animal tried to live up to his name, Pearson wrote,
he had to put a ring in its nose and then send it to market.[19]

Truman's friendship with Vaughan inspired the Alsop brothers to
plan a muckraking article on the military aide and other friends
of the president for the *Saturday Evening Post*. With a working
title of "The Pal Harry Cabinet," the Alsops proceeded until they
concluded that the piece would make them personae non grata with

16. See Oliver Pilat, *Drew Pearson: An Unauthorized Biography.*
17. Drew Pearson, "Confessions of 'an S.O.B.,'" 74.
18. *Editor and Publisher* (February 26, 1949): 10.
19. Ibid.; Pearson, "Confessions of 'an S.O.B.,'" 74ff.

too many members of the administration. They suggested that *SEP* editor Frederic Nelson recruit semi-retired columnist Frank Kent for the piece.[20]

Eventually Kent turned the assignment down, revealing in his letter to Nelson some of the contemporary criticisms of Truman's official family. He described Harry's pals—supplying a different epithet to the individuals named—as being "little," "immature," "coarse," "politically ingrained," "lazy," "bumptious," "completely subservient to the CIO," "radical," and "[un]trustworthy." Nevertheless Kent could not write the piece. "You see," he explained to the *SEP* editor, "I know these fellows are incompetent and inadequate but they are not bad any more than Harry is bad."[21]

Pearson, meanwhile, continued to keep General Vaughan and his friends, especially the mysterious John Maragon, in the news. Maragon, who had wrangled letters of introductions and a passport for travel to Europe immediately after the war through his White House connections with Truman's naval aide, James K. Vardaman, Jr. and General Vaughan, capitalized on one of his trips abroad by bringing back rare oils used in the manufacture of perfume. Vaughan's misplaced friendship with Maragon was only the tip of the iceberg; the general routinely wrote letters of introduction and arranged appointments by telephone for businessmen who wanted to deal directly with government officials whose decisions ranged from the awarding of large contracts to rulings allocating scarce supplies. In the robust postwar business climate and the growing military-industrial complex, lobbyists with friends in government made the most of these connections.[22]

Pearson and the entire news media had a field day with the revelations in the summer of 1949 involving lobbyists who sold their influence with government officials for fees and 5 percent of

20. The idea for the "Pal Harry" piece had evolved from Stewart Alsop's belief that Harry Vaughan, through Democratic National Chairman William Boyle, controlled patronage and thus was responsible for getting Truman to appoint Louis Johnson secretary of defense. Stewart Alsop to Martin Sommers, March 23, 31, April 7, 1949, January–May 1949 folder, Container 26, Joseph Alsop Papers, Library of Congress.

21. Kent to Frederic Nelson, May 2, 1949, Frederic Nelson folder, Box 7, Kent Papers, Maryland Historical Society, Baltimore, Maryland.

22. Dunar, *The Truman Scandals*, 45–51, 40, 70–71, 75–77; Vardaman to Captain D. D. Dupre, August 10, 1945, Chronological File, July–August 1945, Box 1, William M. Rigdon Papers, Truman Library.

the contract. Paul Grindle, a former reporter of the *New York Herald Tribune* turned furniture manufacturer, was instrumental in the disclosures. Grindle told a reporter friend of his dealings with an influence peddler, retired army officer Colonel James V. Hunt. According to Grindle, Hunt claimed that he could land a government contract for the furniture firm through well-placed contacts, including his "closest and dearest friend," General Vaughan. The *Herald Tribune* launched a series of articles that made "five percenters" a household word and prompted the Senate Committee on Expenditures in the Executive Departments to have its Investigations Subcommittee probe the problem. In this roundabout way, Harry Vaughan became the centerpiece of a congressional investigation.[23]

The events surrounding the congressional probe and hearings turned up additional stories of alleged influence-buying through gifts made to General Vaughan. Particularly embarrassing to President and Mrs. Truman was the disclosure that deep freezers had been sent, through Vaughan, to the Truman home in Independence and to a few other Truman officials in late 1945 by the manufacturer as an unsolicited gift of a wealthy businessman. Only one recipient of the freezers, Secretary of the Treasury John Snyder, wisely returned the gift; the others acquiesced in Vaughan's explanation that the deep freezers were experimental or even reject models without commercial value. In fact, the freezers were unreliable, leading to food spoilage and repair bills; within weeks after they were put in use, the freezers at the Truman residence and Vaughan household were hauled to the dump.[24]

The preliminaries to the Senate hearings, as well as the hearings themselves, subjected Vaughan to an accusatory press. He was away from Washington when the *Herald Tribune* first broke the five percenters story that linked his name to Colonel Hunt. Reporters and photographers eagerly awaited his return by train to the capital. The general, irritated with stories that he was in the pay of Hunt and other lobbyists, refused to take reporters' questions at Union Station and dashed away from the cameramen to a waiting car. At the hearings, Vaughan was more composed but still clearly agitated and distraught. After the three-week investigation ended, he returned to the White House and suffered a heart attack. Truman ordered

23. Dunar, *The Truman Scandals*, 58–77.
24. Ibid., 65–66.

Vaughan to go home for rest and helped to keep his illness from the press.[25]

While the subcommittee probe did not prove that Vaughan had done anything illegal, it produced evidence that the president's military aide had crossed the line between referral—a legitimate function—to advocacy, a position that carried the implication of White House interest in the disposition of a case. In the court of public opinion he was convicted of wrongdoing, but in Vaughan's mind, he had been unfairly tried and convicted by political opportunists and a malicious press. Truman shared this belief and for this reason, he refused to accept Vaughan's offer to resign. Consequently, both Vaughan and the president were considered "morally insensitive" by many Americans and members of the press.[26]

Nevertheless, when *Herald Tribune* reporter Jack Steele received the prestigious Raymond Clapper award for his series of articles on the "five percenters," Truman attended the award ceremony and posed for a picture with Steele. In the news caption for the photo, the president was quoted as saying, "Congratulations, Jack, I like good reporting, no matter what it says."[27]

The revival of earlier comparisons of the Truman administration with corruption in the Harding administration appeared once again in the press in 1950 and 1951 when charges of improprieties arose in connection with the Reconstruction Finance Corporation (RFC), the Bureau of Internal Revenue, and the Department of Justice. The first two government agencies prompted investigations in the Senate while, indirectly, the justice department's seemingly lax handling of ballot fraud and criminal activity led to the traveling Senate crime hearings—with its first stop in Kansas City—chaired by Democratic Senator Estes Kefauver of Tennessee.[28]

The RFC investigations led back to the White House and the alleged involvement of Truman's chief personnel officer, Donald Dawson, in influencing a majority of the agency's directors to place

25. McCullough, *Truman*, 746–47; Drew Pearson, "Draft column titled 'Vaughan & Truman,' " undated, Vaughan, Major General Harry folder, Box F 32, 3 of 3, Drew Pearson Personal Papers, Lyndon B. Johnson Library.

26. Dunar, *The Truman Scandals*, 62, 64, 69, 73–77, 56–57. Doris Fleeson leveled the charge that Truman, while personally honest, was "morally insensitive" to the concerns of the public over corruption in government. University of Texas speech, November 21, 1952, News clipping folder, Box 1, Doris Fleeson Papers, University of Kansas.

27. *Editor and Publisher* (April 8, 1950): 35.

28. See Dunar, *The Truman Scandals*, chaps. 5, 6, and pp. 137–38.

loans with firms directed by former RFC officials or companies friendly to the administration. While Dawson effectively refuted the charges against his involvement in RFC affairs, the discredited agency had outlived its usefulness and was abolished at the outset of the Eisenhower administration.

The Senate hearings into the affairs of the RFC produced another powerful symbol of corruption in government with the disclosure that a White House secretary, Mrs. E. Merl Young, had received a $9,600 mink coat billed to a lawyer whose client had received an RFC loan while Mrs. Young's husband had served as an examiner of the agency.[29] Deep freezers, five percenters, and now mink coats were all grist for the mills of the Republican party and the antiadministration press.

An investigation of the Bureau of Internal Revenue by a Senate subcommittee in 1951 unearthed the most damaging evidence of corruption in the Truman administration and led to numerous firings, indictments, and convictions. Ironically, two of the casualties of the administration's own attempt at house cleaning were its chief house cleaners, Newbold Morris, personally selected by Attorney General J. Howard McGrath to conduct an independent investigation into tax fraud, and McGrath himself. The complicated story of McGrath's firing of Morris and Truman's firing of McGrath occupied the front pages of newspapers during the early months of 1952 and kept Truman busy defending his actions and planning reform countermeasures.[30]

Ultimately, the charges of corruption in the administration went well beyond warranted accusations aired in the press. The *Chicago Tribune* outdid itself with vicious editorials assailing Truman directly and personally. The *Tribune* editorial of February 13, 1951, brazenly called for his impeachment for waging "illegal war in Korea" and for instituting "Pendergast spoils in the White House." "Truman is crooked as well as incompetent. That is sufficient ground for the impeachment of any official," the editorial concluded. The newspaper renewed its call for the president's impeachment after the firing of General MacArthur, citing the general's dismissal as evidence of Truman's unfitness, "morally and mentally, for high office."[31]

29. Ibid., 78–95.
30. Ibid., 96–120 and chap. 7.
31. Editorials, *Chicago Tribune*, February 13, April 12, 1951.

William Bradford Huie's May 1951 article on the president for the *American Mercury* was equally derogatory. Huie threw caution and truth to the wind. He took issue with journalists such as David Lawrence who declared, in connection with a piece on corruption in the administration, "Nobody can justly say that Harry Truman is devoid of personal integrity." "We believe," wrote Huie, "that the President, on his record, is a dishonorable man. We believe that he *is* devoid of personal integrity. We believe that he is a fixer among fixers, that his influence in this country is debilitating and evil."[32]

Truman had wanted to file libel charges against the *Chicago Tribune* for its scurrilous editorials, but the justice department's lengthy memorandum on the matter led him to see the futility of that course. For this reason, he never contemplated bringing libel charges against Huie when his derogatory piece appeared later. Privately, though, he took immediate steps to deal with these assaults on his personal integrity and the reputation of his administration.[33]

Truman's handling of the corruption issue in the final year of his administration received, at best, mixed reviews. His appointment of a fair-minded Democrat, James McGranery, as McGrath's successor as attorney general in the spring of 1952 proved to be a good choice. McGranery cooperated with Congress in dealing with tax fraud matters and contributed to the spirit of executive and legislative cooperation that led to acceptance of the administration's plan for reorganization of the Bureau of Internal Revenue. This reform removed the federal tax collection bureaucracy from the patronage system and placed it under civil service. But other reorganization plans to remove political appointments such as postmasters and customs officials from the patronage system to the civil service failed to secure approval in the Senate. These efforts had come too little and too late to satisfy many Americans, and as a result the administration entered the 1952 presidential election year with the albatross of corruption around its neck.[34]

While news stories of five percenters, influence peddlers, and graft unfolded during the Truman years, the news media gave even greater attention to charges leveled at the president and several officials of his administration responsible for carrying out his foreign policies

32. William Bradford Huie, "Is President Truman an Honorable Man?" *American Mercury* 72 (May 1951): 545–50.

33. Dunar, *The Truman Scandals*, 122–27. Truman's efforts to counter and correct the assaults on his integrity and competence are recounted in the following chapter.

34. Ibid., 127–34.

and defense. And, like the early charges of corruption in the Truman administration, press inquiry and reporting on the conduct of foreign affairs and national security were brought into public view, first cautiously and then later with considerable recklessness.

Truman's difficulties with Secretary of State Byrnes are illustrative of the initial caution exercised by the press in reporting on foreign policy formulation. When Truman's correspondence secretary, William Hassett, told *Washington Post* reporter Edward T. Folliard in the winter of 1946 that Truman had dressed down Byrnes for his "go-it-alone policy," Folliard carried the news back to Alexander Jones, managing editor of the *Post*.

Jones nixed the idea of a story at the time. He told Folliard, "Well, Eddie, these are pretty grim times. I don't think we ought to write a story about the President having a quarrel with his Secretary of State. It wouldn't do any good, and it could do some harm, especially abroad." "Just keep it in mind," Jones advised. "If there's some real good reason to write the story, then go ahead and write it."[35]

Folliard waited until Truman provided indirect evidence at a news conference that Byrnes had failed to follow the president's lead in foreign policy. In response to a reporter's question asking if the president supported the state department's policy for Argentina, Truman's eyes flashed as he responded: "The state department doesn't have a policy unless I support it." Folliard's story of a rift between Truman and Byrnes appeared on the front page of the *Post* on March 15, 1946. The *Post* carried their denials the following day, but the quarrel was real and news stories of the rift persisted. Subsequent developments that September placing Commerce Secretary Wallace's views on U.S.-Soviet relations at odds with the president's program led Byrnes to inform the president that he could have only one secretary of state at a time. Truman quickly fired Wallace from his post and bided his time with Byrnes until he resigned in early 1947.[36]

News coverage of Truman's troubles with Secretary of Defense Forrestal in late 1948 and early 1949 greatly surpassed the Truman-Byrnes rift as a focal point of high-level gossip and speculation in

35. Edward T. Folliard oral history, by Jerry N. Hess, 58–59.

36. Ibid., 59; *Public Papers*, 1946, 102; *Washington Post*, March 15, 16, 1946. The reason for the departure of Byrnes and his relationship with Truman received, not unexpectedly, different interpretation by the two men. See Hillman, *Mr. President*, 20–23, for Truman's version and James F. Byrnes, *All in One Lifetime*, 342–48, 399–403.

radio and in the press. Initially, the reports focused on the continuation of Forrestal in the president's cabinet; later reports speculated about the mental stability of the defense secretary.[37] Tragically, the drama between the unstable Forrestal and the patient, protective president, played out over a period of several months, ended with Forrestal's suicide on May 22, 1949.

The tenure of Forrestal in the Truman administration had been problematic from the start because of his conflicting desire to leave government service and yet remain on duty as one of the architects of the postwar navy and the nation's anticommunist policies. Forrestal's ardent advocacy of the navy's interests in the administration's postwar unification of the armed forces made him an almost unmovable force until presidential pressure brought him on board. Truman completed this task in midsummer of 1947 by naming Forrestal the nation's first secretary of defense, a post in which he would have to mediate and administer the interests of the entire armed forces.[38]

Few people, and least of all Truman, realized at the time of Forrestal's appointment that he was a "burnt out case." Forrestal himself could not realize how close he was to a mental collapse. According to his biographers, Forrestal, "stimulated by the scope and complexity of the problems that were now his daily fare, . . . was too absorbed in the process to notice that its wear and tear over seven years had eroded his physical and mental resilience, leaving him more vulnerable than he realized to the continuing risks and pressures of high office."[39]

Nevertheless, by the election of 1948, when Truman seemed to face almost certain defeat, Forrestal's thoughts were of continuing in office—in the cabinet of Thomas E. Dewey. Reports of Forrestal's lack of personal loyalty to Truman arose during the presidential campaign when the defense secretary communicated to Dewey that he would be willing to continue in his post in the Republican administration.[40] Forrestal's belief that Truman would be handily defeated by Dewey in the election reflected, of course, conventional wisdom. Preelection news reports of his inclusion in "President"

37. Townsend Hoopes and Douglas Brinkley, *Driven Patriot: The Life and Times of James Forrestal*, 426–27, 432–33, 435–36.

38. Ibid., passim.

39. Ibid., 350.

40. Ibid., 422–23, 425, 429–30, 435.

Dewey's cabinet must have irritated Truman and, standing by itself, could have been reason enough for his departure from Truman's cabinet.

Paradoxically, Forrestal's mental and physical state worked both for his continuation in government and for his separation from service. Truman despaired over Forrestal's diminished capacity for decision-making. At one point he asked his naval aide, Admiral Robert Dennison, "Do you know who is the Secretary of Defense?" Then answering his own question, he said, "I'm the secretary of defense."[41] Yet when the president tried to provide Forrestal with a graceful exit from government, the defense secretary evaded setting the time for his departure.

Radio broadcasters Walter Winchell and Pearson proved to be enormously influential in the events surrounding the time of Forrestal's retirement and, in the opinion of many, the manner of his death. Winchell, like Pearson, reached a huge listening audience in his Sunday evening broadcasts. Both men, ardent Zionists, interpreted Forrestal's Middle East policies designed to ensure that the nation would have oil for its economic and military policies as inimical to the partition of Palestine for a Jewish homeland. This motivation, Forrestal's biographers have written, led Winchell and Pearson to undertake "a savage campaign of distortion and vilification designed to 'get' Forrestal and drive him from office." Winchell originated a story in early January 1949 that Forrestal had cheated on his income taxes in 1929 and thus was unqualified to command the respect of boys drafted into the army. Pearson reported that when Truman heard Winchell's charge, he hit the ceiling, declaring, "I'm not going to let that little so-and-so tell me who I'm going to keep in my Cabinet."[42]

Pearson circulated his own rumor about Forrestal's unsuitability, dipping back to the 1930s when Mrs. Forrestal had been robbed of her jewelry at gunpoint upon her return home after an evening social engagement. Her husband, according to Pearson's account, "ran out the back door of his house into the alley, leaving his wife to cope with a jewel robbery alone." Although Arthur Krock, a guest of the Forrestals that night, wrote Pearson asking him to retract his false story of Forrestal's alleged cowardice, Pearson refused. Instead, he

41. Ibid., 437.
42. Ibid., 396–97, 437–39.

let his listeners and readers believe that Forrestal "would not appear to have the courage or chivalry to be the best secretary of national defense."[43]

The mental pressures on Forrestal continued to mount to a point where he could not discharge his duties, and on March 2, 1949, he wrote Truman to seek release, a request granted by Truman effective March 31, 1949. On April 1, while in Florida following a post-retirement conference with Truman, Forrestal attempted suicide and was hospitalized five days later at the naval hospital in Bethesda, Maryland. Pearson reported the suicide attempt on his April 9 broadcast.[44]

In the early morning hours of Sunday, May 22, Forrestal plunged to his death from the sixteenth floor of the hospital. That evening Winchell did not comment on Forrestal's demise in his radio broadcast, but Pearson, informing his listeners that Forrestal's death followed three previous suicide attempts, questioned why the former defense secretary had been placed "in a room high above the ground in the tower when all other hospitals place mental patients in rooms near the ground."[45]

Not unexpectedly, Forrestal's death unleashed a storm of criticism of the press and radio commentators within and outside the news profession. Hanson Baldwin of the *New York Times* singled out Pearson for his role in "maligning, traducing, and attacking Forrestal. Radio and the press must bear the burden of the shame for the commentaries," Baldwin wrote. *Editor and Publisher,* in its coverage of the story, noted that "words and phrases such as 'character assassins,' 'professional blatherskites,' 'bloodhounds of the press,' and 'slime mongers' were shot in general directions." Westbrook Pegler, lauding Forrestal's loyalty, bravery, and self-sacrificing service to the nation, charged that he was "a victim of the wanton blackguardism and mendacity of the radio, which has been a professional specialty of Drew Pearson," and promptly drew a quarter-million-dollar lawsuit from Pearson for libel. (The suit was settled out of court by the Hearst Corporation, syndicator of Pegler's column, on terms favorable to Pearson.)[46]

Truman limited his public comments on Forrestal's death to a

---

43. Ibid., 439–40; Krock, *Sixty Years,* 251.
44. Hoopes and Brinkley, *Driven Patriot,* 441–45, 455–56.
45. Ibid., 465; *Editor and Publisher* (May 28, 1949): 5.
46. *Editor and Publisher* (May 28, 1949): 5; Oliver Pilat, *Pegler: Angry Man of the Press,* 238–39.

solemn proclamation and a statement that the late defense secretary was a casualty of the Second World War. Privately, he shared the belief that the attacks on Forrestal in newspapers and on the radio had contributed to the secretary's precarious mental state and ultimate demise.[47]

Forrestal's successor, Louis Johnson, became the center of a subsequent controversy that involved the president, the press, and Secretary of State Dean Acheson. Reports at the outset of Johnson's tenure that he owed his appointment to his large contribution to Truman's presidential campaign were true. But the belief held by some, including columnist Stewart Alsop, that Vaughan had been responsible for Johnson's appointment exaggerated the general's influence with the president on important matters. By the end of Johnson's tenure eighteen months later, Alsop had come to believe that Johnson was worse than a thousand Vaughans.[48]

Johnson quickly ran into trouble with the Alsop brothers, specialists in writing about national security and foreign policy issues, for his ready acquiescence in Truman's stringent defense budgets. The columnists, convinced that Johnson deceived the public with announcements that he was improving the nation's defenses at a savings to the taxpayer, went on the offensive against the blustering secretary. Joseph Alsop angrily wrote a piece for the *Saturday Evening Post* entitled "Johnson is a Liar." Lawyers for the magazine insisted that the wording be changed to "Johnson's Untruths" but let the substance of the piece stand, namely, that the strategic combat design approved by the joint chiefs of staff was not being implemented by the defense secretary. Stewart Alsop quipped that the article on Johnson should be followed by other pieces starting with "Acheson is a Coward, Truman is a Fool, and [Jesse] Donaldson (the postmaster general) is a Son of a Bitch."[49]

The reference to Acheson apparently misinterpreted the reserve and tact that the secretary of state employed in meeting the belittling behavior of the defense secretary. The Alsops had heard of the bizarre treatment meted out to Acheson by Johnson whenever the

47. *Public Papers*, 1949, 179–80; McCullough, *Truman*, 740.

48. Stewart Alsop to Martin Sommers, February 13, 1950, January–June 1950 folder, Container 27, Joseph Alsop Papers, Library of Congress.

49. Ibid; the *Saturday Evening Post* did not publish the piece on Johnson and the criticism of the Alsops of his defense expenditures appeared in their columns syndicated by the *New York Herald Tribune* (Alsop, with Platt, *I've Seen the Best of It*, 302).

two men met to discuss policy. By June 1949 Joseph Alsop reported confidentially to his editor at the *Saturday Evening Post* that Johnson was quarreling with Acheson on matters large and small to the detriment of good cooperation between the two departments.[50] The Alsops eventually resolved their doubts over Acheson by writing more critical columns on Johnson's defense policies.

Johnson counterattacked by attributing the discontent of the Alsops to his shutting off the flow of top-secret information formerly provided to them by Forrestal. He showed reporters a white phone behind his desk that he claimed was a direct line to the columnists. Editors and publishers in turn complained directly to the Alsops on the "ill-tempered tone" and personal nature of their columns about the defense secretary. In response to a Denver publisher upset with the columnists for their critical treatment of Johnson, Stewart Alsop explained that while the defense secretary had angered him and his brother by lying about their direct access to information under Forrestal, their real anger resulted from Johnson's lies about the state of the nation's defense.[51]

The outbreak of the Korean War and the inadequacies in the nation's combat ability gave added urgency to the criticisms that the Alsops had made of Johnson's defense economies and the contretemps between Acheson and the defense secretary. At his August 3, 1950, news conference, a reporter asked Truman his opinion of Congressman Percy Priest's call for the resignation of both Johnson and Acheson. Truman, surprised that this demand originated with the Democratic majority whip in the House, replied, "Just make it plain to him that they are not going to resign, as long as I am president." At the president's news conference on August 31, the lead-off questions for Truman asked for his comment on the assertion of Representative Anthony F. Tauriello that Secretary Johnson had lost the confidence of the people of the country. Truman responded with "no comment." Another reporter tried a different tack by asking

50. Joseph Alsop to Martin Sommers, June 6, 1949, SEP June–December 1949 folder, Container 27, Alsop Papers, Library of Congress.

51. According to Drew Pearson, Johnson had personally witnessed Forrestal telephone the Alsops to tell them both truths and untruths of what was going on (Tyler Abell, ed., *Drew Pearson Diaries, 1949–1959*, 42). When Johnson succeeded Forrestal, and before his falling out with the Alsops, he invited the columnists to call him directly at his Pentagon office, which is something different from a telephone with a "direct line" to the Alsops. Alsop, with Platt, *I've Seen the Best of It*, 303. Stewart Alsop to Edwin P. Hoyt, May 4, 1950, D folder, Container 24, Joseph Alsop Papers, Library of Congress.

if the president was embarrassed by the defense secretary. "No," Truman replied. "If I had been embarrassed everyone would have found it out because I would have announced it." Did the president contemplate making any change? "No," Truman said, to end the discussion for the time being.[52]

However, as criticism of Johnson mounted in Congress and in the press, and as the rift between Johnson and Acheson continued, Truman concluded that he must ask for Johnson's resignation. A damning report had also come to him from high-level sources that Johnson was positioning himself for a presidential bid in 1952 as the candidate of both well-placed Democrats and Republicans.[53]

On September 12, the White House announced the secretary's resignation. A diplomatically worded resignation letter, prepared with the assistance of White House aides, soothed Johnson's bruised feelings by giving him credit for laying the foundation for successful operation of a unified armed forces. It also built a case for his successor, General Marshall, who quickly gained congressional approval to head the civilian agency.[54]

With Johnson gone, right-wing Republicans and the antiadministration press stepped up their demands for the firing or impeachment of Secretary of State Acheson. The impeccably dressed and unflappable secretary, secure in his backing from the president and articulate in his own defense, personified for conservatives the Ivy League New Dealer in government. Senator Hugh Butler (R-Nebr.), moved to anger just by being in Acheson's presence, confessed that he wanted to shout at Acheson, "Get out, Get out. You stand for everything that has been wrong with the United States for years." The Republican right believed that Acheson, in refusing to denounce Alger Hiss when his longtime friend was accused of supplying state secrets to the Soviet Union, made himself unfit for office. Acheson drew even more fire for announcing the "loss" of China in 1949. And his drawing of a defense perimeter in the Far East that excluded

52. *Public Papers*, 1950, 570, 606–7.

53. McCullough, *Truman*, 792–93; Hoopes and Brinkley, *Driven Patriot*, 431. Truman speculated that Johnson's behavior and conflict with Dean Acheson may have been related to a brain tumor removed in subsequent surgery and that may have contributed to Johnson's death. See Paola Coletta's biographical sketch of Johnson in Richard S. Kirkendall, ed., *The Harry S. Truman Encyclopedia*, 189–90.

54. Charles G. Ross, Dictated Notes on Resignation of Secretary of Defense Louis Johnson, September 12, 1950, Official folder, Box 10, Elsey Papers, Truman Library; *Public Papers*, 1950, 632–33.

South Korea, his critics charged, had invited the communist attack there.[55]

When these criticisms reached a crescendo following the rout of American forces in Korea by troops of Communist China, Truman devoted most of his news conference on December 19, 1950, to a strong defense of Acheson. He praised him for his role in shaping the nation's containment policy and for his loyalty to the nation. No official in government, Truman said, "has been more alive to communism's threat to freedom or more forceful in resisting it. . . . If communism should prevail in the world—as it shall not prevail— Dean Acheson would be one of the first, if not the first, to be shot by the enemies of liberty and Christianity." Just as President Abraham Lincoln had refused to accede to the request of critics who clamored for Secretary of State William Seward's dismissal, Truman explained, he would not dismiss Acheson. He appealed for unity, bipartisanship, and the use of "great talents of men like Dean Acheson."[56]

Renewed calls for Acheson's dismissal came after the recall of General MacArthur in April 1951, but Truman remained loyal to his beleaguered secretary. Acheson, in turn, remained steadfastly devoted to the president, and when both moved into retirement, their mutual respect blossomed into an even greater friendship.[57]

Members of the press seemed to miss the significance of loyalty in the president's code of conduct for all members of his administration. Truman allowed a great deal of latitude in the actions of his official family, but once members of his administration had clearly crossed the line between appropriate and inappropriate behavior, dismissal of the errant official occurred resolutely. Wallace, Ickes, Byrnes, Johnson, and MacArthur ultimately fell from the president's grace by their challenges to his authority and to his policies. The repentant, such as the president's personal physician, Wallace Graham, who unwisely purchased grain commodities contracts during the European food crisis of the early postwar period, and the dismissed attorney general, J. Howard McGrath, who bungled both the hiring and firing of special investigator Newbold Morris, never

---

55. *Public Papers*, 1950, 637. 74. Butler is quoted in Eric Goldman, *The Crucial Decade—And After: America 1945–1960*, 125. McCullough, *Truman*, 743–44, 759–61; Ferrell, *Harry S. Truman: A Life*, 317–19.

56. *Public Papers*, 1950, 751.

57. McCullough, *Truman*, 751–56; Douglas Brinkley discusses this friendship and the sources that describe and analyze it in *Dean Acheson: The Cold War Years, 1953–1971*, 14, 332, note 5.

lost Truman's friendship. He remained loyal, too, to Secretary of the Treasury John Snyder and Harry Vaughan when their critics became legion. And, after President Eisenhower's justice department obtained a prison term for Matthew Connelly, convicted in 1956 for taking small gifts in exchange for helping to fix an income tax matter when he was presidential appointment secretary, Truman interpreted the trial as a miscarriage of justice and aided Connelly by successfully lobbying President John F. Kennedy for a pardon.[58]

In an assessment of Truman's personnel problems, the historian Andrew J. Dunar concluded that the president's "dualistic view of people, a facile tendency to divide people into categories . . . Democrats or Republicans, friends or foes, his people or others, was a limited, and limiting perspective."[59]

Yet Truman's code of loyalty, as well as his own personal integrity and his strong sense of honest public service, made it possible for him to retain and enlist men of high ethical standards and purpose for his administration. The list of these officials is impressive: Samuel Rosenman, liberal confidant of Roosevelt held over as special counsel until Clark Clifford (aided by his key lieutenant and later presidential aide, George Elsey) could prove his mettle as the president's closest political strategist and adviser; Charles Murphy, who became special counsel when Clifford left government service in February 1950; John Steelman, presidential assistant for labor-management policies and day-to-day operations; economist Leon Keyserling, Interior Secretary Oscar Chapman, and Secretary of Agriculture Charles Brannan, major contributors to the Truman Fair Deal; George C. Marshall, who, in addition to undertaking the difficult postwar mission to China in a futile attempt to stem the communist victory in the civil war there, gave up retirement twice to serve first as secretary of state and later as secretary of defense; David Lilienthal, who initially misjudged Truman but came to admire him greatly for battling in his behalf when his enemies wanted to drive him from the Tennessee Valley Authority and keep him off the Atomic Energy Commission; Robert Lovett in the Department of Defense and other upper-echelon officials who sacrificed higher-paying jobs in the private sector because they admired Truman

---

58. Dunar, *The Truman Scandals,* 37–39, 119–20, 150–55. Although Snyder's fiscal conservatism matched the fiscal views of Truman, liberals made him and other cabinet officials rather than the president the subject of their criticisms. Phillips, *The Truman Presidency,* 156–57.

59. Dunar, *The Truman Scandals,* 120.

and shared his love for government service; and Charlie Ross, who devoted his few remaining years to serve the president he had come to love as a brother. Perhaps Acheson, the most vilified member of the president's official family, understood best that a man of great integrity had bestowed upon them a priceless gift of trust and friendship.[60]

Although the press from time to time threw bouquets to the competent and dedicated members of Truman's official family, more often than not the journalists lost sight of these capable and devoted government servants. Instead, they pursued sensational stories of alleged and real corruption and assigned blame to ranking members of the administration for perceived and real weaknesses in the nation's defense and foreign policies. Moreover, the reputations of honest and loyal members of the president's official family, like the reputation of the president himself, were linked, as members of the administration, to colleagues whose shortcomings and weaknesses were real.

Some, like General Marshall, accused of being a traitor to his country by Senator Joseph McCarthy, allowed his official biographer to set the historical record straight. Others left extensive oral histories to explain and defend their roles as members of the Truman administration. Acheson and Clifford penned memoirs in the twilight of their years.[61]

Truman, as the head of his official family, joined these efforts in apologia even before he left office. His spirited defense of his personal integrity and the historical reputation of his presidency would become the centerpiece of his relationship with the press during the final months of his administration.

60. Biographical sketches of these individuals are included in Kirkendall, ed., *The Harry S. Truman Encyclopedia,* passim.

61. Forrest Poage wrote a three-volume authorized biography of Marshall. Oral histories of key Truman administration members are in the collection of the Truman Library. Acheson titled his memoirs *Present at the Creation.* Clifford, assisted by Holbrooke, published his memoirs under the title *Counsel to the President: A Memoir.*

11

From the Front Page to the Pages of History

AS HIS PRESIDENCY ENTERED its final months, Truman's relations with the press underwent a series of changes keyed to both day-to-day affairs and the long perspective of history. The former centered around Truman's potential and then real status as a lame duck, with the diminution of presidential power that invariably results as the tenure of the chief executive draws to a close. The latter involved the president's determination that the unfavorable press and radio reports on his administration would not become the verdict of history.

Under the Twenty-second Amendment, adopted in 1951 as a reaction to the four terms accorded by the voters to Franklin D. Roosevelt, Truman was eligible for a second full term. Journalists began to speculate regularly after January 1951 on his decision to seek reelection or retire. Edward T. Folliard led the parade of articles with "Truman Does Not Choose to Run," published in the January 30, 1951, issue of *Look*. When asked about the article at his next news conference, Truman quipped, "Those are Coolidge's words;" he complimented the reporter on the article and refused further comment. Jonathan Daniels, who enjoyed the friendship but not the confidence of the president on his plans for 1952, answered in the affirmative with his piece for *American Magazine* in September

1951. Daniels cast his prediction of Truman's reelection in 1952 in the title of his article: "Truman Can't Lose."[1]

Although the president and the first lady privately decided shortly after his election in 1948 to retire when his term ended in January 1953, announcement of the retirement decision remained under wraps until the appropriate time. Reporters tried numerous variations of the same question about Truman's plans for 1952 at nineteen news conferences of 1951 and at eight news conferences during the election year without success.[2] Truman played the game astutely, holding on to power that he knew would slowly dissipate once he announced his decision not to run again.

Despite his assurances to the White House correspondents that they would be the first to know of his plans for 1952, the manner in which Truman announced that he would not be a candidate suggests that he wanted to give radio and television a break over newspapers. At 11 A.M. on Saturday, March 29, the day of his announcement, press, radio, and television representatives received the text of the president's Jackson Day Dinner speech marked for a 9 P.M. release. The Sunday morning newspapers, reporting that the president was mum on running for reelection, were readied for printing. At 10:57 P.M., in the closing minutes of his speech broadcast on radio and television, Truman picked up his handwritten statement and read the key sentence: "I shall not be a candidate for reelection."[3]

Radio and television scored an instant news break. Newspaper reporters bolted to the door to dictate the news via telephone to their newspapers and wire services, requiring the writing of new leads and heads for already composed front pages. *Editor and Publisher*, recalling Truman's promise that the White House news corps would be the first to be informed of his decision on the 1952 presidential race, commented sarcastically that the correspondents were "at least among the first to know. Only a few million heard it at the same time."[4]

---

1. *Public Papers*, 1951, 113–14; Jonathan Daniels, "Truman Can't Lose," *American Magazine* (September 1951), 29ff in HST file, Box 4, Records of the Democratic National Committee, Truman Library.

2. Harry H. Vaughan oral history, by Charles T. Morrissey, 49. This compilation is derived from reading the president's news conferences from January 1951 until his announcment on March 29, 1952. See *Public Papers*, 1951, 1952–1953, passim. Truman also brushed aside a direct question about seeking reelection 1952 at his press conference on August 25, 1949 (*Public Papers*, 1949, 441).

3. *Editor and Publisher* (April 5, 1952): 13.

4. Ibid., 36.

The slow but still perceptible shift of news media attention from Truman to the prospective presidential candidates in both parties led Stewart Alsop to suggest a dismissing article for the *Saturday Evening Post* entitled "The Forgotten President." His editor at the *Post*, however, noting that Truman would heavily influence the choice of the Democratic nominee and play a large part in the fall campaign, did not take the suggestion.[5]

Truman, in fact, had plans for playing a very active role in the presidential politics of 1952, and he hoped that his choice of candidate would win election and continue Democratic policies. Equally important, he wanted to complete a series of efforts begun earlier during his full term to secure for himself and his presidency an honored place in American history.

In 1949 Truman endorsed the efforts of Jonathan Daniels, former member of the White House Press Office, to write a biography of the president. Daniels, with letters of introduction provided by Truman, conducted extensive interviews and used records made available to him by the Trumans and their kin. *The Man of Independence*, published by Lippincott in September 1950, was not represented by the author as an authorized biography; Truman uncharitably expressed his private opinion that Daniels had written "a lot of bunk." Nevertheless, the book rested on solid research, and in a more balanced opinion, Truman gave it a better review. In a letter to Ethel Noland, he wrote: "I've been reading Jonathan's book and I think the facts are all right but he's not very respectful to my father and mother. But as you say, it is on a much higher plane than most pieces about me."[6]

Next came an autobiographical memoir of Truman compiled and edited by William Hillman, a newspaper reporter and radio correspondent for the Mutual Broadcasting System. The book, *Mr. President*, published by Farrar, Straus and Young in March 1952, preceded Truman's retirement announcement. On the cover of the book Truman wrote, "I want the people to know the presidency as I have experienced it and I want them to know me as I am." In an open letter to his editor published as an afterword of the book, he added,

5. Alsop to Martin Sommers, July 15, 1952, SEP January–August 1952 folder, Container 27, Joseph Alsop Papers, Library of Congress; Ben Hibbs to Alsop, July 18, 1952, ibid.

6. Daniels, *The Man of Independence*, 9; Hechler, *Working with Truman*, 221; Miller, *Plain Speaking*, 60; Truman to Noland, September 24, 1950, in Ferrell, ed., *Off The Record*, 194.

"I expect there will be those who will construe this as a political act. You and I know better."[7]

Indeed, Jonathan Daniels, in his review of *Mr. President* for *Saturday Review*, acknowledged that "it will be widely said and fairly said on the basis of most of its contents that this is the Harry Truman campaign biography for 1952." But Daniels, revising his own earlier prediction that Truman would be in the race, opined that the book offered the best evidence to date that Truman would not run again. According to Daniels, "This book is a volume prepared in farewell by a much lambasted President who wants very much to depart with the understanding and affection of the people of the United States."[8]

In keeping with his desire that the people of the nation should know both him and the presidency, Truman also initiated plans to collect information on his prepresidential business and political affairs by assigning his former aide in the White House Press Office, Eben Ayers, to this research task. Ayers visited the Kansas City area in the spring of 1951 to interview the president's former associates, friends, and acquaintances. He obtained written evidence of Truman's relatively unknown unsuccessful business ventures in banking, oil, and mining when he was still on the farm, and the well-publicized failure of the haberdashery. In addition, Ayers researched Truman's alliance with the Pendergast machine and the tangled business affairs of the family farm. Over the years all had been grist for Truman's political opponents and detractors, and prompted the president's desire to have his side of the story told.[9]

The capstone of these biographical and historical efforts, which Truman hoped would ensure the sound reputation of himself and his administration, involved advance planning for a presidential library. The idea for a library to house his personal and official papers, the papers of members of his administration, and others who knew or associated with him from boyhood onward, did not spring from a single decision. Initially Truman entertained the idea of donating his presidential papers to the University of Missouri, where his prepresidential papers were housed. When officials of the university sought to conclude an agreement with the president for the transfer of his White House papers to its Western Historical Manuscripts Collection, Truman asked instead for the return of his senatorial

---

7. Hillman, *Mr. President*, 1, 251–52.

8. Jonathan Daniel, review of *Mr. President, Saturday Review* 35 (March 22, 1952): 13–14.

9. Dunar, *The Truman Scandals*, 124–27.

and vice-presidential files for a unified collection of his papers in a presidential library, built not on the campus at Columbia, but on the Truman family farm in Grandview.[10]

Presidential assistant George Elsey took the lead in scouting a site for the library on the Truman farm. On his visit there in 1951, the president's brother, Vivian, showed him a remote corner of a field—a depressed swampy area adjacent to a railroad track—as a satisfactory place for the building. Elsey, struck by the attractiveness of a distant prominent slope with a good view in all directions, asked Vivian why the library couldn't be built there. The president's farmer brother replied, "Ain't no use wastin' good farmland on any old dang library."[11]

The importance of the library to the president, however, ensured that the site would be carefully chosen and the building itself would reflect his democratic philosophy and the teaching and research purposes that he envisioned for the institution. An ideal place, an expansive hillside within walking distance of the Truman residence and accessible to the public by U.S. Highway 24 adjacent to the grounds, was donated for the library by the City of Independence in July 1954.[12]

When the library opened in 1957, Truman visited it almost daily except Sundays until his health broke in 1964. There he handled his extensive correspondence and received important visitors. He personally conducted tours of the library for VIPs and spoke to schoolchildren in the auditorium. He believed that the records of his administration housed in the library would allow future historians to accord to him a just place in history.[13]

Indeed, as the Truman administration began to wind down, some historians began to offer their first positive evaluations. *Look* commissioned the eminent historian Henry Steele Commager to evaluate the Truman presidency for its issue of August 28, 1951. Commager gave the administration high marks, noting its achievements in the postwar rehabilitation and security arrangements for Western Europe, the democratization of Japan, and, despite failure to secure

---

10. Truman, *Mr. Citizen,* 188–93; *New York Times,* February 23, 28, 1954. See also G. W. Sand, *Truman in Retirement: A Former President Views the Nation and the World,* 31–40.
11. George Elsey oral history, by Charles T. Morrissey and Jerry N. Hess, 44–45.
12. *New York Times,* July 8, 1954.
13. McCullough, *Truman,* 966–69; Ferrell, *Harry S. Truman: A Life,* 399.

the enactment of the Fair Deal domestic agenda, economic prosperity at home. The editors of *Look*, evidently surprised by Commager's favorable evaluation, prefaced the article with a disclaimer that readers would not likely share the historian's positive assessment. When Senator Ernest McFarland (D-Ariz.) inserted Commager's article in the *Congressional Record*, Truman sent an appreciative note to him. Privately, the historian Allan Nevins wrote Truman to express his high opinion of the Missourian's administration. These early evaluations by historians prefigured an emerging school of historical scholarship that assigned "near greatness" to President Truman in the 1960s, with reaffirmation of that rating in 1996.[14]

But journalists still held center stage in evaluating Truman and his presidency during the closing months of the administration. Their interpretations echoed their initial assessment that he was a "little man" more suited for the courthouse than the White House. Continuing evidence of influence peddling in Washington, corruption in the Bureau of Internal Revenue, and improper loans by the Reconstruction Finance Corporation in 1951 led to the popularization of the Republican charge of a "mess in Washington" in the 1952 presidential election year.[15]

The "mess in Washington" allegation and the general unpopularity of the Truman administration figured significantly in the president's role in shaping the outcome of the Democratic presidential nomination. It angered Truman that Senator Estes Kefauver had tossed his hat into the ring before he had made his retirement decision public, and made him even angrier that the Tennessean had capitalized upon his position as chairman of the Special Senate Crime Investigating Committee to further his bid for the Democratic presidential nomination. After Kefauver won the New Hampshire primary in March and became the front-runner for nomination, Truman joined the anti-Kefauver forces by lining up Governor Adlai E. Stevenson of Illinois for the nomination.[16]

14. Henry Steele Commager, "A Few Kind Words for Harry Truman," 62ff; Truman to MacFarland, August 21, 1951, Mc–General Folder, Box 128, PSF, Truman Papers, Truman Library; Nevins to Truman, December 26, 1952, "N" folder, Box 417 PPF, Truman Papers, Truman Library and the Allan Nevins Papers, Rare Book and Manuscript Library, Columbia University; Franklin D. Mitchell, "Harry S. Truman and the Verdict of History," 264–65; Arthur M. Schlesinger, Jr., "The Ultimate Approval Rating," *The New York Times Magazine*, December 15, 1996, 46–51.
15. Mitchell, "The Verdict of History," 261–62; Dunar, *The Truman Scandals*, 135–36, 144.
16. Dunar, *The Truman Scandals*, 136–40, 143.

But Stevenson proved to be a reluctant candidate, and once nominated, an independent one, too. The Illinois governor's decision to establish his campaign headquarters in Springfield rather than Washington indicated a real and symbolic distancing of the Democratic candidate from the president. Moreover, Stevenson, by responding in August to an Oregon newspaper's query about "the mess in Washington," appeared to be endorsing the Republican charge of widespread wrongdoing in the Truman administration. The news media, to Truman's distress, gave prominent coverage to Stevenson's blunder.[17]

The incident so provoked Truman that he wrote an angry letter to Stevenson, charging him with "trying to beat the Democratic President instead of the Republicans and General of the Army who heads their ticket." "There is no mess in Washington," Truman asserted, "except the sabotage press in the nature of Bertie Mc-Cormick's *Times-Herald* and the anemic Roy Howard's snotty little *News.*" Stevenson's public claim of being indebted to no one for his nomination was untrue, Truman asserted. "Had I not come to Chicago when I did, [Kefauver] the squirrel headed coonskin cap man . . . , who has no sense of honor, would have been the nominee. Best of luck to you from a bystander who has become disinterested." The letter, unmailed, went instead to the files.[18]

Truman, with a larger and long-standing quarrel with the news media and Republicans, had no intention of sitting on the sidelines in the fall campaign. Determined to defend both the twenty-year record of the Democratic party and his own leadership and character, he thrust himself into the presidential campaign with gusto. For more than six weeks after the traditional Labor Day opening of the campaign, he traveled more than eighteen thousand miles in a railroad tour of the East, Midwest, and West, delivering more than two hundred speeches ranging from formal addresses to whistlestop remarks.[19]

Several themes emerged in Truman's campaign talks. In Montana he defended politics as the democratic expression of the people and as an honorable calling. Proud of his long career that had carried him from a precinct office to the presidency, he proclaimed that "the most honorable profession in the country is politics—and politics in the sense that it is government [which] is, in my opinion, the

17. Ibid., 143–45.
18. Poen, ed., *Strictly Personal and Confidential*, 120–21.
19. *Public Papers*, 1952–1953, 1031.

most honorable career that a man can have."[20] This belief, essential as a defense against the attacks upon both him and his administration, also contrasted with Republican presidential candidate Eisenhower's long career in the military.

Truman kept the heat on the press for distorting his record as president. He could not let the opportunity pass while speaking in Spokane, Washington, to lambaste his nemesis there, the *Spokesman-Review*, repeating his charge of 1948 that the newspaper was "the second worst paper in the United States." According to the president, the Spokane newspaper "never told the truth in politics in its life, and it wouldn't know the truth if it met it coming down the road." He hammered away at the distortion or omission of his record in press reports and in the speeches of Republican politicians. The voting record of Republicans against the Democratic legislative successes of the past twenty years, he said, could be found in the *Congressional Record* but not in Republican newspapers.[21]

Truman's charge of a one-party press, made so often during the campaign, began to sound like a one-song musical. He first tore into the Republican-favored newspapers of New York State, charging in early October that the state's newspapers were biased 12 to 1 in favor of the GOP.[22] On October 22, he declared that General Eisenhower was saying "one thing in the East. He says another thing in the West. What he says in the North is different from what he says in the South." But, Truman added, "The true facts finally get out to the people, no matter how much the one-party press tries to cover them up or distort." The large crowds that turned out for his speeches gave proof, he believed, that he was getting his story out to the people over the heads of the newspapers.

The friendly turnout for him, he asserted, "shows that the great attempt to misrepresent me and my administration has not been successful. If the people believed what they read in the one-party press, they would regard me as a sort of horrible monster with horns and a tail." But people did not regard him as the devil because "they know I have been standing up for their interests, for the interests of the common, everyday man . . . no matter what it costs." They know, too, Truman added, "that any President who does that is going

20. Ibid., 643.
21. *Editor and Publisher* (June 12, 1948): 13; *Public Papers*, 1952–1953, 667, 852.
22. *Public Papers*, 1952–1953, 776.

to be vilified and slandered by the rich men who control the press and the opposition party."[23]

He elaborated upon his charge of a one-party press throughout the fall campaign, even stating that the "present press set-up . . . [is] against us 100 percent, and they try to make it appear that everything we do is wrong." He added, "It is all right for the other side to call me a liar and a traitor—and there's nothing wrong with that, if you will read the press, but when I nail down a few lies on the other side, why that's something awful."

"Well," he added, "I have been called everything—I have had as much abuse, I reckon, as any other President; but they haven't hurt me yet, and I'm not through, I want to tell you, until the 4th day of November."[24]

Truman's spirited campaigning and his ability to attract large crowds wherever he went led Bess to quip to her husband: "Have I been asleep, and are you running for President?"[25]

In fact, Truman was defending his honor and his place in history. In Chicago for a major speech in behalf of Adlai Stevenson on October 29, Truman charged that the newspapers had not reported on his discussion of the issues during his railroad campaign tour. When he had stayed in Washington and took no part in the campaign, Truman explained, Eisenhower and "the one-party press felt free to vilify me as a traitor and a corruptionist. When I replied and carried a campaign of truth around the country, their only retort was to accuse me of slander and abuse." Moreover, Truman charged, "The Republican leaders and the Republican press are desperate in this campaign. From the beginning, they had planned to win by using the 'big lie' and the 'big doubt.' When these tactics were exposed," he said, "there was nothing they could do but cry 'foul.' "[26]

Truman coupled his campaign efforts to his place in history in a television and radio address in Detroit in the closing week of the campaign. "I hope you will forgive me if I talk a little bit about the accomplishments of my administration," he said. An explanation was necessary because "History doesn't begin to be kind to a President for about 50 years after he has served. If there is anything good about me, you will never find it out from the newspapers of today. Jefferson, Lincoln, Jackson, Cleveland, Woodrow Wilson, Franklin

23. Ibid., 926.
24. Ibid., 944.
25. Ibid., 954.
26. Ibid., 989.

Roosevelt were treated in exactly the same way, so you see I am in pretty good company."[27]

Truman's contemporary standing remained close to its lowest level in the final days of the campaign. In a Gallup Poll taken the previous November to evaluate the public's opinion of the president's performance, only 23 percent of those polled approved of his performance. The low rating reflected the public's dissatisfaction with the stalemated war in Korea, allegations of communism in government, and charges of corruption in the administration. Sixty-seven percent of the nation's newspapers gave editorial endorsement to Dwight Eisenhower.[28]

In the November general election, the electorate accorded Eisenhower a resounding popular victory over Stevenson by a vote of 34 million to 27 million. Both houses of Congress came under Republican control, too, but by slender margins. Some newspapers interpreted the election as more than a loss for Adlai Stevenson; it was a rebuke of Truman as well.[29]

Truman's final efforts to fix his place in history came in the time-honored "State of the Union" message and a "Farewell Address to the American People" in January 1953. In the former the president emphasized his record in domestic and foreign affairs in a ten-thousand-word review of his administration, and the press took note of his allusions to the historical record. Arthur Krock, however, found the significance of the departing president's message in the warning to Joseph Stalin that Lenin's prophecy of war between communism and capitalism as a stage of communist development had been rendered obsolete by the nature of war itself. War in the atomic age, Truman said, meant the devastation of the Soviet lands and of its hegemony. The president's solemn reminder of the nature of nuclear warfare, Krock opined, "was a final act of statescraft for which Harry S. Truman will be remembered when much else in his record has been forgotten."[30]

Truman offered his own fuller assessment of how history would remember the times and statescraft of his presidency in his farewell address on radio and television to the American people on January

27. Ibid., 1008.
28. Dunar, *The Truman Scandals,* 127, 135–36; Senator Karl Mundt (R–S.D.), popularized these charges with the formula C2K1: Communism, Corruption, and Korea. *Editor and Publisher* (November 8, 1952): 40.
29. *Editor and Publisher* (November 1, 1952): 9.
30. *Public Papers,* 1952–1953, 1114–28; *Washington Post,* January 8, 1953; Arthur Krock, "In the Nation," *New York Times,* January 11, 1953.

15, 1953. He reported that he had done his best during the past two months for an orderly transfer of power to the incoming Eisenhower administration, and had established, he hoped, a precedent for the future.

He was confident that the larger course of history had been set by the actions he had taken during his administration. "I suppose that history will remember my term in office as the years when the 'cold war' began to overshadow our lives," he said. "But when history says that my term of office saw the beginning of the cold war, it will also say that in those 8 years we have set the course that can win it."

> We have succeeded in carving out a new set of policies to attain peace—positive policies, policies of world leadership, policies that express faith in other free people. We have averted World War III up to now, and we may already have succeeded in establishing conditions which can keep that war from happening as far ahead as man can see. . . .
>
> Some . . . may ask, when and how will the cold war end? The Communist world has great resources, and it looks strong. But there is a fatal flaw in their society. Theirs is a godless system, a system of slavery; there is no freedom in it, no consent. The Iron Curtain, the secret police, the constant purges, all these are symptoms of a great basic weakness—the rulers' fear of their own people.

There would have to be a time when change would come to the Soviet world, Truman concluded.

> Nobody can say for sure when that is going to be, or exactly how it will come about, whether by revolution, or trouble in the satellite states, or by a change inside the Kremlin. . . . Whether the Communist rulers shift their policies of their own free will— or whether the change comes about in some other way—I have not a doubt in the world that a change will occur.

The president contrasted the burden of costly defense with the prospects of economic development at home and abroad in an era of peace. The American workforce of more than sixty million people enjoyed the blessings of high living standards. He held out the prospect of achieving "equal economic opportunities, equal rights of citizenship, and equal educational opportunities for all our people, whatever their race or religion or status of birth." He envisioned for the free peoples of the world a golden age ushered in by using the peaceful tools of science to attack poverty and human misery.

His prophetic address that envisioned the end of Soviet Communism and the bright future of democracy was a splendid valedictory of the people's president.[31]

The president's leave-taking in these historic messages commanded the headlines of front pages and the editorial pages of the nation's newspapers, but Truman had yet another strategy to engage the press in highlighting the historical record of his administration. He invited eleven Washington correspondents to the White House for exclusive exit interviews. The privileged reporters—Anthony Leviero of the *New York Times*, Carleton Kent of the *Chicago Sun-Times*, Raymond "Pete" Brandt of the *St. Louis Post-Dispatch*, Jack Costello of the *New York Daily News*, Edward Folliard and Jerry Klutz of the *Washington Post*, Doris Fleeson for the Bell Syndicate, John Erling of the *Washington Star*, and the three wire service reporters, Merriman Smith, Ernest Vacarro, and Robert Nixon—had all taken Truman to task for giving an exclusive interview to Krock in 1950. Apparently rationalizing that they functioned as a "pool" of reporters representing all of their colleagues in journalism, each kept the appointment with the president. The stories they filed garnered for the president the front pages of their respective newspapers and prominent attention in other news sources when he could still command interest as the nation's most important news maker.[32]

Truman, in seeking a retrospective view of his presidency, invited questions on all aspects of his administration ranging from key decisions to major regrets. His greatest accomplishment, he told Kent, was avoiding a third world war. His hardest decision, he informed the *Sun-Times* reporter, was not the order for the use of atomic bombs in Japan to bring World War II to a swift end; rather it was the decision to commit ground troops in Korea. He cited the Soviet Union's support for North Korea's invasion of South Korea as Stalin's biggest mistake in that it led to the vital rearmament of the United States for its defense of the free world. The president credited his administration's economic policies for the continuing and widespread postwar prosperity. He defended his official family and his loyalty to those falsely accused of corruption and disloyalty to the nation. He admitted, somewhat ruefully, that he had lost his temper and good decorum by writing an angry letter to the music

31. *Public Papers*, 1952–1953, 1197–1202.
32. These interviews and newspaper clippings are gathered in Box 131, PSF, Truman Papers, Truman Library.

critic who had written a review critical of his daughter Margaret's singing performance.[33]

David Lawrence, who had written his share of critical columns for *U.S. News and World Report,* went to the heart of the significance of the farewell interviews by stating that Truman was consciously playing to his place in history.[34]

On January 20, 1953, the presidential inauguration of Dwight D. Eisenhower marked the end of the Truman presidency and the beginning of a new administration. The historic dynamics of the president and the press now engaged the new chief executive as the dynamics of history engaged the old president. Eisenhower moved to the front page of newspapers, and Truman moved on to the pages of history.

33. Ibid.

34. David Lawrence, "Last Days of Truman," *U.S. News and World Report* 34 (January 16, 1953): 24–26.

HARRY AND BESS TRUMAN succeeded to some extent in re-establishing the private character of their lives during their long retirement. Secret Service protection ended on Inauguration Day with the transfer of power to President Eisenhower. Frequent news coverage of the former president and first lady, however, continued for awhile, and when the Trumans boarded the train for their return to Missouri, they were accompanied by a few reporters, including Bob Nixon of International News Service and Tony Vacarro of Associated Press.[1]

In Independence an enthusiastic crowd of ten thousand gathered at the railroad station to greet Harry and Bess, while a few thousand more waited outside their house to welcome them home. The demonstration of affection by the townsfolk visibly moved the couple and left each with a feeling that the warm homecoming had made the efforts of his presidency worthwhile. It was the payoff, Truman recorded in his diary, for "thirty years of hell and hard work."[2]

In the ensuing days and months the Trumans made the transition from public to private life with relative ease. Both drove their own automobile and ran their own errands until advancing old age caught up with them. Harry visited the barber shop regularly and Bess

1. Truman, *Mr. Citizen*, 17–18. After the assassination of President John F. Kennedy in 1963, Congress appropriated funds for Secret Service protection for former presidents. With reluctance, and then later with appreciation, the Trumans accepted the protection. Margaret Truman, *Bess W. Truman*, 418–19. Robert G. Nixon oral history, by Jerry N. Hess, 975–76.

2. Truman, *Mr. Citizen*, 18–19. Diary entry, January 21, 1953, Box 298, PSF, Truman Papers, Truman Library.

kept a weekly appointment at the hairdresser. She also visited the dry cleaners, shopped for groceries, and checked out books at the Independence Public Library for herself and Harry. Both moved about Independence with a minimum of fuss from the townspeople.[3]

Nevertheless, the claim that the public made on the former president and first lady could never be completely relinquished, thus ensuring intermittent news coverage of them. Reporters queried Truman for his opinion on breaking international news developments and his postpresidential perspective on the events of his administration. His views were sought on the performance of his presidential successors, his preference for the Democratic presidential nomination during election years, the civil rights movement, black activism, the war in Vietnam, and other issues.[4]

Truman created a news fury soon after leaving office by stating to wire service reporter Nixon his belief that the Soviet Union did not possess atomic bombs. Truman had first piqued Nixon's interest when he announced in September 1949 that the Soviets had produced an "atomic explosion." Now, three and a half years later, he explained to Nixon that he did not believe the Soviets had accomplished the necessary "know-how" to "make an A-bomb work. I am not convinced they have the bomb." Although reporters elicited concurring views from physicist Arthur Compton and Lieutenant General Leslie Groves, both intimately involved in the building of the nation's first atomic weapons, President Eisenhower laid the matter to rest by stating that the United States had "incontrovertible evidence" that the Soviet Union had atomic bombs.[5]

Truman also made news with retrospective accounts of his presidency. The publication of his two-volume memoirs in 1955 and 1956 by Doubleday and its serialization in *Life* rekindled some of the controversies of his administration, including his troubled relations with Ickes, Wallace, Byrnes, and MacArthur.[6]

---

3. Truman, *Mr. Citizen*, 19–21. This account is based on the author's chance and unobtrusive observation of the Trumans in the summer of 1969. Bess, with an armful of books, stood in line at the Independence Public Library; outside, sitting in the family Chrysler, was Harry. A young woman pushing a baby stroller carrying a small child passed by the Truman car without giving the former president so much as a glance.

4. See Harry S. Rosenthal's account of his coverage of Truman in retirement for the Associated Press, "Covering Truman: A Reporter's Story," *Whistle Stop* 12, no. 5 (1984).

5. *New York Times*, January 27, 1953; *Newsweek* (February 9, 1953): 24.

6. McCullough, *Truman*, 946–49.

Later, the publication of Truman's speeches delivered before college and university audiences and essays written originally for the
American Weekly under the title *Mr. Citizen* in 1960 elicited only
mild public interest. His occasional pieces for the North American
Newspaper Alliance written during the mid-1950s through the early
1960s did not always meet the expectations of the publisher.[7]

During the Eisenhower administration, a newspaper editor took
note of Truman's diminishing role as a national news maker with a
humorous apocryphal story of thinly disguised admiration:

> The nation has once more been treated to the unedifying spec-
> tacle of a former President of the United States shooting off his
> mouth in a rash, ill-timed remark characterized by unbridled
> partisanship and profanity.
>
> When reporters accosted Mr. Truman on his morning stroll
> yesterday, they inquired what he thought about the weather.
> In his cockiest, shooting-from-the-hip manner Mr. Truman told
> the astonished group, "Boys, I think it's going to rain like hell."
>
> The Missouri politician could hardly have been unaware of
> the fact that his intemperate statement ran directly counter to
> the official weather forecast, which was Clear and Sunny. He
> was, in effect, casting aspersions upon the present Administra-
> tion, under which the Weather Bureau operates, and, indeed,
> upon the Press, which faithfully published the Bureau's forecast.
>
> His words were apparently calculated to spread gloom and
> promote panic among the thousands who planned picnics and
> other outdoor diversions, and to lessen public confidence in the
> President, who was already on his way to the golf course. We
> can well imagine the glee with which the masters of the Kremlin
> must have greeted this latest attempt to create division and sow
> disunity among Americans.
>
> To be sure, we did have some fourteen inches of rain yes-
> terday. But to belabor the coincidence would be to miss the
> essential point of the matter. Mr. Truman is not an authorized
> weather prognosticator and, in fact, he no longer holds any
> public position whatsoever. Furthermore, nobody is interested
> in what private-citizen Truman thinks; and the next time we
> send out reporters to interview him we hope he will have the
> good grace to remember that.[8]

Television brought the Trumans back into public view with a
first-time visit of the cameras inside their house for a telecast in

7. Ibid., 969. See the North American Alliance Collection, Boxes 921–924,
Post Presidential File, Truman Papers, Truman Library.

8. "Wet Blanket," Unidentified, undated editorial, James E. Bailey, Correspondence Number 3 folder, Box 6, Postpresidential Name file, Truman Papers,
Truman Library.

the mid-1950s. With daughter Margaret hosting the interview for Edward R. Murrow, the regular host of the popular CBS program "Person to Person," Harry and Bess commented candidly on their retirement lifestyle. But when television producer David Susskind attempted to find a market for a series on the Truman presidency, the networks were not interested.[9]

Still, the public's and the news media's growing admiration and affection for Old Harry, visible to some during his presidency, hinted during his remaining years that he was destined to become a national hero. The liberal columnist Max Lerner had captured the essence of Truman in his March 1952 review of *Mr. President:*

> I see a man who is in the most genuine sense an American primitive. He is what Grandma Moses would paint if she were to paint an American President, or stitch him into a quilt. He has all the Puritan virtues, and he believes in them unstintedly. He believes in thrift and self-reliance and self-discipline, in getting up early and working hard and going to bed early at night and sleeping the dreamless sleep of the just. He believes in Mom and "my sweetheart and my baby." He believes in understanding the motives of his enemies, and in sticking by his friends ("to the last drop of mercy"). He defends his daughter against criticism as a father should. He believes in utter honesty, and above all, what he thinks is right. He practices the homey maxims of the copybook and the sampler.
>
> He thinks the Supreme Court should stick to its judicial last, and that all should be right and orderly in a right and orderly universe.[10]

Lerner admitted that this appealing portrait, in being two-dimensional, resembled Truman's revealing but incomplete diary and papers gathered for publication under the title *Mr. President.* What was missing, Lerner stated, was

> how the Missouri and small-town boy turned into the man on whose shoulders an empire fell, and how those shoulders proved somehow strong enough to carry it without crumbling its power or destroying its freedom. And how a man rooted in all the virtues of order was able to survive in a chaotic world. That

9. *New York Times*, May 28, 1955; McCullough, *Truman*, 977. For an earlier effort by then President Truman to secure future income from television see Martin Stone, "Could Truman Pay His Bills?" *New York Times*, August 5, 1989.

10. Max Lerner, "Portrait of Harry Truman," *New York Post*, March 18, 1952, in HST File folder, Box 3, Records of the Democratic National Committee, Truman Library.

is not only Truman's story, but in the deepest sense the story of a democracy.[11]

By the early 1960s, historians and biographers sensitive to the strengths and weaknesses of American democracy had written liberal, affirmative interpretations of Truman and his presidency. During the same decade revisionist scholars, disillusioned with the Cold War, the perils of the nuclear age, flawed liberalism, and the war in Vietnam found the source of their discontent in Truman and his administration. It appeared then that the mixed historical accounts, as the written record and interpretation of the past, would not bear out Truman's belief that history would assign to him an honorable place among American statesmen.[12]

Yet an even more powerful folk history that affirmed the goodness and greatness of Harry Truman was being written, not in scholarly texts, but in the hearts and minds of the people. The pilgrimages of several presidents to the Truman home and library both acknowledged and promoted the growing affection and respect of Americans for Harry and Bess. The highlight of the presidential visits occurred in the summer of 1965 when President Lyndon B. Johnson and Lady Bird Johnson, along with Vice President and Mrs. Hubert Humphrey, staged the signing of Medicare into law at the auditorium of the library. As live television broadcast the late afternoon ceremony to news watchers around the nation, President Johnson presented Medicare cards numbers one and two to a beaming Harry and Bess in honor of Truman's advocacy of a national health insurance program during his administration.[13]

When the news media returned to Independence with President and Mrs. Richard M. Nixon in early 1969 for a presentation of a White House grand piano to the Truman Library, they found that time had caught up with the old Missourian. After Nixon had enthusiastically played "The Missouri Waltz" on the gift piano, the failing former president asked Bess in a voice loud enough for the viewing audience to hear, "What did he play?" It was Truman's last ceremonial visit to the library.[14]

11. Ibid.

12. Mitchell, "Harry S. Truman and the Verdict of History," 260–66.

13. Margaret Truman, *Bess W. Truman*, 419–20; Ferrell, *Harry S. Truman: A Life*, 400. The author viewed the signing on television.

14. Margaret Truman, *Bess W. Truman*, 420; McCullough, *Truman*, 984; author's recollection of the television coverage of the event. Truman's final

Thereafter Harry and Bess met members of the family, a few old friends, and distinguished visitors at home. The news media recorded their few remaining public appearances together on the front porch of their Victorian house: On June 28, 1969, for a fiftieth wedding anniversary photograph, and again on July 4 as honored observers of the city's Independence Day parade. A chair provided for a much enfeebled Harry allowed him to view the parade sitting down, but he respectfully rose from his seat with the passing of the color guard. Each group of riders and marchers carried the American flag, and Truman, soon worn out after rising several times, remained seated until the parade had passed.[15]

Truman died a day after Christmas in 1972 at the age of eighty-eight. In deference to the wishes of his family, he received a simple funeral in the foyer of the Truman Library. Through television, millions observed the Episcopal service, complemented by a solemn rite of the Masonic Order and a prayer of a Baptist minister, and the interment ceremony in the inner courtyard of the library. Field artillerymen fired six howitzers in a final twenty-one-gun salute. A distant bugler sounded Taps.[16]

The eulogies and memorial tributes to Truman penned by journalists, historians, and others marked, in their own way, a benediction that reverberated across the nation and around the world. Some of the newspaper editorials recounted the old controversies and did not gloss over honest differences with the former president. Many editorials observed, as did the *St. Louis Post-Dispatch,* that "Mr. Truman was overwhelmingly a man of the people—earthy, gregarious, stubborn, courageous, honest and a mixture of pride and humility." The *Wall Street Journal* struck one of the central themes of the editorial eulogies, noting that "His contemporaries judged him harshly. . . . Yet now, these twenty years later, it grows increasingly hard to remember what Harry Truman did wrong, and increasingly hard to dispute that he did most of the big things right."[17]

---

visit to the library occurred in 1971 when he returned to inspect an addition to the building. Ferrell, *Harry S. Truman: A Life,* 399.

15. McCullough, *Truman,* 986; *Independence Examiner,* June 28, 1969; author's observation of the July 4, 1969, parade.

16. McCullough, *Truman,* 988–89; Margaret Truman, *Bess W. Truman,* 421–23.

17. The editorials and other tributes memorializing Truman are published in *Memorial Services in the Congress of the United States and Tributes in Eulogy of Harry S Truman, Late a President of the United States,* 105–6 and passim.

The *Journal*'s editorial echoed one of Truman's favorite sayings, penned years before by another famous Missourian. "Always do right!" Mark Twain advised. "This will gratify some people and astonish the rest."[18] Truman surely would have liked the journalistic "thirty" of his life and presidency.

18. Hillman, *Mr. President*, 225.

SELECTED BIBLIOGRAPHY

MANUSCRIPTS

Alsop, Joseph. Papers. Manuscript Division, Library of Congress, Washington, D.C.

Ayers, Eben A. Papers and diary. Harry S. Truman Library, Independence, Mo.

Barnett, Claude A. Papers (microfilm of original deposited in the Chicago Historical Society, Chicago, Ill.). Manuscript Division, Library of Congress.

Brandt, Raymond P. Papers. Western Historical Manuscript Collection, University of Missouri–Columbia.

Clifford, Clark M. Papers. Harry S. Truman Library.

Craig, Elizabeth May. Papers. Manuscript Division, Library of Congress.

Cull, Richard, Jr. Papers. Harry S. Truman Library.

Daniels, Jonathan. Papers. Southern Historical Collection, Wilson Library, University of North Carolina, Chapel Hill.

Democratic National Committee. Papers. Harry S. Truman Library.

Elsey, George M. Papers. Harry S. Truman Library.

Fleeson, Doris. Papers. Kenneth Spencer Research Library, University of Kansas, Lawrence.

Furman, Bess W. Papers. Manuscript Division, Library of Congress.

Halverstadt, Dallas C. Files. Harry S. Truman Library.

Hannegan, Robert E. Papers. Harry S. Truman Library.

Heslep, Charter. Papers and diary. Harry S. Truman Library.

Howard, Roy B. Papers. Manuscript Division, Library of Congress.

Keeley, Mary Paxton. Papers. Harry S. Truman Library.

Kent, Frank R. Papers. Maryland Historical Society, Baltimore.

Lockett, Edward B. Papers. Harry S. Truman Library.

Luce, Clare Boothe. Papers. Manuscript Division, Library of Congress.

McDonough, Gordon L. Papers. Regional Cultural History Center, University of Southern California, Los Angeles.

Niles, David. Papers. Harry S. Truman Library.

Noland, Mary Ethel. Papers. Harry S. Truman Library.

Odum, Reathel. Papers. Harry S. Truman Library.

Pearson, Drew. Papers. Lyndon B. Johnson Library, University of Texas, Austin.

Prattis, Percival. Papers. Moreland Library, Howard University, Washington, D.C.

Pulitzer, Joseph, II. Papers. Manuscript Division, Library of Congress.

Rigdon, William M. Papers. Harry S. Truman Library.

Rosenman, Samuel I. Papers. Harry S. Truman Library.

Ross, Charles G. Papers. Harry S. Truman Library.

Smith, Harold D. Diary (photocopy of original deposited in the Franklin D. Roosevelt Library, Hyde Park, New York). Harry S. Truman Library.

Truman, Harry S. Papers and diary. Harry S. Truman Library.

ORAL HISTORIES

All oral histories cited are deposited in the Harry S. Truman Library.

Ayers, Eben A., by Jerry N. Hess. 1967–1970.

Cull, Richard, Jr., by Niel M. Johnson. 1988.

Elsey, George M., by Jerry N. Hess. 1969.

———, by Charles T. Morrissey and Jerry N. Hess. 1974.

———, by William Smiley and Jerald L. Hill. 1976.

Folliard, Edward T., by Jerry N. Hess. 1970.

Greene, Charles J., by Jerry N. Hess. 1971.

McKim, Edward D., by J. R. Fuchs. 1964.

Nixon, Robert G., by Jerry N. Hess. 1979.

Perlmeter, Irving, by Charles T. Morrissey. 1964.

Reinsch, J. Leonard, by J. R. Fuchs. 1967.

Rowe, James H., Jr., by Jerry N. Hess. 1979.

Tames, George, by Benedict K. Zobrist. 1984.

Truman, Margaret, by Ron Cockrell. 1985.

Truman, Mary Jane, by Stephen and Cathy Doyal and Fred and
    Audrey Truman. 1975.
————, by Jerald L. Hill and William D. Stilley. 1976.
Tubby, Roger, by Jerry N. Hess. 1970.
Vaughan, Harry H., by Charles T. Morrissey. 1963.

PHOTOGRAPHIC ARCHIVAL SOURCES

Harry S. Truman Library

NEWSPAPERS

Unless indicated otherwise, newspapers cited were examined in
the Clipping File, Records of the Democratic National Committee,
the Vertical File, and the Microfilm Collection, Harry S. Truman
Library.

Baltimore Sun
Belton [Missouri] *Herald.* State Historical Society of Missouri, Co-
    lumbia.
Chicago Tribune. Elmer Ellis Library, University of Missouri–
    Columbia.
Christian Science Monitor
Independence Examiner
Los Angeles Times. Doheny Library, University of Southern Cali-
    fornia, Los Angeles.
Louisville Courier-Journal
Kansas City Star
Kansas City Times
Portland [Maine] *Press-Herald.* Scrapbook, Elizabeth May Craig
    Papers. Manuscript Division, Library of Congress.
[Santa Monica, Calif.] *The Daily Breeze/Outlook/News Pilot.* Santa
    Monica Public Library, Santa Monica, Calif.
St. Louis Post-Dispatch
New York Daily News
New York Herald Tribune
New York Post
New York Times
Philadelphia Record
Washington Daily News
Washington Post

Washington Star
Washington Times-Herald

MAGAZINES

All magazines were consulted in the Graduate Research Library and the Undergraduate Library, University of California, Los Angeles.

American Heritage
Broadcasting
Collier's
The Crisis
Editor and Publisher
Fortune
Look
Life
Nation
New Republic
Newsweek
Saturday Evening Post
Television Daily
Time
U.S. News
U.S. News and World Report

BOOKS, ARTICLES, DISSERTATIONS, THESES

Abell, Tyler, ed. *Drew Pearson Diaries, 1949–1959.* New York: Holt, Rinehart and Winston, 1974.

Alsop, Joseph W., with Adam Platt. *I've Seen the Best of It: Memoirs.* New York: Norton, 1992.

Alsop, Stewart. *The Center: People and Power in Political Washington.* New York: Harper and Row, 1961.

Barnouw, Erik. *Tube of Plenty: The Evolution of American Television.* New York: Oxford University Press, 1975.

Baughman, James L. *Henry R. Luce and the Rise of the American News Media.* Boston: Twayne, 1987.

———. *The Republic of Mass Culture: Journalism, Filmmaking, and Broadcasting in America since 1941.* 2d ed. Baltimore: Johns Hopkins University Press, 1997.

Beasley, Maurine H. *Eleanor Roosevelt and the Media: A Public Quest for Self-Fulfillment.* Urbana: University of Illinois Press, 1987.

————. "Bess Truman and the Press: A Case Study of a First Lady as Political Communicator." In *Harry S. Truman: The Man from Independence,* edited by William F. Levantrosser. Westport, Conn.: Greenwood, 1986, 207–16.

Blair, Clay. *The Forgotten War: America in Korea, 1950–53.* New York: Times Books, 1987.

Bliss, Edward, Jr. *Now the News: The Story of Broadcast Journalism.* New York: Columbia University Press, 1991.

Bluford, Lucile. "Missouri 'Shows' the Supreme Court." *Crisis* 46 (August 1949): 230–32, 242.

Brayman, Harold. *The President Speaks Off-the Record: Historic Evenings with America's Leaders, the Press, and Other Men of Power, at Washington's Exclusive Gridiron Club.* Princeton, N.J.: Dow Jones, 1976.

Brinkley, Douglas. *Dean Acheson: The Cold War Years, 1953–1971.* New Haven: Yale University Press, 1992.

Byrnes, James F. *All in One Lifetime.* New York: Harper, 1958.

Childs, Marquis W. *Witness to Power.* New York: McGraw-Hill, 1975.

Clifford, Clark M., with Richard Holbrooke. *Counsel to the President: A Memoir.* New York: Random House, 1991.

Cockrell, Ron. *The Trumans of Independence: Historic Recourse Study.* Omaha: National Park Service, 1985.

Coffin, Tris. *Missouri Compromise.* Boston: Little, Brown, 1947.

Commager, Henry Steele. "A Few Kind Words for Harry Truman." *Look* 15 (August 28, 1951): 62–69.

Cornwell, Elmer E., Jr. *Presidential Leadership of Public Opinion.* Bloomington: Indiana University Press, 1965.

Dalfiume, Richard M. *Desegregation of the Armed Forces: Fighting on Two Fronts, 1939–1953.* Columbia: University of Missouri Press, 1969.

Daniels, Jonathan. *The Man of Independence.* Philadelphia: Lippincott, 1950.

Davies, Richard O. *Housing Reform during the Truman Administration.* Columbia: University of Missouri Press, 1966.

Dingman, Roger. "Atomic Diplomacy during the Korean War." In *Nuclear Diplomacy and Crisis Management,* edited by Sean M. Lynn-Jones, Steven E. Miller, and Stephen Van Evera, 114–55. Cambridge: MIT Press, 1990.

Donovan, Robert J. *Conflict and Crisis: The Presidency of Harry S. Truman, 1945–1948.* New York: Norton, 1977.

———. *Tumultuous Years: The Presidency of Harry S Truman, 1949–1953.* New York: Norton, 1982.

Dorsett, Lyle W. *The Pendergast Machine.* New York: Oxford University Press, 1968.

Dunar, Andrew J. *The Truman Scandals and the Politics of Morality.* Columbia: University of Missouri Press, 1984.

Dunnigan, Alice A. *A Black Woman's Experience: From Schoolhouse to White House.* Philadelphia: Dorrance, 1974.

Edwards, Julia. *Women of the World: The Great Foreign Correspondents.* Boston: Houghton Mifflin, 1988.

Elson, Robert T. *The World of Time Inc.* Vol. 2, *The Intimate History of a Publishing Enterprise, 1941–1960.* New York: Atheneum, 1973.

Emery, Michael, and Edwin Emery. *The Press and America: An Interpretive History of the Mass Media.* 7th ed. Englewood Cliffs, N.J.: Prentice-Hall, 1992.

Erskine, Helen Worden. "The Riddle of Mrs. Truman." *Collier's* 129 (February 9, 1952): 11, 61–62.

Farrar, Ronald T. *Reluctant Servant: The Story of Charles G. Ross.* Columbia: University of Missouri Press, 1969.

Ferrell, Robert H. *Choosing Truman: The Democratic Convention of 1944.* Columbia: University of Missouri Press, 1994.

———. *Harry S. Truman: A Life.* Columbia: University of Missouri Press, 1994.

———. *Harry S. Truman: His Life on the Family Farms.* Worland, Wyo.: High Plains, 1991.

———, ed. *The Autobiography of Harry S. Truman.* Boulder: Colorado Associated University Press, 1980.

———, ed. *Dear Bess: The Letters from Harry to Bess Truman, 1910–1959.* New York: Norton, 1983.

———, ed. *Off the Record: The Private Papers of Harry S. Truman.* New York: Harper and Row, 1980.

———, ed. *Truman in the White House: The Diary of Eben A. Ayers.* Columbia: University of Missouri Press, 1991.

Ferrell, Robert H., and Francis H. Heller. "Plain Faking?" *American Heritage* 46 (May/June 1995): 14–16.

Fielding, Raymond. *The American Newsreel, 1911–1967.* Norman: University of Oklahoma Press, 1972.

Fuller, Wayne E. *RFD: The Changing Face of Rural America.* Bloomington: Indiana University Press, 1964.

Furman, Bess W. "The Independent Lady from Independence." *New York Times Magazine,* June 9, 1946, 20, 47.

Gies, Joseph. *The Colonel of Chicago.* New York: E. P. Dutton, 1979.

Giglio, James N., and Greg G. Thielen. *Truman: In Cartoon and Caricature.* Ames: Iowa State University Press, 1984.

Goldman, Eric. *The Crucial Decade—and After: America, 1945–1960.* New York: Random House, 1961.

Gore, Albert, Jr. "The Impact of Television on the Conduct of the Presidency." Master's thesis, Harvard College, 1969.

Hamby, Alonzo L. *Beyond the New Deal: Harry S. Truman and American Liberalism.* New York: Columbia University Press, 1973.

———. *Man of the People: A Life of Harry S. Truman.* New York: Oxford University Press, 1995.

Harper, Alan D. *The Politics of Loyalty: The White House and the Communist Issue, 1946–52.* Westport, Conn.: Greenwood, 1969.

Harris, Eleanor. "May Craig: TV's Most Unusual Star." *Look* 26 (April 29, 1962): 109–14.

Harry S. Truman, Late a President of the United States: Memorial Tributes Delivered in Congress. Washington: Government Printing Office, 1973.

Hechler, Ken. *Working with Truman: A Personal Memoir of the White House Years.* New York: Putnam, 1982.

Heller, Francis H., ed. *The Truman White House: The Administration of the Presidency, 1945–1953.* Lawrence: Regents Press of Kansas, 1980.

Hersey, John. *Aspects of the Presidency.* New Haven and New York: Ticknor and Fields, 1980.

Hess, Stephen. *The Washington Reporters.* Washington: Brookings Institution, 1981.

Higgins, Marguerite. *War in Korea: The Report of a Woman Combat Correspondent.* Garden City, N.Y.: Doubleday, 1951.

Hillman, William. *Mr. President.* New York: Farrar, Straus and Young, 1952.

Hoopes, Townsend, and Douglas Brinkley. *Driven Patriot: The Life and Times of James Forrestal.* New York: Knopf, 1992.

Jenkins, Roy. *Truman.* New York: Harper and Row, 1986.

[Keeley], Mary Gentry Paxton. *Mary Gentry and John Gallatin Paxton.* Chillicothe, Mo.: Privately printed, 1967.

Kirkendall, Richard S. "Election of 1948." In *History of American Presidential Elections,* edited by Arthur M. Schlesinger, Jr.,

Fred L. Israel, and William P. Hansen, vol. 4, 3099–211. New York: Chelsea House, 1971.

———. *A History of Missouri: Volume V, 1919 to 1953.* Columbia: University of Missouri Press, 1986.

———, ed. *The Harry S. Truman Encyclopedia.* Boston: G. K. Hall, 1989.

Krock, Arthur. *Memoirs: Sixty Years on the Firing Line.* New York: Funk and Wagnalls, 1968.

Lawrence, Bill. *Six Presidents, Too Many Wars.* New York: Saturday Review Press, 1972.

Lee, R. Alton. *Truman and Taft-Hartley: A Question of Mandate.* Lexington: University Press of Kentucky, 1966.

Leuchtenburg, William E. "The Conversion of Harry Truman." *American Heritage* 42 (November 1991): 55–68.

Liebling, A. J. "The Press." *Holiday* (February 1950): 98–101, 124, 127–28.

Liebovich, Louis. *The Press and the Origins of the Cold War, 1944–1947.* New York: Praeger, 1988.

Lilienthal, David E. *The Journals of David E. Lilienthal.* Vol. 2, *The Atomic Energy Years, 1945–1950.* New York: Harper and Row, 1964.

McClendon, Sarah. *My Eight Presidents.* New York: Wyden, 1978.

McCoy, Donald R. *The Presidency of Harry S. Truman.* Lawrence: University Press of Kansas, 1984.

McCoy, Donald R., and Richard T. Ruetten. *Quest and Response: Minority Rights and the Truman Administration.* Lawrence: University Press of Kansas, 1973.

McCullough, David. *Truman.* New York: Simon and Schuster, 1992.

McLellan, David S., and David C. Acheson, eds. *Among Friends: Personal Letters of Dean Acheson.* New York: Dodd, Mead, 1980.

[Marble, Joan]. "Washington's Armchair Correspondents by One of Them." *Harper's Magazine* 198 (February 1949): 49–52.

Marcus, Maeva. *Truman and the Steel Seizure Case: The Limits of Presidential Power.* New York: Columbia University Press, 1977.

Marzolf, Marion. "Marguerite Higgins." In *Notable American Women: The Modern Period, A Biographical Dictionary,* edited by Barbara Sicherman and Carol Hurd Green, with Ilene Kantrov and Harriette Walker, 340–41. Cambridge: Belknap Press of Harvard University Press, 1980.

———. *Up from the Footnote: A History of Women Journalists.* New York: Hastings House, 1977.

Miller, Merle. *Plain Speaking: An Oral Biography of Harry S. Truman.* New York: Berkley, 1974.

Miller, Richard Lawrence. *Truman: The Rise to Power.* New York: McGraw-Hill, 1986.

Mitchell, Franklin D. "An Act of Presidential Indiscretion: Harry S. Truman and the Marine Corps Incident of 1950." *Presidential Studies Quarterly* 11 (fall 1981): 565–75.

———. *Embattled Democracy: Missouri Democratic Politics, 1919–1932.* Columbia: University of Missouri Press, 1968.

———. "Harry S. Truman and the Verdict of History." *South Atlantic Quarterly* 85 (summer 1986): 261–69.

———. "Who is Judge Truman?: The Truman-for-Governor Movement of 1931." *Mid-Continent American Studies Journal* 7 (fall 1966): 3–15.

Montgomery, Ruth. *Hail to the Chiefs: My Life and Times with Six Presidents.* New York: Coward-McCann, 1970.

Nagel, Paul C. *Missouri: A Bicentennial History.* Nashville: American Association for State and Local History. New York: Norton, 1977.

Pearson, Drew. "Confessions of 'an SOB' Part II: My Life in the White House Doghouse." *Saturday Evening Post* 229 (November 10, 1956): 38–39, 72–76.

Perrett, Geoffrey. *Days of Sadness, Years of Triumph: The American People, 1939–1945.* Baltimore: Penguin, 1974.

Pfaff, Daniel W. *Joseph Pulitzer II and the Post-Dispatch.* University Park: Pennsylvania State University, 1991.

Phillips, Cabell. *The Truman Presidency: The History of a Triumphant Succession.* New York: Macmillan, 1966.

Phillips, Cabell, Duncan Aikman, Homer Joseph Dodge, William C. Bourne, and William A. Kinney. *Dateline: Washington: The Story of National Affairs Journalism in the Life and Times of the National Press Club.* Garden City, N.Y.: Doubleday, 1949.

Pilat, Oliver. *Drew Pearson: An Unauthorized Biography.* New York: Harper's Magazine Press, 1973.

———. *Pegler: Angry Man of the Press.* Boston: Beacon, 1963.

Poen, Monte M. *Harry S. Truman versus the Medical Lobby.* Columbia: University of Missouri Press, 1979.

———, ed. *Letters Home by Harry S. Truman.* New York: Putnam, 1984.

————, ed. *Strictly Personal and Confidential: The Letters Harry Truman Never Mailed.* Boston: Little, Brown, 1982.

Pogue, Forrest C. *George C. Marshall.* Vol. 4, *Statesman.* New York: Viking, 1987.

Pollard, James E. *The Presidents and the Press.* New York: Macmillan, 1947.

————. *The Presidents and the Press: From Truman to Johnson.* Washington: Public Affairs Press, 1964.

Prendergast, Curtis, with Geoffrey Colvin. *The World of Time Inc.* Vol. 3, *The Intimate History of a Changing Enterprise, 1961–1980.* New York: Atheneum, 1986.

Public Papers of the Presidents: Harry S. Truman, 1945–1953. 8 vols. Washington: Government Printing Office, 1961–1966.

Reid, Loren. *Hurry Home Wednesday: Growing Up in a Small Missouri Town, 1905–1921.* Columbia: University of Missouri Press, 1978.

Reinsch, J. Leonard. *Getting Elected: From Radio and Roosevelt to Television and Reagan.* New York: Hippocrene, 1988.

Robbins, Jhan. *Bess and Harry: An American Love Story.* New York: Putnam, 1980.

Rosenman, Samuel I., and Dorothy Rosenman. *Presidential Style: Some Giants and a Pygmy in the White House.* New York: Harper and Row, 1976.

Ross, Irwin. *The Loneliest Campaign: The Truman Victory of 1948.* New York: New American Library, 1968.

Rowan, Carl T. *Breaking Barriers: A Memoir.* Boston: Little, Brown, 1991.

Sand, G. W. *Truman in Retirement: A Former President Views the Nation and the World.* South Bend, Ind.: Justice, 1993.

Schmidtlein, Eugene F. "Truman the Senator." Ph.D. diss., University of Missouri, 1962.

Smith, A. Merriman. *The Good New Days: A Not Entirely Reverent Study of Native Habits and Customs in Modern Washington.* Indianapolis: Bobbs-Merrill, 1962.

————. *Thank You, Mr. President: A White House Notebook.* New York: Harper, 1946.

Smith, Richard Norton. *Thomas E. Dewey and His Times.* New York: Simon and Schuster, 1982.

Steel, Ronald. *Walter Lippmann and the American Century.* New York: Random House, 1980.

Steinberg, Alfred. *The Man from Missouri: The Life and Times of Harry S. Truman.* New York: Putnam, 1962.

Taft, William H. *Missouri Newspapers.* Columbia: University of Missouri Press, 1964.

Tames, George. *Eye on Washington: The Presidents Who've Known Me.* New York: HarperCollins, 1990.

Thompson, Kenneth W., ed. *Ten Presidents and the Press.* Washington, D.C.: University Press of America, 1983.

Trohan, Walter. *Political Animals: Memoirs of a Sentimental Cynic.* Garden City, N.Y.: Doubleday, 1975.

Truman, Harry S. *Memoirs.* Vol. 1, *Year of Decisions.* Vol. 2, *Years of Trial and Hope.* Garden City, N.Y.: Doubleday, 1955, 1956.

———. *Mr. Citizen.* New York: Geis, 1960.

———. *Truman Speaks.* New York: Morrow, 1973.

Truman, Margaret. *Bess W. Truman.* New York: Macmillan, 1986.

———. *Harry S. Truman.* New York: Morrow, 1973.

———, ed. *Letters from Father: The Truman Family's Personal Correspondence.* New York: Arbor House, 1981.

Underhill, Robert. *The Truman Persuasions.* Ames: Iowa State University Press, 1981.

Wade, Betsy, comp. and ed. *Forward Positions: The War Correspondence of Homer Bigart.* Fayetteville: University of Arkansas Press, 1992.

Wendt, Lloyd. *Chicago Tribune: The Rise of a Great American Newspaper.* Chicago: Rand McNally, 1979.

White, Graham J. *FDR and the Press.* Chicago: University of Chicago Press, 1979.

Williams, Herbert Lee. *The Newspaperman's President: Harry S. Truman.* Chicago: Nelson-Hall, 1984.

———. "Truman and the Press." Ph.D. diss., University of Missouri, 1954.

Winfield, Betty Houchin. *FDR and the News Media.* Urbana and Chicago: University of Illinois Press, 1990.

Wolseley, Roland E. *The Black Press, U.S.A..* 2d. ed. Ames: Iowa State University Press, 1990.